RUSSIAN GRAMMAR

The original publication of this Russian
Grammar was the French edition which is
Volume V of the series *Les Langues du Monde*
published in Editions I. A. C., Lyons-Paris

RUSSIAN GRAMMAR

BY

B. O. UNBEGAUN

Professor of Comparative Slavonic Philology
in the University of Oxford
and Fellow of Brasenose College

OXFORD
AT THE CLARENDON PRESS

Oxford University Press, Amen House, London E.C.4

GLASGOW   NEW YORK   TORONTO   MELBOURNE   WELLINGTON
BOMBAY   CALCUTTA   MADRAS   KARACHI   LAHORE   DACCA
CAPE TOWN   SALISBURY   NAIROBI   IBADAN   ACCRA
KUALA LUMPUR   HONG KONG

FIRST PUBLISHED 1957
REPRINTED LITHOGRAPHICALLY IN GREAT BRITAIN
BY D. R. HILLMAN & SONS LTD., FROME
FROM CORRECTED SHEETS OF THE FIRST IMPRESSION
1960, 1962

PREFACE

THIS descriptive grammar is the outcome of my experience as a teacher at the Universities of Strasbourg, Brussels, and Oxford. It contains only the minimum necessary for the understanding of the mechanism of modern literary Russian, to the exclusion of any historical perspective.

The task I have set myself has been not so much to expound Russian grammar in the greatest possible detail as to bring out the main lines of the general pattern of the language. This pattern is that of every living language in which an ancient heritage passed down from age to age is combined with innovations which unceasingly modify and enrich it. The essential purpose of this book has accordingly been to bring to light the precise relations between these two elements of modern Russian. Their co-existence renders necessary a clear distinction between the living, productive forms of the language and those which are dead and unproductive. This distinction is constantly stressed in the present work.

As the most vital and productive elements of the Russian language are the processes of word-formation, these have been accorded more than the inadequate degree of attention usually devoted to them in Russian grammars.

A peculiarity of Russian, which it shares with the other Slavonic languages, is the close interdependence of inflexion and word-formation. These are therefore treated conjointly for each part of speech. At the same time, it is necessary to distinguish between the principles of the two processes, which are quite different in nature, and, in the case of word-formation, between its several functions. It is for this reason that, in the verb, for example, aspectual and purely lexical word-formation are discussed separately from the morphology of verbal forms and from the purely practical problem of the classification of verbs.

The present English version differs from the French edition in two respects: (*a*) the text has been adapted to the requirements of the English student; (*b*) the exposition has been improved in some places.

In this work of adaptation I have been greatly assisted by Professor D. P. Costello, who has not only produced a faithful English version of my grammar but, by his judicious observations and suggestions, has contributed to render it less imperfect than it would otherwise have been. I am most sincerely grateful to him for his collaboration.

I should like to thank Professor C. L. Wrenn who took the trouble to read the manuscript and who let me profit by his valuable observations, as well as Mr. M. C. C. Wheeler, M.A., for his kind help and advice.

My thanks are also due to the Delegates of the Clarendon Press for undertaking the publication of this book and for the accuracy and typographical elegance with which they have accomplished it.

B. O. U.

CONTENTS

INTRODUCTION   xxiii

I. ORTHOGRAPHY AND PHONOLOGY   1

I. ORTHOGRAPHY   1

    1. The Alphabet   1

    2. Observations on Alphabet and Orthography   3
       1. The Letters е, ё, ю, я   3
       2. The Letters ь, ъ   4
       3. Orthographical Incompatibilities   5

II. PHONOLOGY   5

    A. CONSONANTS   6

    1. Voiced and Voiceless   7

    2. Hard and Soft   7
       1. Consonants which may be either Hard or Soft in all Positions   8
       2. Consonants which may be Soft in Certain Positions only   10
       3. Consonants which are always Hard or always Soft   10
       4. Use of ь and о/ё after the Letters ж, ш, ц, ч, and щ   11

    3. Simplification of Groups of Consonants   13
       1. Assimilation of Sonority   13
       2. Assimilation of Palatalization   14
       3. Optional Simplifications   14

    B. VOWELS   15

    1. General Observations   15
    2. Stress   17
       1. General Characteristics   17
       2. Pronunciation of Unstressed Vowels   18
         (a) The vowels ы and y   19

(*b*) The vowels a and o after a hard consonant   19

(*c*) The vowels и, e, ё, and я (a) after a soft consonant   20

(*d*) The vowel e after a hard consonant   21

(*e*) Grammatical analogies   22

C. ALTERNATIONS   22

1. Consonantal Alternations   23

    1. Labials   23

    2. Dentals   23

    3. Velars   24

    4. Isolated Alternations   25

    5. Alternation of Consonant/Zero   25

    6. The Consonant *yod*   26

2. Vocalic Alternations   26

    1. Alternation é/ë (*é*/'*o*)   26

    2. Other Alternations   27

    3. Alternation of Vowel/Zero   28

II. DECLENSION AND WORD-FORMATION   29

I. DECLENSION   29

    1. The Cases   30

    2. Gender and Declension   31

    3. Singular and Plural   32

    4. Stress   33

II. WORD-FORMATION   33

III. NOUNS: DECLENSION   37

I. GENERAL CHARACTERISTICS   37

II. FIRST DECLENSION   38

    1. Example   38

    2. Observations   39

    3. Accusative Plural   40

    4. Mobile Vowel   41

Contents

    5. Stress   41
      (a) Fixed stress   41
      (b) Mobile stress   42

III. SECOND DECLENSION   44
 1. Masculine   44
    1. Example   44
    2. Observations   45
    3. Accusative Singular and Plural   45
    4. Mobile Vowel   45
    5. Stress   46
      (a) Fixed stress   46
      (b) Mobile stress   50
    6. Double Endings   51
      (a) Genitive singular   51
      (b) Locative singular   52
      (c) Nominative plural   53
      (d) Genitive plural   55
    7. Suppletive Plurals   56
      (a) Nouns of hard type in singular forming plurals of soft type   56
      (b) Plural in -ья   56
      (c) Plural of nouns in -ин   57
 2. Neuter   58
    1. Example   58
    2. Observations   59
    3. Mobile Vowel   60
    4. Stress   61
      (a) Fixed stress   61
      (b) Mobile stress   61
    5. Suppletive Plurals   62
      (a) Plural in -ья   62
      (b) Isolated Nouns   63
      (c) Nouns in -ёнок, -ята   63

IV. THIRD DECLENSION 64

1. Feminine 64
    1. Example 64
    2. Observations 65
    3. Mobile Vowel 65
    4. Stress 65
        (a) Fixed stress 65
        (b) Mobile stress 66

2. Masculine 67

3. Neuter 67

V. PLURALIA TANTUM 68

VI. INDECLINABLE NOUNS 69

IV. NOUNS: WORD-FORMATION 72

I. NON-SUFFIXAL DERIVATIVES 72

II. SUFFIXAL DERIVATIVES 72

1. Nouns denoting Persons 72
    1. Masculine 72
        (a) Nouns of agent, nouns of occupation, and attributive nouns 73
        (b) Nouns of origin 74
    2. Feminine 75

2. Abstract Nouns 77
    1. Nouns of Action 77
    2. Abstract Nouns Proper 78

3. Collective and Singulative Nouns 80
    1. Collectives 80
    2. Singulatives 80

4. Concrete Nouns 81

5. Diminutives and Augmentatives 83

    A. Diminutives 83
    1. First Degree 83

2. Second Degree 84
    (a) Suffixes of endearment 85
    (b) Pejorative suffixes 85
3. Third Degree 86
4. Emancipation of Diminutives 86

B. Augmentatives 87
6. Diminutives of Christian Names 87
    1. Suffixes of Endearment 88
        (a) First degree 88
        (b) Second degree 88
        (c) Other forms 89
    2. Pejorative Suffix 89

III. COMPOUND NOUNS 89
    1. Compounds with Connecting Vowel 90
        1. Compounds with Second Element of Verbal Origin 90
            (a) Non-suffixal compounds 90
            (b) Suffixal compounds 90
            (c) Compounds with an independent word as second element 91
        2. Compounds with Second Element of Substantival Origin 91
            (a) Non-suffixal compounds 91
            (b) Suffixal compounds 91
            (c) Compounds with an independent word as second element 92
    2. Other Types of Compounds 92
        1. Compounds with a Numeral as First Element 92
        2. Compounds with an Invariable First Element 92
            (a) With a prefix as first element 92
            (b) With a negative particle as first element 93
            (c) With a foreign word as first element 93
        3. Compounds formed by Abbreviation 93

V. ADJECTIVES   95

I. DECLENSION   95

1. General Characteristics   95

2. Normal Declension   96
   1. Example   96
   2. Observations   96
   3. Stress   97

3. Short Form   97
   1. General Observations   97
   2. The Force of the Short Form   98
   3. Mobile Vowel   99
   4. Stress   99

4. Adjectives of Mixed Declension   100
   1. Relative Adjectives in *yod*   100
   2. Possessive Adjectives in -ин and -ов   101

5. Surnames in -ов/-ев and -ин   102

6. Substantivized Adjectives   103

II. DEGREES OF COMPARISON   104

1. Comparative   104
   1. The Analytical Comparative   104
   2. The Suffixal Comparative   105
   3. Use of the Comparative   107

2. Superlative   108

III. WORD-FORMATION   109

A. SUFFIXAL DERIVATIVES   109

1. Adjectives with the Suffix -н-   110
   1. Denominative Adjectives   110
   2. Deverbal Adjectives   110
   3. Russification of Foreign Adjectives   111

2. Relative Adjectives   111
   1. Suffixes with General Value: -ск- and -ов-   111
   2. Suffixes with Special Value   112

3. Descriptive Adjectives   113
    1. Denominative Adjectives   113
    2. Deverbal Adjectives   115
      (*a*) Suffixes of participial origin   115
      (*b*) The suffix -к-   116

4. Possessive Adjectives   116
    1. Adjectives in -ов and -ин   116
    2. Surnames in -ов/-ев and -ин   117

5. Diminutive and Augmentative Adjectives   117
    1. Diminutives   117
    2. Augmentatives   118

B. COMPOUND ADJECTIVES   118

    1. Compound Adjectives with Connecting Vowel   118
      1. Compound Adjectives with Second Element of Verbal Origin   118
      2. Compound Adjectives with Second Element of Substantival or Adjectival Origin   119

    2. Other Types of Compound Adjectives   119
      1. Compound Adjectives with a Numeral as First Element   119
      2. Compound Adjectives with an Invariable First Element   120
        (*a*) With a preposition or a prefix as first element   120
        (*b*) With a negative particle as first element   120
        (*c*) With a foreign prefix as first element   121

VI. PRONOUNS   122

I. PERSONAL PRONOUNS   122

    1. Pronouns of the First and Second Persons and the Reflexive Pronoun   122
    2. The Pronoun of the Third Person   123

II. NON-PERSONAL PRONOUNS   125

    1. Classification   125
      1. Possessive Pronouns   125

2. Demonstrative Pronouns   127
3. Determinative Pronouns   127
4. Interrogative-Relative Pronouns   128
5. Negative Pronouns   129
6. Indefinite Pronouns   129

2. Declension   130
   1. First Declension   131
    (a) Hard type   131
    (b) Soft type   132
   2. Second Declension   133
    (a) Hard type   133
    (b) Soft type   134
   3. Pronouns with Abnormal Declension   135

VII. NUMERALS   136
I. CARDINALS   136
   1. Declension   137
    (a) General observations   137
    (b) The numerals два, три, четы́ре, and о́ба   138
    (c) Other numerals   139
   2. Use of the Cardinal Numerals   140

II. COLLECTIVES   143
   1. Declension   143
   2. Use of the Collectives   143

III. ORDINALS   145

VIII. ADVERBS   147
I. PRODUCTIVE TYPES   147
   1. Adverbs in -o/-e   147
   2. Adverbs in -и   148
   3. Adverbs formed from по-+Dative   149

II. UNPRODUCTIVE TYPES   149
   1. Fossilized Noun and Verb Forms   149

   1. Substantivized Adjective with Preposition   149

   2. Noun with Preposition   150

   3. Noun without Preposition   150

   4. Repetition of the same Noun in Different Cases   151

   5. Numerals   152

   6. The Gerund   152

   7. General Observations   153

 2. Primary Adverbs   153

   1. Adverbs of Time   153

   2. Adverbs of Place   154

   3. Adverbs of Manner   155

   4. Adverbs of Quantity   155

III. USE OF THE ADVERBS   155

IX. VALUES OF THE CASES   158

   1. General Observations   158

   2. Nominative   159

   3. Accusative   159

   4. Dative   159

   5. Instrumental   160

   6. Genitive   162

     (a) With verbs   162

     (b) With nouns   163

     (c) With adjectives   163

     (d) With numerals   164

   7. Locative   164

X. VERBS: FORMS   165

I. GENERAL OBSERVATIONS   165

II. PRESENT GROUP   167

   1. Present   167

     (a) Forms   167

     (b) Stress   168

   2. Present Participle Active   169

3. Present Participle Passive   170
4. Present Gerund   170
5. Imperative   171

III. INFINITIVE GROUP   172

1. Infinitive   173
2. Past Tense   173
   (*a*) Forms   173
   (*b*) Stress   175
3. Past Participle Active   176
4. Past Participle Passive   176
   (*a*) The suffix -нн-   176
   (*b*) The suffix -т-   177
5. Past Gerund   178
6. Compound Future   179

XI. VERBS: CLASSIFICATION   181

I. GENERAL OBSERVATIONS   181

II. FIRST CLASS: VERBS IN -e- WITH CONSONANTAL STEM   182

  A. INFINITIVE STEM WITHOUT SUFFIX   183

    1. Present and Infinitive Stems Identical in Structure   183
    2. Present and Infinitive Stems of Different Structure   184
    3. Stress   187

  B. INFINITIVE STEM WITH SUFFIX -a-   188

    1. Present and Infinitive Stems Identical in Structure   188
    2. Present and Infinitive Stems of Different Structure   188
    3. Stems whose Final Consonants differ through Alternation   189
    4. Stress   191

III. SECOND CLASS: VERBS IN -не-/-ну-   191

  A. VERBS WHICH RETAIN THE SUFFIX -ну- IN ALL FORMS OF THE INFINITIVE STEM   191

  B. VERBS WHICH MAY DROP THE SUFFIX -ну- IN CERTAIN FORMS OF THE INFINITIVE STEM   193

IV. THIRD CLASS: VERBS IN -e- WITH VOCALIC STEM 194

A. INFINITIVE STEM WITHOUT SUFFIX 195

1. Present and Infinitive Stems Identical in Structure 195
2. Present and Infinitive Stems of Different Structure 196
3. Stress 196

B. INFINITIVE STEM WITH SUFFIX 196

1. The Suffix -я- 196
2. The Suffix -ва́- 196
3. Verbs in -у-/-ова- 197

V. FOURTH CLASS: VERBS IN -и- 198

A. INFINITIVE STEM WITH SUFFIX -и- 198

1. Consonantal Stem 198
2. Vocalic Stem 200

B. INFINITIVE STEM WITH SUFFIX -e- 200

C. INFINITIVE STEM WITH SUFFIX -a- 201

1. Consonantal Stem 201
2. Vocalic Stem 202

VI. VERBS WHICH COMBINE FEATURES OF DIFFERENT CLASSES 202

1. The Two Stems belong to Different Classes 202
2. The Combination occurs within the Present Tense 203

VII. ISOLATED VERBS 204

XII. VERBS: ASPECTS 206

I. THE NOTION OF ASPECT 206

II. FORMATION OF ASPECTUAL PAIRS 210

III. IMPERFECTIVE/PERFECTIVE PAIRS 211

1. Simple Imperfective/Perfective with Prefix 211
2. Simple Imperfective/Perfective with Suffix 213

IV. PERFECTIVE/IMPERFECTIVE PAIRS 213

1. Perfective with Prefix/Imperfective with Suffix 213
1. The Suffix -á-/-я́- 215

    (*a*) Classes I and II   215
    (*b*) Class IV   216
  2. The Suffix -вá-   217
  3. The Suffix -ыва-/-ива-   218
    (*a*) Class III   218
    (*b*) Class IV   218
    (*c*) Class I   219
    (*d*) Class II   220
    (*e*) The alternation o/á in the root   220
  2. Simple Perfective/Imperfective with Suffix   220

V. SUPPLETIVE PAIRS   222
  1. Perfective: Determinate with Prefix/Imperfective: Indeterminate with Prefix   222
  2. Formation of Aspectual Pairs from Verbs with the Same Root   224
  3. Formation of Aspectual Pairs from Entirely Different Verbs   225

VI. VERBS WHICH DO NOT FORM ASPECTUAL PAIRS   225
  1. Imperfectives without Perfectives   225
    1. Simple Verbs   225
    2. Verbs with Prefix   226
  2. Perfectives without Imperfectives   227

VII. VERBS WHICH MAY BE EITHER PERFECTIVE OR IMPERFECTIVE   228
  1. Verbs in -овать   228
  2. Verbs in -ить   228

XIII. TENSE, MOOD, VOICE   229
I. TENSES   229
  1. The Present   229
    1. The Present Imperfective   229
    2. The Present Perfective   230
  2. The Past   231
    1. The Past Imperfective   231
    2. The Past Perfective   232

3. The Future Imperfective 232

4. Gerund and Participle 232
   1. Gerund 233
     (*a*) Present gerund 233
     (*b*) Past gerund 233

   2. Participle 234
     (*a*) Present participle 234
     (*b*) Past participle 234

II. MOODS 235
  1. Indicative 236

  2. Imperative 236
   1. Imperative Force Proper 236
   2. Inclusive Form 237
   3. Special Modalities of the Imperative 238
     (*a*) Arbitrarily imposed obligation 238
     (*b*) Arbitrary action (sudden and instantaneous) 238
     (*c*) Hypothetical action 239

  3. Infinitive 239

  4. Words and Particles with Modal Force 239
   1. The Particle бы 240
   2. The Word бывáло 241
   3. The Word бы́ло 241
   4. The Particle -ка 242
   5. The Words дай, давáй 243
   6. The Words пусть, пускáй 243
   7. The Particle да 243
   8. The Word как 244
   9. The Verb взять 244
   10. The Verbal Interjection 245

III. VOICES 245
  1. Transitive and Intransitive 245

2. Active and Passive   246
    1. The Passive expressed by a Reflexive Verb   246
    2. The Passive expressed by a Past Participle Passive 246

3. Reflexive and Non-reflexive Verbs   247

XIV. VERBS: WORD-FORMATION   251

VERBS FORMED FROM OTHER VERBS   251
1. Suffixion   251
    1. Frequentative Suffixes   251
    2. Suffixes of Istantaneous Action   252

2. Prefixion   253
    1. Productive Prefixes   253
    2. Unproductive Prefixes   262

II. DENOMINATIVE VERBS   262
1. Suffixion   262
    1. Productive Suffixes   263
    2. Unproductive Suffixes   265

2. Prefixion   265

XV. AUXILIARY WORDS   268

I. PREPOSITIONS   268
1. Primary Prepositions   268
    1. Accusative   268
    2. Genitive   270
    3. Dative   271
    4. Instrumental   271
    5. Locative   272
    6. Use of the Primary Prepositions   273

2. Secondary Prepositions   275
    1. Prepositions of Adverbial Origin   275
    2. Prepositions of Nominal Origin   276
    3. Prepositions of Verbal Origin   276
    4. Compound Prepositions   276

Contents

II. CONJUNCTIONS   277
    1. Primary Conjunctions   277
    2. Secondary Conjunctions   277
    3. Compound Conjunctions   277

III. PARTICLES   278

XVI. THE SENTENCE   281

I. THE SUBJECT   281
    1. Subject in First or Second Person   281
      1. Indicative   281
      2. Imperative   282
    2. Subject in Third Person   283

II. PREDICATE   284
    A. PERSONAL STATEMENT   284
    1. Verbal Predicate   284
    2. Non-Verbal Predicate   285
      1. Complement in the Nominative   285
      2. Complement in the Instrumental   287
      3. Other Forms of the Complement   289
      4. Omission of the Verbal Predicate 290

    B. IMPERSONAL STATEMENT   291
    1. Verbal Predicate   291
      1. Impersonal Verbs   291
      2. Personal Verbs used Impersonally 291
      3. Verbs in -ся   292
      4. Impersonal Use of the Past Participle Passive 292
      5. Negative Statement   292
      6. Infinitive   293

    2. Non-Verbal Predicate   293
      1. Adverbs in -o   293
      2. Nouns and other Words   294

III. SECONDARY ELEMENTS OF THE SENTENCE   294
    1. Direct Object   294
    2. Extensions of the Verb   295

IV. WORD-ORDER   296
    1. The Ordinary Sentence   296
        1. Subject and Predicate   297
        2. Secondary Elements of the Sentence   298
            (a) Words dependent upon nouns   298
            (b) Words dependent upon verbs   301
            (c) Negation   302
            (d) Enclave   302
    2. Questions   303

V. PUNCTUATION   304
    1. Comma   304
        1. General Observations   304
        2. Subordinate Clauses introduced by Conjunctions   305
        3. Subordinate Clauses introduced by Interrogative-Relative Pronouns and Adverbs   306
        4. Phrases introduced by Participles   307
        5. Phrases introduced by Gerunds   307
        6. Co-ordinate Clauses   307
    2. Dash   308
        1. General Observations   308
        2. Nominal Statements   309
        3. Statements with Verb omitted   309
        4. Co-ordination instead of Subordination   309
        5. Resumption of Enumerations   310
        6. Direct Speech   310

BIBLIOGRAPHY   313
INDEX   317

INTRODUCTION

MODERN literary Russian, which is described in this grammar, is a mixed language. Its composite character can be understood only in the light of its historical evolution.

The earliest surviving texts written in Russia do not go further back than the eleventh century. From that period, one spoken and two written languages are found in Russia.

The spoken language was the medium of communication of all the inhabitants of the then Russian lands. This *Old Russian*, or, more exactly, *East Slavonic*, which was the common ancestor of modern Russian, Ukrainian, and White Russian (or Byelorussian), already included slight dialectal variations; on the other hand, it was already at this remote period distinct from *West Slavonic* (comprising Polish, Czech, Slovak, Lusatian, and a few now extinct dialects of eastern Germany) and from *South Slavonic* (comprising Bulgarian, Serbo-Croat, and Slovene).

The *first written language* of Russia was, originally, nothing more than an ecclesiastical language, and it was not Russian. The Russians, who had received Christianity from Byzantium, did not translate the Scriptures into their own language. They received them from Bulgaria which, having been converted some hundred and thirty years before Russia, already possessed a Christian tradition. These books were written in Old Bulgarian, the dialect into which, about the year 863, St. Cyril and St. Methodius had translated from the Greek a number of ecclesiastical works, thereby inaugurating the literary tradition in the Slav world. Old Bulgarian became the ecclesiastical language of all the Slavs of the Greek rite and, at the beginning, also of some Slavs of the Latin rite. In this universal function Old Bulgarian is commonly known as *Old Church Slavonic*. Old Church Slavonic is thus only one of the several Slavonic languages, the first of them to have been recorded in writing.[1] In no case should it be confused with *Common Slavonic*, the hypothetical ancestor of all the Slavonic languages, which is presumed to have been spoken as late as in the first centuries of the Christian era and of which no text is known to exist.

Old Church Slavonic, imported into Russia as the ecclesiastical language, was adopted there as the language of literature, which in the Middle Ages was essentially religious. While it was a South Slavonic language and consequently different from the Old Russian which was the language of the country, it was none the less readily intelligible to the Russians. As a foreign book language employed by Russians, it underwent certain changes which became accentuated with time. This modified Old Church Slavonic is known as *Russian Church Slavonic*.

Almost simultaneously, the *Cyrillic* alphabet in which the Old Church Slavonic texts were written was employed by the Russians to record their own spoken language. Thus, the *second written language* of old Russia was none other than the native language of the country. Unlike Church Slavonic, which was reserved for the Church and for literature, written Russian was used only in legal and administrative texts of no literary pretensions: laws, licences, ordinances, reports, bills of sale and lease, &c. It was the *chancery language* (приказный язык). It was employed also for diplomatic and private correspondence.

This dualism in the written usage, opposing *literary Church Slavonic* to *non-literary Russian*, lasted, roughly, to the end of the seventeenth century. The distinction was not lost, despite the continued existence side by side of the two

---

[1] This language has been called by different names. The traditional Russian and German names (древне-церковно-славянский язык, *Altkirchenslavisch*) are identical with the English name used here. In French it is called *vieux slave* (i.e. Old Slavonic), which corresponds to the modern Russian term старославянский язык. The term *Old Bulgarian* (German *Altbulgarisch*) is also sometimes used.

written languages; and their inevitable interpenetration and the creation of certain mixed literary forms, as in the *Chronicles*, had only a limited extension.

Each of the two written languages has its own separate history. Religious writers strove, naturally, to maintain Church Slavonic, as a language that was both holy and dead, in its original state of purity. They succeeded, more or less as their counterparts in the West succeeded in preserving medieval Latin from excessive alteration. It is to be emphasized that Church Slavonic was never employed in Russia as a spoken language.

The Russian *chancery language*, employed solely for practical and utilitarian purposes, followed generally the evolution of the spoken language of which it was the written expression. With time local variations reflecting the dialectal divisions of Russian arose within this written language. In the sixteenth century the language of the Moscow chanceries began to win acceptance throughout Russia.

The intense Europeanization of Russia which began in the second half of the seventeenth century shook the foundations of this linguistic dualism. Neither Church Slavonic nor the chancery language was any longer capable of satisfying the requirements of the new Russian civilization. The resultant linguistic anarchy came to an end towards the middle of the eighteenth century, when the two fused into what was henceforth a single language. Modern Russian literature dates from this period. The credit for its creation belongs to Mikhail Lomonosov (1711–65).

The amalgam of Russian and Church Slavonic by no means constitutes a mechanical or arbitrary mixture. Each of the two elements performs a definite function of its own. As a general rule, in the fabric of the literary language, Russian forms the foundation, Church Slavonic the superstructure.

The *phonology* of modern literary Russian is entirely Russian and owes nothing to Church Slavonic. It was based originally on the Moscow pronunciation, which was particularly acceptable to the Russian population as a whole for the reason that, being current in a transitional zone between the dialects of the north and those of the south, it possessed certain features of both, without exhibiting the more extreme characteristics of either. Moscow pronunciation was standard until the end of the nineteenth century. From the beginning of the twentieth century, it encountered the competition of a developed type of pronunciation shorn of the most salient Moscovite features and closer to the written word. This process of neutralization has been appreciably accelerated since 1917, so that today the more marked Moscovitisms are already felt as provincialisms and avoided accordingly.

The adoption of the *Cyrillic alphabet* was accompanied by the adoption in its entirety of the Old Church Slavonic system of *orthography*. The Church Slavonic form of the printed letters was slightly modified at the beginning of the eighteenth century and brought somewhat closer to that of the Latin letters. With this reform the modern Russian alphabet was born. On the other hand, orthography, in its general principles, has remained Church Slavonic down to our own day, although it has undergone a few minor changes, notably in 1917.

The *morphology* of the language is essentially Russian and Moscovite in its origins. It has hardly changed since the beginning of the nineteenth century. The few modifications which have occurred have tended to eliminate certain irregular forms for the benefit of the general system. In the field of morphology Russian is moving steadily towards a greater systematization of forms. The only important innovation has been the uninterrupted development of the nominative plural masculine in -á. Church Slavonic had no influence on the inflection of nouns. It did affect the verb to some slight extent by supplying it with the system of participles and by influencing, through its alternations, the conjugation of the present tense.

The contribution of Church Slavonic was most decisive

in the field of *vocabulary*. As a general rule, Church Slavonic
words are used to express notions of an abstract, learned,
lofty, figurative or, in some cases, poetic character. In a
word, they form the superstructure of the Russian vocabulary. Russian scientific terminology is for the greater
part composed of Church Slavonic terms or terms formed
from Church Slavonic elements. The semantic distinction
between Russian and Church Slavonic words is particularly striking when it manifests itself in elements which are
parallel if not identical, as for example:

Russian:	передать письмо 'to forward a letter'
C.S.:	предать отечество 'to betray one's country'
Russian:	вылить воду 'to pour out water'
C.S.:	излить душу 'to pour out one's heart'
Russian:	вожак слепого 'the blind man's guide'
C.S.:	вождь народа 'the leader of the people'

It will be apparent what rich stylistic possibilities are
offered by such a duality of linguistic structure. The number of Church Slavonic words in Russian is considerable;
it becomes immense when one takes into account the fact
that Church Slavonic has provided literary Russian not
only with ready-made words but also with elements of
word-formation, notably, with a good number of suffixes
which make it readily possible to create words which are
in part, if not entirely, of Church Slavonic origin. In all,
the Church Slavonic elements of the literary vocabulary
are not inferior in number to the Russian; they are superior
to them in cultural value.

In the *syntax*, the primary combinations (rules governing
the use of the cases, the use of prepositions, predicative
constructions, &c.) are Russian. On the other hand, the
structure of the sentence, particularly the treatment of
subordinate clauses and, above all, participial constructions, are derived either from the Church Slavonic system
(which in turn was modelled largely on the Greek) or
from the corresponding constructions in the Western

languages: the influence of French and German on Russian was extremely strong in the eighteenth century and was still perceptible in the nineteenth.

The Church Slavonic elements in literary Russian, although completely assimilated by the language, none the less continue the phonetic traditions of Old Church Slavonic, which are distinct from those of Russian. It is for this reason that, in morphology and word-formation, certain alternations are limited exclusively to the Church Slavonic elements, for example the alternations т/щ, д/жд; on the other hand, the alternation е/ё does not affect words of Church Slavonic origin. The mechanism of alternations in Russian cannot be systematized or understood unless account is taken of these interventions of Church Slavonic. In this grammar they are accordingly pointed out in each case.

Church Slavonic in its pure state, eliminated from literature, continues to perform its original functions as a liturgical language in the Russian Orthodox Church.

What is the position of the *spoken language*, as distinct from literary Russian?

Literary Russian, formed by the fusion of Russian and Church Slavonic and influenced by French and German phraseology, became, as from the end of the eighteenth century, the *spoken language of cultivated society*. From this period, the evolution of the written language is inseparable from that of the language spoken by educated people. Any innovation in the latter now passes automatically into the literary language. The most important consequence of this has been the final break between the literary language, whether written or spoken, and the speech of the peasants in its various forms.

Peasant speech at the present time consists not so much of sharply defined dialects as of a mass of local speech types which differ little from one another. They may be divided roughly into a northern group, linguistically more conservative, and a southern group in which development has proceeded further. The principal difference between the two lies in the treatment of the vowels: in the south the quality of the vowel depends on the position of the stress within the word; in the north it is generally independent of the stress. The central, transitional types of speech, including that of Moscow, on which the literary pronunciation is based, tend towards the southern treatment of the vowels without exhibiting its extreme characteristics. In general, Russian peasant speech is much closer to the literary language than are the dialects of western languages. By the townspeople, and normally also by those who themselves employ the peasant forms of speech, these are now felt only as incorrect Russian. For this reason, the speech of the towns tends to exercise an ever stronger assimilatory influence upon that of the country-side.

Standard literary Russian is the normal spoken language of only a section of the town population, the lower strata of which generally use a mixed idiom which might be termed the *vulgar language of the towns*. The peasant speech which forms its original basis has been subjected to the strong influence of trade terms and slang. In addition, those who speak this mixed idiom have always tried to imitate as far as possible (often without success) the norms of the standard literary language. After the Revolution of 1917 this vulgar language for a short time invaded literary Russian itself. Little by little, however, literary Russian has returned to its old tradition, retaining, however, certain elements of slang in its vocabulary and phraseology.

This vulgar language and the speech of the peasants, to which I have felt it necessary to refer since they are a living element of Russian, do not, naturally, come within the scope of the present grammar. This work will, then, be exclusively a description of the modern literary language as it is written and spoken by those who today represent traditional Russian culture.

I

Orthography and Phonology

I. ORTHOGRAPHY

1. The Alphabet

Printed form		Cursive form		Transliteration	Value
А	а	*A*	*a*	a	North-country a in *lad*, or French a in *patte*
Б	б	*Б*	*б*	b	b
В	в	*В*	*b*	v	v
Г	г	*Г*	*v*	g	g in *get*
Д	д	*Д*	*g, д*	d	d
Е	е	*8*	*e*	e, je	e, ye in *yet*
Ё	ё	*ё*	*ё*	o, jo	o, yo (as Italian open o)
Ж	ж	*Ж*	*ж*	ž	z in *azure*
З	з	*З*	*з*	z	z in *zinc*
И	и	*U*	*u*	i	Italian i
Й	й	*Й*	*й*	j	y in *yet*
К	к	*К*	*к*	k	k
Л	л	*Л*	*л*	l	l

5493   B

Printed form		Cursive form		Trans-literation	Value
М	м	*М*	*м*	m	m
Н	н	*Н*	*н*	n	n
О	о	*О*	*о*	o	Italian open o
П	п	*П*	*п*	p	p
Р	р	*Р*	*р*	r	r (trilled)
С	с	*С*	*с*	s	s
Т	т	*Т*	*т*	t	t
У	у	*У*	*у*	u	oo in *tool*
Ф	ф	*Ф*	*ф*	f	f
Х	х	*Х*	*х*	ch	ch in *loch*
Ц	ц	*Ц*	*ц*	c	ts
Ч	ч	*Ч*	*ч*	č	ch in *church*
Ш	ш	*Ш*	*ш*	š	sh
Щ	щ	*Щ*	*щ*	šč	see pp. 6–7
Ъ	ъ	*Ъ*	*ъ*	—	see p. 4
Ы	ы	*Ы*	*ы*	y	see p. 16
Ь	ь	*Ь*	*ь*	'	see p. 4
Э	э	*Э*	*э*	e	e in *let*
Ю	ю	*Ю*	*ю*	u, ju	oo, yoo
Я	я	*Я*	*я*	a, ja	a, ya

Before the 1917 reform of the orthography, the Russian alphabet included four more letters: i (equivalent to и), ѣ (equivalent to е), ѳ (equivalent to ф), and ѵ (equivalent to и). The last letter occurred only in certain rare ecclesiastical terms of Greek origin and had been virtually eliminated before 1917.

The same reform abolished the use of the letter ъ after a final consonant.

The use of the letter ё, while remaining optional, is at the present time becoming more frequent, particularly since 1945. Thereby the ambiguity occasioned by the use of the letter e with the value of ё is tending to disappear.

2. Observations on Alphabet and Orthography

Russian orthography is an historical orthography, the principles of which were established in the Middle Ages, and does not normally take account of the changes which the sounds have undergone in the course of the centuries. In particular, it does not indicate the phonetic alternations due to the position of the sound in the word, whether it be the position of the vowel relative to the stress (see p. 18) or of the consonant relative to other consonants (see p. 13).

Although, however, certain words which are pronounced the same way, may, theoretically at least, be spelt differently (thus, *rot* may be either рот 'mouth', or род 'kind'), a written word may, as a general rule, be pronounced only one way, provided always that the position of the stress is known. Homographs such as exist in English (e.g. he will *read*, he has *read*) do not occur in Russian.

1. THE LETTERS е, ё, ю, я

The letters е, ё, ю, я possess a twofold phonetic value:

(*a*) After a consonant they are equivalent to *e, o, u, a* respectively and at the same time indicate that the preceding consonant is soft (for soft consonants, see pp. 7 ff.):

> нет (*n'et*) 'no'
> пёс (*p'os*) 'dog'
> нюх (*n'uch*) 'scent'
> взял (*vz'al*) 'he took'

(*b*) At the beginning of a word and after a vowel they are preceded in pronunciation by a *yod* (indicated phonetically by *j*) and are equivalent respectively to *je, jo, ju, ja*:

ест (*jest*) 'he eats'

заем (*zajem*) 'I shall eat after'

ёрш (*jorš*) 'ruff' (fish)

заём (*zajom*) 'loan'

юный (*junyj*) 'young'

мою (*moju*) 'I wash'

ямы (*jamy*) 'ditches'

маяк (*majak*) 'lighthouse'

2. THE LETTERS ь, ъ

The letter ь, known as the 'soft sign' (ерь or мягкий знак), has no *independent* phonetic value. It can stand only after a consonant:

(1) If the consonant is one which may be either hard or soft, and if it is not followed by a vowel, the letter ь indicates the softening (palatalization) of the consonant in question: конь (*kon'*) 'horse' (see pp. 8 ff.);

(2) If the consonant is one which may be only hard or only soft, the use of the letter ь at the end of the word is governed entirely by morphological considerations (for details, see p. 11);

(3) If the letter ь is followed by the letters и, е, ё, ю, я, it indicates both that the preceding consonant is soft (provided that it is capable of being softened) and that the vowels in question are pronounced respectively *ji, je, jo, ju, ja*:

статьи (*stat'ji*) 'articles'

пьесы (*p'jesy*) 'plays'

льёт (*l'jot*) 'he pours'

бью (*b'ju*) 'I beat'

судья (*sud'ja*) 'judge'

In foreign borrowings and in them alone the combination *jo* is indicated not by ё but by ьо or йо. Thus,

бульон (*buljon*) 'bouillon'   район (*rajon*) 'district'

The letter ъ, known as the 'hard sign' (ер or твёрдый знак), may stand only after a consonant before the letters е, ё, ю, я, and that only after a prefix or in foreign words. It then has exactly the same value as the letter ь:

съест (*s'jest*) 'he will eat'

адъютант (*ad'jutant*) 'aide-de-camp'

съёмки (*s'jomk'i*) 'surveys'
изъян (*iz'jan*) 'defect'

From what has been said it will be seen that the consonant *j* (*yod*) is represented by the letter й (after a vowel, whether at the end of a word or before a consonant), but may also be included in the letters е, ё, и, ю, я.

3. ORTHOGRAPHICAL INCOMPATIBILITIES

There are a few orthographical incompatibilities which in some cases correspond to the pronunciation and in others are at variance with it. These concern the use of the vowels after those consonants which are always hard or always soft (see pp. 10–13), namely:

After ж, ш, ч, and щ one does not write я, ю, ы, but а, у, и.

After ц one does not write я, ю, but а, у; one normally writes и, but ы is allowed in certain words and is obligatory in all the appropriate endings of the declension of nouns.

After ц one does not write ё but о.

After ж, ш, ч, and щ one may write either ё or о without the pronunciation being affected. After the same consonants and ц one does not write о in an unstressed syllable, but е. For details see pp. 11–13.

The orthographical incompatibilities apply only to Russian words and to Russified words in common use. They do not apply to the rendering into Russian letters of the unfamiliar sounds of foreign words.

II. PHONOLOGY

Unlike English, in which it is perfectly possible to study the consonant and vowel systems separately, in Russian the two are closely associated and together form a complex mechanism. For this reason, the two following sections will contain numerous cross-references.

A. *CONSONANTS*

The articulation of Russian consonants is comparable to that of French consonants: the position of the tongue is horizontal, whereas in the articulation of English consonants the tip of the tongue is in a vertical position. Moreover, Russian consonants are articulated further forward in the mouth than English. The difference is most perceptible in the case of the dentals *t* (т) and *d* (д).

Russian consonants are pronounced less energetically than English or French, more energetically than German.

Where the lips are employed they play a more important part than in English but a less important part than in French. Their role is comparable to that which they play in German.

No consonant in Russian is subject to aspiration, as is the case with *p*, *t*, and *k* in English.

A number of consonants call for special observations.

Russian *r* (р) is a trilled *r* produced by the vibration of the tip of the tongue. The trill is moderate: one or two beats of the tongue. The other variants of *r* found in English, French, German, &c., do not occur in Russian.

Russian hard *l* (л) is articulated with the tip of the tongue touching the limit of the upper front teeth and the gums, with the middle of the tongue lowered and the breath escaping from both sides of the buccal cavity. An *l* of the same type occurs in Polish (ł). Russian hard *l* resembles acoustically the English dark *l* in *full*, *able*, and the American *l*. Hard *l* should not be replaced by a sound similar to English *w*.

The sound *ch* (x) resembles the Scottish *ch* (*loch*) and the German *ch* (*lachen*) but is formed a little farther forward in the mouth.

The sound c (ц) does not represent *t-s*, but a single sound.

The sound represented by the letter щ may be pronounced either as a long, soft ш (š̌′), in which case it

resembles the English *sh* in *should*, or as the combination
шч (*šč*), also soft. Both pronunciations are correct. The
combinations сч and зч have the same phonetic value as
щ. The transcription *šč* adopted in this book is therefore
purely conventional.

*The Russian consonantal system is dominated by two major
divisions: that into voiced and voiceless, and that into hard and
soft.*

1. Voiced and Voiceless

Twelve consonants form six pairs of voiced and voiceless
consonants:

> Voiced: б, в, д, з, ж, г
> Voiceless: п, ф, т, с, ш, к

At the end of a word a voiced consonant is pronounced
like the corresponding voiceless consonant, as in German:

> хлеб (*chl'ep*) 'bread'. But dat. хлебу (*chl'ebu*)
> крив (*kr'if*) 'crooked'. But кривой (*kr'ivoj*)—same
>   meaning
> суд (*sut*) 'law-court'. But gen. суда (*suda*)
> глаз (*glas*) 'eye'. But pl. глаза (*glaza*)
> муж (*muš*) 'husband'. But dat. мужу (*mužu*)
> враг (*vrak*) 'enemy'. But pl. враги (*vrag'i*)

It follows that words spelt differently may be pronounced
the same, e.g. род 'kind' and рот 'mouth' are both pronounced *rot*.

The voiceless consonants х, ц, and ч have no corresponding voiced consonants; the voiced consonants л, р, м, н,
and *j* have no voiceless partners, although they may occasionally be pronounced voiceless at the end of a word.

2. Hard and Soft

*The most outstanding characteristic of the Russian consonantal
system is the division into hard and soft (palatalized) consonants.*

The articulation of the hard consonants is in general the same as in English (apart from the differences indicated on pp. 6, 10–11).

In the articulation of soft consonants the middle of the tongue rises towards the front or middle of the hard palate. The contact between the tongue and the roof of the mouth is greater in the case of soft consonants than in that of the corresponding hard consonants. The zone of production of the soft consonants is the middle region of the palate. The tip of the tongue is lowered and touches the lower front teeth.

In English the distinction between hard and soft consonants does not exist, while in French it exists only in the case of the consonant *n*: the members of each of the following pairs of words are distinguished from each other acoustically only by the quality of the *n*, which is hard in the first, soft in the second:

> colonne/Cologne   reine/règne   anneau/agneau

In Russian this division into hard· and soft extends to almost all the consonants. It is particularly clear-cut in the case of the dentals and *l*; it is less pronounced in the case of the labials and *r*. Nevertheless, for a Russian the difference between hard and soft consonants is essential; it may serve to distinguish two words whose phonetic forms are in other respects identical.

I. CONSONANTS WHICH MAY BE EITHER HARD OR SOFT IN ALL POSITIONS

The following consonants may be either hard or soft in all positions: б, п, в, ф, м, д, т, з, с, н, л, р (in transcription softening is indicated by an acute accent immediately after the particular consonant).

In Russian orthography softening is indicated in several ways.

(1) At the end of a word or before a consonant softening is indicated by the letter ь:

стан (*stan*) 'stature, camp'	стань (*stan′*) 'become, stand up'
брат (*brat*) 'brother'	брать (*brat′*) 'to take'
лес (*l′es*) 'forest'	лезь (*l′es′*) 'climb'
стал (*stal*) 'he has become'	сталь (*stal′*) 'steel'
кров (*krof*) 'roof'	кровь (*krof′*) 'blood'
жар (*žar*) 'heat'	жарь (*žar′*) 'cook!'
галки (*galk′i*) 'jackdaws'	гальки (*gal′k′i*) 'pebbles'

(2) Before the sounds *a, o, u, i*, softening is indicated by the letters я, ё, ю, и, while its absence is indicated by the letters а, о, у, ы:

рад (*rat*) 'pleased'	ряд (*r′at*) 'row'
нос (*nos*) 'nose'	нёс (*n′os*) 'he was carrying'
лук (*luk*) 'onion, bow'	люк (*l′uk*) 'hatch'
выть (*vyt′*) 'to howl'	вить (*v′it′*) 'to twist'
валы (*valy*) 'waves'	вали (*val′i*) 'throw down'

Thus, the four following words are distinguished from one another only by the softening of their consonants:

мат (*mat*) 'mate' (in chess)	мать (*mat′*) 'mother'
мять (*m′at′*) 'to crumple'	мят (*m′at*) 'crumpled'

In the case of the pair ы/и, the two vowels are not completely identical (*y/i*—see p. 16), but the relation between them in respect of the softening of consonants is exactly the same as that between а and я, о and ё, у and ю.

The incompatibility between и and a hard consonant is such that when they meet the и (*i*) is pronounced, and sometimes even written, as ы (*y*):

с иглой (*sygloj*) 'with the needle'
в Италии (*vytal′ii*) 'in Italy'
исход (*ischot*) 'way out', but безысходный (*b′ezyschodnyj*) 'from which there is no way out' (adj.)

(3) As a general rule the consonant preceding the sound *e* must be soft. Thus, нет (*n'et*) 'no'. A hard consonant may occur before *e* only in borrowings which retain their foreign pronunciation. In the latter case the letter э is sometimes, but not always, used. Thus, мэр (*mer*) 'mayor', отель (*otel'*) 'hotel'. It goes without saying that the consonant preceding an initial э remains hard. Thus:

с этим (*set'im*) 'with this'

в эру (*veru*) 'in the era'. Cf. Веру (*v'eru*), acc. case of the name Вера 'Vera'.

The junction of a soft consonant and a vowel takes place without any glide. *Care must be taken in particular not to pronounce the sound* yod, *however faintly, after the soft consonant.* Thus, дя is *d'a*, never *dja*, *dịa*, or *dia*.

2. CONSONANTS WHICH MAY BE SOFT IN CERTAIN POSITIONS ONLY

These are the velars г, к, and х.

They are always soft before *i* and *e* :

ноги (*nag'i*)	ноге (*nag'e*)
руки (*ruk'i*)	руке (*ruk'e*)
блохи (*blach'i*)	блохе (*blach'e*),

the gen. and dat. sing. respectively of нога 'foot', рука 'hand', блоха 'flea' (but see p. 97 for pronunciation of adjectives in -кий).

On the other hand, before *a*, *o*, and *u* and at the end of a word the gutturals are always hard. Final *g'* and the combinations *g'a*, *g'o*, *g'u*, &c., do not occur in Russian, at least in Russian words.

Orthographically, the result is that ы, я, ё, ю, and ь may not follow the velar consonants.

3. CONSONANTS WHICH ARE ALWAYS HARD OR ALWAYS SOFT

The following consonants are always hard: ж, ш, and ц (it is to be observed that the English equivalents of the first two, *s* in *measure* and *sh* in *should*, respectively, have a softer sound than the Russian consonants). They may precede the sounds *a, o, u, y, e,* but not *i*.

The following consonants are always soft: ч and щ. They may precede the sounds *a, o, u, i, e,* but not *y*.

By an anachronism of spelling, after these five consonants a and y are always written instead of я and ю (even after the soft consonants) and и and e instead of ы and э (even after the hard consonants). Thus чай 'tea', плачу 'I weep', сгущать 'to condense', ищу 'I seek'.

After the hard consonants of this group и is pronounced *y*. Thus: лыжи (*lyžy*) 'skis', шина (*šyna*) 'tyre', цирк (*cyrk*) 'circus'. In certain words modern usage admits the use of ы after ц: цыган 'gipsy'. Moreover, ы is regularly written after ц in the case-endings of nouns: птица 'bird', gen. sing. птицы.

4. USE OF ь AND O/ё AFTER THE LETTERS Ж, Ш, Ц, Ч, AND Щ

As the consonants ж, ш, ц, ч, and щ remain invariably hard or soft as the case may be, whatever be the letter which follows them, the use of the letter ь at the end of the word, as well as the choice between o and ё, is governed solely by morphological considerations.

(*a*) *Use of* ь

After ц, ь is never written.

After ж, ш, ч, and щ, ь is not written at the end of the word:

(1) in the nom. sing. masc.:

    нож 'knife'   плач 'weeping'
    ваш 'your'   плащ 'cloak, raincoat'

(2) in the gen. pl. fem. and neut.:

краж (from кража 'theft')   лож (from ложе 'couch')
крыш (from крыша 'roof')   плеч (from плечо 'shoulder')
тысяч (from тысяча 'thousand')
    рощ (from роща 'grove')
кладбищ (from кладбище 'cemetery')

After ж, ш, ч, and щ, ь is written at the end of the word:
(1) in the nom. sing. fem.:

ложь 'lie'	ночь 'night'
мышь 'mouse'	вещь 'thing'

(2) in the following verb forms:

infinitive: лечь 'to lie down'

2nd pers. sing. of the present tense: несёшь 'thou carriest'

imperative: режь 'cut', плачь 'weep'

(3) in the adverbs: настежь 'open', прочь 'away'.

(b) Use of о/ё

After ц, о is always written.
After щ, ё is always written.
After ж, ш, and ч it is normal to write о in the noun forms and ё in the verb-endings:

жолудь 'acorn'	стрижёт 'he clips'
кружок 'small circle'	сражённый 'struck down'
шорник 'saddler'	
большой 'big'	пришёл 'he came'
чопорный 'affected'	сушёный 'dried'
плечо 'shoulder'	течёт 'it flows'
мечóм 'with the sword'	точёный 'turned' (on the lathe)

Compare the noun поджог 'arson' with the verb поджёг 'he set fire to'.

Several nouns, for the most part belonging to the class in which the alternation е/о occurs (see p. 26), admit the letter ё: жёны 'wives', шёлк 'silk', пчёлы 'bees', &c.

* * * * * *

The following table illustrates both the orthographical rules and the pronunciation of the four groups of consonants which have been under discussion. In each case the group is represented by one consonant:

т	(*t*)	ть	(*t'*)	к	—	(*k*)	ж	жь	(*ž*)	ч	чь	(*č'*)
та	(*ta*)	тя	(*t'a*)	ка	—	(*ka*)	жа	—	(*ža*)	ча	—	(*č'a*)
то	(*to*)	тё	(*t'o*)	ко	—	(*ko*)	жо	жё	(*žo*)	чо	чё	(*č'o*)
ту	(*tu*)	тю	(*t'u*)	ку	—	(*ku*)	жу	—	(*žu*)	чу	—	(*č'u*)
ты	(*ty*)	ти	(*t'i*)	—	ки	(*k'i*)	—	жи	(*žy*)	—	чи	(*č'i*)
—	—	те	(*t'e*)	—	ке	(*k'e*)	—	же	(*že*)	—	че	(*č'e*)

3. Simplification of Groups of Consonants

I. ASSIMILATION OF SONORITY

Assimilation of sonority is in Russian as rigorous as it is systematic. It takes place whenever two consonants of different series form a group, whether within a word or between a preposition and the following noun:

(1) *Voiced before voiceless become voiceless:*

рубец (*rub'ec*) 'scar'	gen. sing. рубца (*rupca*)
плавить (*plav'it'*) 'to melt' (trans.)	плавкий (*plafk'ij*) 'fusible'
гвозди (*gvoz'd'i*) 'nails'	гвоздь (*gvos't'*) 'nail'
в бой (*vboj*) 'into battle'	в пруд (*fprut*) 'into the pond'

(2) *Voiceless before voiced become voiced:*

просит (*pros'it*) 'he asks'	просьбы (*proz'by*) 'requests'
так (*tak*) 'thus'	также (*tagžy*) 'also'
отклик (*otkl'ik*) 'echo'	отзыв (*odzyf*) 'expressed opinion'

The voiced consonants р, л, м, н, в, and *j* do not exert an assimilating action on a preceding voiceless: твой (*tvoj*) 'thy', &c.

Assimilation of sonority is reflected in spelling only in one case. The prefixes вз- (воз-), из-, раз-, низ- are written with an -c- if they precede a voiceless consonant. Thus, избить 'to beat', but испечь 'to bake'. It is to be observed that this assimilation was not indicated before c in the old orthography. Thus, восстать 'to revolt' (new orthography), as against возстать (old orthography).

2. ASSIMILATION OF PALATALIZATION

Assimilation of palatalization is much less regular than that of sonority.

Hard consonants never assimilate a preceding soft. Thus, нянька (*n'an'kə*) 'nursemaid'.

On the other hand, there is a tendency for a hard consonant to be softened by a succeeding soft. This assimilation is not obligatory except in the groups ст, зд, нт, нд, нч, and нщ. Thus:

стих (*s't'ich*) 'a line of verse'
гвоздик (*gvoz'd'ik*) 'a small nail'
зонтик (*zon't'ik*) 'umbrella'
Индия (*in'd'ijə*) 'India'
кончить (*kon'č'it'*) 'to end'
банщик (*ban'šč'ik*) 'bath-house attendant'

In all other groups of consonants the assimilation is either optional (ловкий 'dexterous': *lof'k'ij* or *lofk'ij*) or absent (мелкий 'small, shallow': *m'elk'ij*).

3. OPTIONAL SIMPLIFICATIONS

All the remaining simplifications, which until recently were obligatory, are now only optional: pronunciation in accordance with the spelling, although less usual, is now accepted as correct. This applies to the following cases:

(1) Groups of three consonants: известный 'well-known' (*izv'esnyj* and *izv'estnyj*), солнце 'sun' (*soncə* and *solncə*);
(2) The pronoun and conjunction что 'what, that' (*što* and *čto*);

(3) The group чн in certain words: конечно 'of course' (*kan'ešnə* and *kan'ečnə*);
(4) The groups гд and кт: когда 'when': *kaɣda* (with voiced *ch*), *kagda* and *kada*; никто 'nobody' (*n'ichto* and *n'ikto*).

B. *VOWELS*

1. General Observations

Russian vowel articulation is most closely related to the German and has some affinity with the French, although less distinct than the latter. On the other hand, it differs considerably from English vowel articulation. Russian does not possess two of the typical features of English:

(1) the vowels of 'intermediate' type, such as *æ* in *cat* (between *e* and *a*) and *ɔ* in *hot* (between *o* and *a*);
(2) the tendency to articulate the vowels from the middle region of the mouth (except in the case of the sound *ə* in the production of unstressed vowels, see p. 20).

No distinction according to quantity occurs in Russian: vowels are not divided into long and short. Vowels bearing the stress are of medium length—shorter than long vowels in English, French, or German, longer than the short vowels in these languages. The stressed vowel in Russian, while lengthened, never tends to become a diphthong as is the case in English.

Vowels bearing the stress (see p. 17) are always a little longer than unstressed vowels. Quantity, however, plays no grammatical or semantic role. It is impossible to imagine two Russian words differing from each other only in the quantity of their vowel as do, for example, Fr. *mettre* and *maître*, Ger. *Kamm* and *kam*, &c.

Russian attributes no grammatical function to the distinction between open and close vowels, any more than it does to that between long and short. Nevertheless, the two variants, open and close, exist in all the vowels, although in differing degrees.

The distinction is greatest in the case of the vowel *e*, to such an extent that it is possible to speak, physiologically, of open *e* and close *e* in Russian.

The vowel *e* is close (more so than the English *e* in *get*) before a soft consonant: имели (*im'el'i*) 'they had', есть (*jes't'*) 'to eat', эти (*et'i*) 'these'.

It is open (more so than *e* in *get*), in all other positions, namely:

(1) before a hard consonant: имел (*im'el*) 'he had', ест (*jest*) 'he eats', это (*etə*) 'this, that';

(2) at the end of the word: нигде (*n'igd'e*) 'nowhere', уже (*uže*) 'already'.

There cannot, therefore, be any two Russian words differing only in the degree of openness of their *e*, as there may be in French: *mes* (close *e*) and *mais* (open *e*).

The difference between the open and close variants is much less appreciable with the other vowels than it is with *e*. It is, however, to be observed that it is greater for the vowels of the back series (*a*, *o*, *u*); for *i* and *y* it is negligible. All these vowels are rather more close if they are followed by a soft consonant; they are still more close if they are also preceded by a soft consonant. Thus, the vowel *a* is progressively more close in the following three words: мат (*mat*), мать (*mat'*), мять (*m'at'*).

Russian *a* is a medium *a*; Russian *o*, *u*, and *i* are open vowels.

The vowel *y* (represented by the letter ы) is pronounced with the middle part of the tongue raised into a position intermediate between that for *i* and that for *u*. Unlike the vowel *u*, *y* involves no labialization. It is a sound of the same type as the English short *i*, which, however, is formed farther forward in the mouth than the Russian *y*. The pronunciation of Russian сын (*syn*) 'son' is not very far from that of the English *sin*. The sound of the Russian ы

may be produced by putting the tongue into the position
for *u* (у) and the lips into that for *i* (и).

2. Stress

I. GENERAL CHARACTERISTICS

The Russian vowel system is dominated by the stress accent.

*Every word in Russian has an accented syllable which is more
forcibly articulated than the other syllables.* This energetic articulation is accompanied by *two secondary phenomena: raising of
the pitch and lengthening of the stressed syllable.* In this grammar.
the stress will be indicated by an acute accent over the
stressed vowel.

The stress in Russian is free: it may fáll on any syllable
of the word, as it may in English. Secondary stresses, common in English and German, do not occur in Russian.
However long a Russian word, it can have only one stress:
присоединя́ющиеся 'those who attach themselves'.

The stress alone suffices to distinguish different words
the phonetic form of which is in other respects identical:

мука́ 'flour'	му́ка 'torment'
атла́с 'satin'	а́тлас 'atlas'
жила́ 'she lived'	жи́ла 'vein'
по́лка 'shelf'	полка́ 'of the regiment'
ледни́к 'glacier'	ле́дник 'ice-house'
вы́купать 'to bathe'	выкупа́ть 'to redeem'
во вре́мя 'during'	во́ время 'in time'

The Russian stress is mobile, that is, it may fall on
different syllables of the same word in the course of inflection. Sometimes different forms of the same word, possessing identical endings, are distinguished from each other
only by the stress:

стены́ (gen. sing.) / сте́ны (nom. pl.) of стена́ 'wall'
головы́ (gen. sing.) / го́ловы (nom. pl.) of голова́
    'head'

óстрова (gen. sing.) / островá (nom. pl.) of óстров 'island'

нóсите 'you carry' / носи́те 'carry!'

To perform adequately its manifold functions, the Russian stress must be clearly heard; and in fact it is appreciably more distinct than in languages in which the stress is fixed and in which, consequently, it has no semantic value, as in French (on the last syllable), Czech (on the first), or Polish (on the penultimate).

Some analogies to this function of the Russian stress can be found in English, in which in some cases the stress alone serves to distinguish the verb from the noun or from the adjective, as in *presént*/*présent*, *incréase*/*íncrease*.

Monosyllabic prepositions and the negative particles не and ни have no stress of their own. They are attached to the following word in such a way that the combination *preposition or negative particle + noun* or *negative particle + verb* carries only one stress. This stress, in the great majority of cases, falls on the noun or the verb:

от руки́ (*atruk'i*) 'from the hand' (gen. sing.)

не знáл (*n'iznál*) 'he did not know'

In some cases, however, it falls on the preposition or the negative particle: the noun or the verb is then unstressed:

нá руки (*náruk'i*) 'onto the hands' (acc. pl.)

нé дал (*n'édəl*) 'he did not give'

2. PRONUNCIATION OF UNSTRESSED VOWELS

As has been seen, Russian vowels may occur in two forms: *stressed or strong* and *unstressed or weak*.

In comparison with the stressed vowels, the unstressed are reduced vowels. This reduction is accompanied, to a varying extent according to the particular vowel, by a change of quality resulting from a shift of articulation towards the middle of the buccal cavity.

The unstressed vowels of a word are not all reduced to

the same extent: the pretonic vowel (that which immediately precedes the accented syllable) is stronger than the
other unstressed vowels. In this respect Russian differs
notably from English, in which the pretonic vowel is the
weakest in the word.

Russian spelling, which does not indicate the stress or
the effects of the stress, gives no indication of the pronunciation of the unstressed vowels.

(a) *The vowels* ы *and* у

The postpalatal vowels of the high series (*y*, *u*) when unstressed undergo no notable change of quality, apart from
reduction and a certain increased openness. Accordingly,
unstressed ы and у are throughout pronounced *y* and
u respectively (though reduced and more open) in the
words

> рýку (*rúku*) 'hand' (acc. sing.)
> дымы́ (*dýmy*) 'columns of smoke'
> сундýк (*sundúk*) 'trunk'
> вырыва́ть (*vyryvát'*) 'to pull out'

The same is true of the third vowel of the high series,
и (*i*) which, while undergoing reduction and becoming
more open, continues to be an *i*. It will be considered along
with other vowels which are pronounced *i* when unstressed
(see p. 20).

(b) *The vowels* a *and* o *after a hard consonant*

After a hard consonant the vowels a and o are phonetically distinct from each other only when they bear the stress:

> рад (*rat*) 'pleased'   род (*rot*) 'kind'

Whenever they occur in an unstressed syllable, a *and* o *represent
the same sound.*

In the pretonic syllable *o* becomes *a*, while *a* is un-
changed:

> во́ды (*vódy*) 'the waters'   вода́ (*vadá*) 'water'
> сад (*sat*) 'garden'   сады́ (*sadý*) 'the gardens'

In all other unstressed syllables (preceding the pretonic
syllable or following the stressed syllable) *a* and *o* are both
reduced to a neutral vowel of medium character in respect
both of the elevation of the tongue and of its situation on
the horizontal axis of the Russian vowel system (see p. 21).
In this book this vowel will, in accordance with common
practice, be indicated by the symbol *ə* (*e* reversed). It may
be compared to the similarly unstressed vowels in the
English words *aloud* (*əláud*), *radius* (*réidiəs*), and in the German *Gabe* (*gábə*).

For example:

> мáло (*málə*) 'little' / малодýшно (*məladúšnə*) 'pusillanimously'
>
> гóлос (*góləs*) 'voice' / голосá (*gəlasá*) 'voices' / голосовáть (*gələsavát'*) 'to vote'
>
> э́та (*étə*) 'this' (fem.) / э́то (*étə*) 'this' (neut.) / э́тот (*étət*) 'this' (masc.)

The vowel *ə* cannot occur at the beginning of a word;
its place is taken by an unaccented *a*:

óстров (*óstrəf*) 'island'	островá (*astravá*) 'islands'
Áфрика (*áfrikə*) 'Africa'	Африкáнский (*afrikánsk'ij*) 'African'

Care must be taken not to pronounce the sound *ə* instead
of *a* in the pretonic syllable. This mistake is often made by
English people, precisely because in English the pretonic
syllable is the weakest syllable in the word.

(c) *The vowels* и, е, ё, *and* я (a) *after a soft consonant*

The vowels и, е, ё, and я (a) when unstressed and preceded by soft consonants are all pronounced as an open *i*
the articulation of which, as compared with that of the
stressed *i*, shifts slightly in the direction of *e*. This takes
place in all the unstressed positions; in other words, there

is no noticeable difference between the pretonic and the other unstressed syllables:

извини́тельный (*izv'in'it'il'nyj*) 'pardonable'

пи́лит (*p'íl'it*) 'he is sawing' / перепили́ть (*p'ir'ip'il'it'*) 'to saw through'

ле́бедь (*l'éb'it'*) 'a swan' / лебеди́ный (*l'ib'id'ínyj*) 'of swans' (adj.)

ве́чер (*v'éč'ir*) 'evening' / вечера́ (*v'ič'irá*) 'evenings' / вече́рний (*v'ič'érn'ij*) 'of evening' (adj.)

вёл (*v'ol*) 'he led' / вели́ (*v'il'í*) 'they led' / вы́вели (*výv'il'i*) 'they led out'

грязь (*gr'as'*) 'mud' / в грязи́ (*vgr'iz'í*) 'in the mud' / грязево́й (*gr'iz'ivój*) 'mud' (adj.).

часть (*č'as't'*) 'part' / у́часть (*úč'is't'*) 'fate' / части́чно (*č'is't'íč'nə*) 'partly'

(d) *The vowel* e *after a hard consonant*

The vowel e after the hard consonants ж, ш, and ц is, naturally, pronounced not *i* (see above), but *y*:

же́нщина (*žén'šč'inə*) 'woman' / жена́ (*žyná*) 'wife'

лише́нье (*l'išén'jə*) 'privation' / лишена́ (*l'išyná*) 'deprived'

цел (*cel*) 'whole' (masc.) / цела́ (*cylá*) 'whole' (fem.) / целико́м (*cyl'ikóm*) 'wholly'

*　*　*　*　*　*　*

The two systems of Russian vowels may be represented schematically as follows:

Stressed vowels				*Unstressed vowels*		
i	y	u		i	y	u
e		o			ə	
	a				a	

The modifications undergone by the vowels when in unstressed positions are summed up in the following table:

Stressed	Pretonic	Unstressed other than pretonic
y		*y*
u		*u*
a, o after a hard consonant	*a*	*ə*
i, e, o, a after a soft consonant		*i*
e after *ž, š, č*		*y*

(*e*) *Grammatical analogies*

Grammatical analogy imposes certain modifications on the rigidity of the system outlined above. For example, as the soft declension of nouns is today modelled on the hard declension (see p. 31), the vowel *ə*, not *i*, occurs in the case-endings of the soft declension in the majority of cases where, in the corresponding endings of the hard declension, the same vowel *ə* occurs. Thus:

Nom. sing. пу́ля (*púl'ə*) 'bullet'; dat. pl. пу́лям (*púl'əm*); loc. pl. пу́лях (*púl'əch*); instr. pl. пу́лями (*púl'əm'i*). Nom. sing. пла́тье (*plát'jə*) 'dress'; gen. sing. пла́тья (*plát'jə*); nom. pl. пла́тья (*plát'jə*), &c.

The same sound *ə* occurs in place of the expected *i* in certain other grammatical forms. This pronunciation will be indicated in each case in the sections dealing with morphology.

C. *ALTERNATIONS*

By the term 'alternation' is meant the faculty possessed by the consonants and the vowels of a root or suffix of appearing sometimes in one form, sometimes in another.

1. Consonantal Alternations

The most frequent consonantal alternations are those arising from the divisions of consonants into *voiced* and *voiceless* (see p. 7) and *hard* and *soft* (see p. 8).

Apart from these, which are still living and which are governed automatically by the phonetic context, there are other alternations which occur in certain forms of conjugation and in word-formation. These latter are in general survivals from the period of Common Slavonic. They arise usually from the contact of a consonant with a prepalatal vowel or with an original *yod* (*j*). Some of these alternations may be extended by analogy to modern words and may thereby exhibit a certain vitality. Some alternations are limited to words of Church Slavonic origin.

All the consonants except р, л, and *j* are subject to alternation.

I. LABIALS

Labials alternate with labials + *l'*, viz:

б/бл, п/пл, в/вл, ф/фл, м/мл

This alternation is found most frequently in conjugation (see pp. 190–1, 199) but occurs also in word-formation:

> любить 'to love' / люблю 'I love'
> земно́й 'terrestrial' / земля́ 'the earth'

In the verb it has a certain vitality:

> офо́рмить 'to regularize'
> офо́рмлю 'I shall regularize'

2. DENTALS

Dentals alternate with ж, ш, ч, щ. These alternations are fairly frequent in the conjugation and in word-formation:

д/ж   ходи́ть 'to walk' / хожу́ 'I walk'
       медве́дь 'bear' / медве́жий 'of a bear' (**adj.**)

д/жд победи́ть / побежда́ть 'to conquer'
жа́дный / жа́жда 'thirst'
> *This alternation occurs only in words of Church Slavonic origin*

т/ч пати́ть 'to pay' / плачу́ 'I pay'
добы́ть 'to acquire / добы́ча 'booty'

This alternation has a certain vitality:
намагни́тить/намагни́чивать 'to magnetize'

т/щ трепета́ть 'to tremble' / трепещу́ 'I tremble'
пита́ть 'to feed' / пи́ща 'food'
> *This alternation occurs only in words of Church Slavonic origin.*

з/ж ре́зать 'to cut' / ре́жу 'I cut'
францу́з 'a Frenchman' / францу́женка 'a French-woman'

с/ш пляса́ть 'to dance' / пляшу́ 'I dance'
весна́ 'spring' / ве́шний 'of spring' (adj.)

ст/щ пусти́ть 'to allow' / пущу́ 'I shall allow'
густо́й 'thick' / гу́ще 'thicker'

ц/ч лицо́ 'face, person' / ли́чный 'personal'
> *This alternation does not occur in the verb.* It still operates in word-formation, particularly in the type переселе́нец 'settler' / переселе́нческий 'of settlers' (adj.).

3. VELARS

Velars alternate with ж, ш, ч, щ *and* ц. This series of alternations is unproductive in the verb but is still operative in word-formation:

г/ж бегу́ 'I run' / бежи́шь 'thou runnest'
стро́гий 'strict' / стро́же 'stricter'
флаг 'flag' / флажо́к 'pennon'

к/ч   пеку́ 'I bake' / печёшь 'thou bakest'
      каза́к 'Cossack' / каза́чий 'Cossack's' (adj.)
      фрак 'tail-coat' / фра́чный 'appertaining to a tail-coat' (adj.)

х/ш   паха́ть 'to plough' / пашу́ 'I plough'
      дух 'spirit' / душа́ 'soul'

ск/щ   иска́ть 'to seek' / ищу́ 'I seek'

к/ц   *This alternation does not occur in verbs. It is limited almost exclusively to adjectives formed from nouns:*
      дура́к 'fool' / дура́цкий 'idiotic'

4. ISOLATED ALTERNATIONS

In addition to the above alternations, occurring in groups of words which are often of considerable size, there are some which are limited to a few words:

т/с   плету́ 'I plait' / плести́ 'to plait' (see p. 173)

д/с   веду́ 'I lead' / вести́ 'to lead' (see p. 173)

б/с   гребу́ 'I row' / грести́ 'to row' (see p. 173)

г/з   друг 'friend' / друзья́ 'friends'
      княги́ня 'princess' / князь 'prince'

ск/ст пуска́ть/пусти́ть 'to let'
      блеск 'brilliance' / блесте́ть 'to shine'

н/ш   only in diminutives: ко́рень 'root' /корешо́к (dim.)
      бара́н 'ram, sheep' / бара́шек (dim.).

5. ALTERNATION OF CONSONANT/ZERO

л disappears in the past tense masculine:
      нёс 'he carried' / несла́ 'she carried' (see p. 174)

д, т disappear in the past tense:
      веду́ 'I lead' / вёл 'I led'
      мету́ 'I sweep' / мёл 'I swept' (see p. 174)

б, п, д, т, г, к may elide, in certain roots, before the suffix -н-:
      ги́бнуть 'to perish' / сги́нуть 'to disappear'
      тро́гать/тро́нуть 'to touch'

6. THE CONSONANT *yod*

In certain positions the consonant *yod* (*j*) may be weakened or may even disappear completely.

Postvocalic *j* disappears before *i*: моя (*majá*) 'my' (fem.), but мой (*mai*) 'my' (pl.); брею (*breju*) 'I shave', but бреет (*bréit*) 'he shaves'; пояс (*póis*) 'belt'.

It tends to disappear before *i* (originating from unstressed vowels) at the beginning of a word: язык (*jizýk* and *izýk*).

It is weakened to the point of becoming almost imperceptible in unstressed final syllables after ы, и: новый, ранний.

It maintains itself in all other positions, although it is weakened when it occurs in an unstressed syllable in an intervocalic or final postvocalic position, as in делаю, делая, делай.

2. Vocalic Alternations

1. ALTERNATION é/ë (*é/'o*)

This alternation, which occurs only under the stress (since both e and ë when unstressed are pronounced *i*—see p. 20) takes place in two sets of conditions:

(1) é before soft consonant becomes ë before hard consonant:

плеть (*pl'et'*) 'whip' / плётка (*pl'ótkə*)—same meaning
весéлье (*v'is'él'jə*) 'gaiety' / весёлый (*v'is'ólyj*) 'gay'
чернь (*č'er'n'*) 'rabble' / чёрный (*č'órnyj*) 'black'
ель (*jel'*) 'fir-tree' / ёлка (*jólkə*)—same meaning

This alternation occurs, generally speaking, only in word-formation. It is extremely rare in inflexion:

чéрти (*č'ért'i*) 'devils' / чорт (*č'ort*) 'devil'
жечь (*žeč'*) 'to burn' / жёг (*žok*) 'he burned'

For the orthographical convention on the representation of the *o* sound after ж, ш, ч, щ, see pp. 12-13.

(2) At the end of a word é alternates with ë only in certain cases of the declension of nouns and adjectives:

все (*fs'e*) 'all' (pl.) / всё (*fs'o*) 'all' (neut. sing.)

копьé (*kap'jé*) loc. sing. of копьё (*kap'jó*) 'lance'

The alternation é/ë before a consonant which is hard in both cases is extremely rare:

жéнский (*žénsk'ij*) 'feminine' / жёны (*žóny*) 'wives'

It need hardly be said that, alternation notwithstanding, é *may* precede a hard consonant. This occurs in particular:

(*a*) in foreign words:

> газéта (*gaz'é'tə*) 'newspaper'
> лéнта (*l'éntə*) 'ribbon'

(*b*) in Church Slavonic or assimilated words:

> крест (*kr'est*) 'cross'   предмéт (*pr'idm'ét*) 'object'

(*c*) in words in which the e replaces a previous ѣ:

> нет (*n'et*) 'not'   лес (*l'es*) 'forest'

(*d*) in a few words in which the hard consonant following e was once soft:

> серп (*s'erp*) 'sickle'   купéц (*kup'éc*) 'merchant'

Conversely, ë may precede a soft consonant. In practically all such cases what is involved is palatalization occasioned by inflection:

> берёза (*b'ir'ózə*) 'birch' / берёзе (*b'ir'óz'i*) dat.-loc. sing.
> несёт (*n'is'ót*) 'he carries' / несёте (*n'is'ót'i*) 'you carry'

2. OTHER ALTERNATIONS

Vowel alternations in Russian, apart from those due to the stress and from the mutation e/ë, are not numerous, and constitute survivals from the period of Common Slavonic:

o/á   *This alternation occurs only in verbs in* -ыва- *and those from which they respectively derive*: сбрóсить / сбрáсывать 'to throw off' (see p. 220)

и/е	брить 'to shave' / брéю 'I shave' (see p. 196)
ы/о	мыть 'to wash' / мóю 'I wash' (see p. 196)
и/о	бить 'to beat' / бой 'battle'
	собирáть 'to gather' / сбор 'gathering'
у/о	глухóй 'deaf' / глóхнуть 'to become deaf'
у/ы, и	дух 'spirit' / дыхáние 'breath'
	губить 'to ruin' / гибнуть 'to perish'
е/о	петь 'to sing' / пой 'sing!'
	звенéть 'to ring' / звон 'ringing'
	ведёт/вóдит 'he leads'
е/я, а	лечь 'to lie down' / ля́гу 'I shall lie down'
	сесть 'to sit' / ся́ду 'I shall sit' / осáда 'siege'

3. ALTERNATION OF VOWEL/ZERO

The alternations o/*zero*, e/*zero* present the phenomenon of the *mobile vowel*. They are frequent in the declension of nouns (see p. 37) and in word-formation:

лóжный 'false' / лжи́вый 'lying'
веснá 'spring' / весéнний 'of spring' (adj.)

The alternations и/*zero*, ы/*zero* are limited almost entirely to the word-formation and conjugation of verbs:

начинáю 'I begin' / начнý 'I shall begin'
посылáть/послáть 'to send'
бить 'to beat' / бью 'I beat'
оди́н 'alone' (masc.) / однá 'alone' (fem.)

II

Declension and Word-Formation

MORPHOLOGY includes both inflexion (creation of syntactical categories) and word-formation (creation of lexical categories).

The principles of the two processes are distinct. Nevertheless, at every step one may observe the effects exercised by word-formation upon inflexion; in the verbal system the result may fairly be termed a morphological amalgam.

Because of this interpenetration of the two processes, it is desirable not to treat the whole question of word-formation in a separate chapter, but to break it up in such a way as to combine the appropriate section with the description of the inflection of the different parts of speech.

I. DECLENSION

Russian distinguishes five types of declension:

(1) Nouns.
(2) Adjectives.
(3) Pronouns other than personal pronouns.
(4) Personal pronouns.
(5) Numerals.

The difference between the declension of adjectives and that of pronouns other than personal pronouns is very slight indeed; the two declensions are built upon the same principles. The declension of numerals is distinguished by the absence of unity.

I. THE CASES

There are two numbers, *singular* and *plural*. Certain nouns have only the plural form; these are termed *pluralia tantum*. On the other hand, there are no singular nouns from which a plural may not be formed, even though this plural may, in many cases, rarely, if ever, occur.

In each number there are six cases: *nominative, accusative, genitive, dative, locative,* and *instrumental*. Their general value may be illustrated by the following table, which gives the singular of the word го́род 'town':

Nominative:	го́род покупа́ет 'the town buys'
Accusative:	я ви́жу го́род 'I see the town'
Genitive:	у́лицы го́рода 'the streets of the town'
Dative:	дать го́роду 'to give to the town'
Locative:	в го́роде 'in the town'
Instrumental:	ку́пленный го́родом 'bought by the town'

There is no vocative in Russian, except Бо́же (from Бог 'God') and Го́споди (from Госпо́дь 'Lord'), both borrowed from Church Slavonic.

For details of the values of the cases see Chapter IX.

The mechanism of declension consists of the addition of a case-ending beginning with a vowel to a stem which normally is invariable and ends in a consonant: nom. sing. э́т-а но́в-ая доро́г-а 'this new road', gen. sing. э́т-ой но́в-ой доро́г-и, &c. Very rarely, and only in the instrumental of the Third Declension of nouns, the ending may begin with a consonant (*j* or *m*): ко́сть-ю (*kós't'-ju*) 'by the bone', лю́дь-ми́ (*l'ud'-m'í*) 'by the people'.

Certain classes of nouns in certain cases have no case-endings at all and are reduced to the stem; the word is then said to have a *zero*-ending. The mark of the particular case is then the absence of a case-ending. Thus, in the example quoted, the nom. sing. го́род has a zero-ending. Similarly, the gen. pl. of доро́га is доро́г.

In all nouns, adjectives, and pronouns, the accusative, except in the feminine singular, has no form special to itself. In the neut. sing. it is always identical with the nominative (except for personal pronouns—see next paragraph). In the masculine singular and in the plural of all declensions it is identical with the nominative if it denotes something inanimate (object or abstract notion) and with the genitive if it denotes something animate (person or animal).

In the personal pronouns the accusative is always identical with the genitive, in all three genders and both numbers.

Nouns, adjectives, and pronouns, in almost all the declensions, may be grouped in two series, *hard type* and *soft type,* according to the character of the final consonant of the stem. In both types the endings are normally phonetically identical but orthographically distinct (it has already been seen that the softening of the consonant is indicated in Russian by the following vowel).

In the spelling of case-endings account must be taken of the orthographical incompatibilities, particularly in the use of the vowels after г, к, х, ж, ш, ч, щ.

2. GENDER AND DECLENSION

There are three genders in Russian: masculine, feminine, and neuter.

In English, gender is expressed morphologically only in the personal, relative, and interrogative pronouns (*he, she, it; who, which; who? what?*).

In Russian, gender has morphological value not only in the pronoun, but also in the adjective and the noun. It is, indeed, associated with their form and declension. Apart from one exception which will be indicated below, Russian does not possess words with identical declensions but of different genders, such as are found in Latin (*manus,* fem. and *exercitus,* masc.; *facilis,* masc. and fem., &c.) and Greek.

Usually, in Russian, the form of the nom. sing. is

sufficient to indicate both the gender and the type of declension of a noun, adjective, or pronoun.

Thus, in the noun, *every word ending in a hard consonant is masculine*; *in* -a, -я, *feminine*; *in* -o, -e, -мя, *neuter* (the -я of a feminine word is never preceded by -м-). *The only category comprising both masculine and feminine words is that of nouns ending in a soft consonant*; with these, it is necessary to know the form of another case in order to determine the type of declension and the gender. The gender of words ending in ж, ш, щ, ч is indicated by the absence (for the masc.) or the presence (for the fem.) of a soft sign the value of which is purely morphological, as was explained above (p. 11).

There are very few exceptions to these rules. The two most important are the following:

(1) masculine nouns in -a, -я; their gender, however, is determined by their meaning; they are words denoting persons of the male sex (cf. Latin words of the type *agricola*);

(2) indeclinable nouns, the gender of which is determined by semantic considerations (see p. 71).

Isolated exceptions will be pointed out as they are encountered.

In the adjective and the pronoun the form is associated even more closely with the gender and the type of declension.

3. SINGULAR AND PLURAL

Russian declension is characterized by *a clear disparity between the singular and plural forms.*

In adjectives and pronouns the three genders and, consequently, the three types of declension, are distinguished from one another only in the singular:

masc. но́вый fem. но́вая neut. но́вое

As against this triple declension in the singular, the plural possesses only one type of declension: но́вые.

In this respect, therefore, the Russian adjective behaves

in the same way as the German adjective and the French definite article.

Nouns, without going so far, nevertheless show a similar tendency: while genders and types of declension are rigorously distinguished in the singular, the plural shows a complete absence of the notion of grammatical gender and a confusion of types of declension resulting therefrom.

Thus, the dative, locative, and instr. pl. of the various types of declension have each of them only a single ending (-ам, -ах, and -ами respectively); in the nom.-acc. the use of the various endings (-ы, -и, -а) overlaps the different types of declension; only the genitive endings show a certain stability.

It may be said that the noun, which has several distinct types of declension in the singular, has in the plural a single declension with a few variants in the nominative and genitive.

4. STRESS

The stress forms an important part of declension. It is essential to know the stress of each word. The stress may be fixed and fall always upon the same syllable in all the cases. This is the rule for all adjectives and pronouns and for the majority of nouns.

It may also, however, be mobile and fall upon different syllables in different grammatical cases: this occurs in a certain number of nouns. Each declension includes both nouns with fixed stress and nouns with mobile stress. This mobility itself is of several types which may vary from one class of words to another.

II. WORD-FORMATION

Word-formation, i.e. the creation of new words with the aid of elements already existing in other words, is a process which is always going on in Russian. Thanks to it, the vocabulary is being continuously enriched.

The basic element of a Russian word is a *stem* which usually ends in a consonant. It is normally followed by suffixes (*suffixion*) and often preceded by prefixes or other elements (*composition*). A Russian word may consist of the stem alone, but such cases are rather unusual. A word whose suffix is no longer felt to be such is normally regarded as being without a suffix.

Suffixes may be divided into the *dead* or *unproductive*, limited to a fixed number of words, and the *living* or *productive*, which continue to give rise to new words. The degree of vitality varies from suffix to suffix. But even a dead suffix, so long as it may be detected as such, may on occasion be employed to form a new word. Russian is in general highly sensitive to the relative vitality of its means of word-formation.

Since words are normally formed from one another, it is possible for two suffixes juxtaposed to combine to form a composite suffix.

Apart from the normal processes of suffixion and composition, word-formation entails alternation (particularly of consonants, rarely of vowels) as well as shifts of stress.

The very absence of a suffix (like the absence of case-endings in declension) may in certain cases constitute an element of word-formation as characteristic as the suffix itself.

The principles of Russian word-formation may be illustrated by the following example:

(1) The noun го́род 'town' is today a non-suffixal noun;

(2) при́-город 'suburb';

(3) город-о́к 'little town' is the diminutive form; the same word, in the plural, denotes a Russian national game;

(4) город-и́ш-ко is both a diminutive and a pejorative form;

(5) город-и́ще is an augmentative form and also denotes a 'prehistoric city';

(6) горож-а́н-ин 'town-dweller';

(7) горож-а́н-ка 'town-dweller' (fem.);

(8) город-н-и́ч-ий 'town-prefect' (before 1860);

(9) город-н-и́ч-иха 'town-prefect's wife';

(10) город-н-и́ч-ество 'the post of town-prefect';

(11) город-ск-о́й 'of a town' (adj.);

(12) по город-ск-и́ 'after the town manner' (adv.);

(13) город-ов-о́й 'of a town' (adj.) but usually in the sense 'police constable';

(14) As the original meaning of го́род was 'enclosure, construction', a factitive verb город-и́-ть 'to enclose, to construct' has been derived from it (this verb is now employed only in a few phrases such as городи́ть вздор 'to talk nonsense');

(15) город-ьба́, a noun denoting the action of the verb городи́ть, is now a dialect word;

(16) The verb городи́ть may receive verbal prefixes which modify or specify its meaning: о-город-и́-ть 'to enclose', за-город-и́-ть 'to block', пере-город-и́-ть 'to partition off', &c.;

(17) Each of these verbs may take the imperfective suffix -ива-: о-гора́ж-ива-ть 'to enclose', &c.;

(18) Each of these verbs may form derivative nouns, such as пере-горо́д-ка 'partition wall', &c.; the unsuffixed derivative о-горо́д 'kitchen garden, market garden' will be taken as example;

(19) о-горо́д-н-ый 'of a market garden' (adj.);

(20) о-горо́д-н-ик 'market gardener';

(21) о-горо́д-н-ица 'market gardener' (fem.);

(22) о-горо́д-н-ич-еск-ий 'of a market gardener' (adj.);

(23) о-горо́д-н-ич-ество 'market gardening';

(24) о-горо́д-н-ич-а-ть 'to practise market gardening';

(25) по-о-горо́д-н-ич-а-ть 'to do a bit of market gardening';

(26) Finally, the first part of the word го́род may go to form modern compound words, such as горсове́т 'town council'.

This example gives some idea of Russian fertility in word-formation. Nouns, adjectives, adverbs, and verbs are formed one from another with the aid of prefixes and suffixes, often composite in character (горож-а́нин, огоро́д-ник, огоро́д-ничать) and combined with shifts of stress (го́род, городо́к, огоро́д, при́город) and with phonetic alternations (го́род/горож-а́нин, огоро́дник/ огоро́днич-а-ть, огороди́ть/огора́живать).

The number of Russian suffixes is extremely great. Normally, a particular suffix is reserved for a particular function. It is not unusual, however, for one suffix to have several functions, to such an extent that it is often possible to speak of homonymous suffixes. On the other hand, suffixes may extend their field of application by analogy. Thus, suffixes indicating the agent (person) may become suffixes indicating the instrument (thing). Abstract nouns, becoming concrete, may combine their suffixes with those of nouns indicating objects, and so on.

Without going into detail, the general principles of Russian word-formation will be given. For each part of speech, word-formation will be examined after inflexion.

III

Nouns: Declension

I. GENERAL CHARACTERISTICS

NOUNS may be divided into three declensions. This classification is based upon the various systems of case-endings.
In consequence of the close connexion which exists between
declension and gender, each declension corresponds
broadly to a particular gender, namely:

the *First Declension* to feminines ending in -a, -я;

the *Second Declension* to masculines and neuters (it comprises, therefore, two types of noun);

the *Third Declension* to feminines ending in a consonant.

Nouns which do not fit in with the above scheme are to
be regarded as exceptions or survivals.

Normally each case has only one ending. Certain cases,
however, have two. These double endings may exist simultaneously in the same word or they may be restricted each
to a particular category of nouns.

In some nouns the plural differs from the singular in
respect of some supplementary feature, usually the presence
or absence of a suffix. In such cases the process of word-
formation overlaps that of declension. To this type of
plural we give the name *suppletive*. In some archaic nouns
or groups of nouns the same difference is to be observed
between the nom. sing. and the rest of the declension.

In cases which have a zero-ending and which therefore
have been reduced to the stem alone, when this stem ends
in two or more consonants, a vowel known as the *mobile*

vowel, which may be -o- or -e- (-ё- under the stress before a hard consonant), is normally inserted before the last consonant of the stem.

A feature of the declension of nouns which is as important as it is difficult to master is the stress. This may be fixed or mobile. *Living classes of nouns generally have a fixed stress.* Certain living classes have, nevertheless, a mobile stress, but the mobility is then of a simple type: *contrast between the singular and the plural as a whole.* The more complex systems of mobile stress, those in which the stress shifts within the singular and within the plural, are restricted to the closed groups, certain of which, it should be observed, include some of the commonest nouns.

With the exception of a few groups of nouns, the stress of the nominative singular gives no clue to that of the rest of the declension. There is, however, one rule which applies to all the declensions and to which there are almost no exceptions: any noun of three or more syllables whose nominative singular takes the stress on a syllable other than the first or the last has a fixed stress:

собáка 'dog'   спасѝтель 'saviour'
болóто 'swamp'   опáсность 'danger'

A common exception is the word дерéвня 'village', the gen. pl. of which is деревéнь; other exceptions are certain masculines with plural in -á, as дирéктор 'director', pl. директорá (see p. 53). As a general rule, all nouns in Russian are declinable. There are, however, a considerable number of recent borrowings which are indeclinable and keep the same form in every case.

Substantivized adjectives keep the form and declension of adjectives. They will be considered along with the latter.

II. FIRST DECLENSION

1. EXAMPLE

This declension includes all nouns ending in -a and -я (except -мя). These are:

(1) feminines, which form the great majority: вода́ 'water', забо́та 'care', ды́ня 'melon';

(2) certain masculines denoting persons of the male sex (same type as Lat. *agricola*), such as слуга́ 'servant', ю́ноша 'lad', дя́дя 'uncle', as well as the diminutives in -ишка (мальчи́шка, dim. of ма́льчик 'boy') and -ушка (де́душка dim. of дед 'grandfather').

To these may be added such proper names as Фома́ 'Thomas', Илья́ 'Elijah', and above all the numerous diminutive forms of proper names: Ко́ля, Ва́ня, Са́ша, Ми́тя, &c.;

(3) numerous nouns of common gender (masc. or fem. as the case may be) denoting persons, usually with a pejorative shade of meaning: сирота́ 'orphan', пья́ница 'drunkard', пла́кса 'cry-baby'.

This declension is the most regular of all. It contains very few exceptions or abnormal forms.

According as the final consonant of the stem is hard or soft, the vowel of the case-ending may appear in one or other of two forms: а/я, у/ю, ы/и, о/ё. The declension, however, is the same, since phonetically the difference lies only in the final consonant of the stem. Examples: шко́ла 'school' (hard type), ба́ня 'bath' (soft type).

	Singular			*Plural*	
N.	шко́ла	ба́ня	N.	шко́лы	ба́ни
A.	шко́лу	ба́ню	A.	шко́лы (= N.)	ба́ни (= N.)
G.	шко́лы	ба́ни	G.	школ	бань
D.	шко́ле	ба́не	D.	шко́лам	ба́ням
L.	шко́ле	ба́не	L.	шко́лах	ба́нях
I.	шко́лой	ба́ней	I.	шко́лами	ба́нями

2. OBSERVATIONS

The instr. sing. of the soft type has an -e- instead of the -o- of the hard type, *e* being the regular equivalent of *o* (ё) after a soft consonant in an unstressed position. On the other hand, wherever this ending is stressed, *'o* (ё) occurs. Thus, nom. земля́ 'earth', instr. землёй. In nouns of which the final syllable in the singular is stressed, the correspondence between the hard and soft types is complete.

Alongside the current ending -ой, -ей (-ёй) of the instr. sing., is found the ending -ою, -ею (-ёю), which is confined to the written language.

Nouns the stems of which end in *yod* follow the regular declension of the soft type: nom. иде́я (*id'éjə*) 'idea', acc. иде́ю (*id'éju*), &c. Their gen. pl. naturally has a zero-ending: иде́й (*id'éj*). Such of these nouns as have an -и- before the *yod* take -и instead of -е in the ending of the dat.-loc. sing. This is due to orthographical convention, not to any difference of sound. Example: ли́ния 'line'.

Singular	*Plural*
N. ли́ния	N. ли́нии
A. ли́нию	A. ли́нии (= N.)
G. ли́нии	G. ли́ний
D. ли́нии	D. ли́ниям
L. ли́нии	L. ли́ниях
I. ли́нией	I. ли́ниями

A very few nouns have in the gen. pl., instead of the zero-ending, the ending -ей, by analogy with the third declension: дя́дей, from дя́дя 'uncle'; ноздре́й, from ноздря́ 'nostril'; ю́ношей, from ю́ноша 'lad'; вожже́й, from вожжа́ 'rein'.

3. ACCUSATIVE PLURAL

The acc. pl. has no special form of its own. It has the form of the nominative (known as 'nominative-accusative') for inanimate things (names of objects and abstract nouns) and that of the genitive (known as 'genitive-accusative') for animate things (names of persons and animals). Thus:

он лю́бит ка́рты (nom.-acc. of ка́рта) и соба́к (gen.-acc. of соба́ка) 'he is fond of cards and dogs'.

4. MOBILE VOWEL

In the first declension the mobile vowel occurs only in the gen. pl., which is the only case with a zero-ending.

After a hard consonant the mobile vowel is normally -о-:

> скáзка 'fairy-tale', gen. pl. скáзок
>
> иглá 'needle', gen. pl. и́гол

On the other hand, соснá 'pine-tree', pl. сóсен.

After a soft consonant or after ж, ш, it is normally -е-:

> тюрьмá 'prison', gen. pl. тю́рем
>
> дéньги 'money', gen. pl. дéнег
>
> лóжка 'spoon', gen. pl. лóжек
>
> ви́шня 'cherry', gen. pl. ви́шен

It should be noted that nouns in -ня which have a consonant (including *yod*) before this ending have a hard -н in the gen. pl. (with the exception of дерéвня 'village' and бáрышня 'young lady', which form gen. pl. деревéнь and бáрышень respectively).

When the mobile vowel is inserted after or before a *yod* its mechanism is somewhat obscured by the orthography; it is, nevertheless, perfectly regular:

> чáйка (*čájkə*) 'seagull', gen. pl. чáек (*čájek*, pronounced *čáik*)
>
> бóйня (*bójn'ə*) 'slaughter-house', gen. pl. бóен (*bójen*, pronounced *bóin*)
>
> статья́ (*stat'já*) 'article', gen. pl. статéй (*stat'éj*)
>
> свинья́ (*sv'in'já*) 'pig', gen. pl. свинéй (*sv'in'éj*)

The few nouns in -ья with an unstressed final syllable take -и- instead of -е- as the mobile vowel, by a pure convention of orthography:

> гóстья 'visitor' (fem.), gen. pl. гóстий

5. STRESS

(a) Fixed stress

The stress on nouns in -a, -я is always fixed when it does not fall on the final syllable.

ме́ра 'measure'   охо́та 'hunting'   вы́ставка 'exhibition'

It *may* also be fixed when it does fall on the last syllable, but this occurs in a rather small number of current words, like:

госпожа́ 'lady, Mrs.'   скамья́ 'bench'
жара́ 'heat'   статья́ 'article'
кайма́ 'edging'   тесьма́ 'braid, tape'
клевета́ 'slander'   черта́ 'line'

(b) Mobile stress

The stress is normally mobile when it falls on the last syllable. This mobility may be of three types.

(1) Contrast of singular and plural: final stress in the singular moving back by one syllable in the plural (becoming initial, therefore, in the plural of disyllabic words):

игра́ 'game', pl. и́гры   красота́ 'beauty', pl. красо́ты

Similarly:

вдова́ 'widow'   изба́ 'peasant's hut'   сосна́ 'pine-tree'
весна́ 'spring'   коза́ 'goat'   страна́ 'country'
вина́ 'fault'   коса́ 'scythe; plait'   струна́ 'string'
дыра́ 'hole'   метла́ 'broom'   толпа́ 'crowd'
жена́ 'wife'   оса́ 'wasp'   трава́ 'grass'
змея́ 'snake'   пчела́ 'bee'   труба́ 'pipe, trumpet'
игла́ 'needle'   слуга́ 'servant'   тюрьма́ 'prison'
                 глубина́ 'depth'   высота́ 'height'

The words

овца́ 'sheep'   сестра́ 'sister'
свинья́ 'pig'   судья́ 'judge'
семья́ 'family'

which belong to the same group, have a final stress in gen. pl.: ове́ц, свине́й, семе́й, сестёр, суде́й.

This is the commonest type of mobility and the only one which is still living. It has a tendency to extend at the expense of the two following types, which are only survivals limited to a small number of nouns in current use.

The mobility of stress in these survivals is preserved by the frequency with which they occur.

(2) Final stress in singular and plural except in nom.-acc. pl., where it is initial:

> губа́ 'lip', acc. губу́, pl. гу́бы, dat. губа́м

Similarly:

блоха́ 'flea'	свеча́ 'candle'
волна́ 'wave'	слеза́ 'tear'
копна́ 'rick'	строка́ 'line'
ноздря́ 'nostril'	тропа́ 'path'

(3) Final stress in singular and plural except in acc. sing. and nom.-acc. pl., where it is initial:

рука́ 'hand, arm'	голова́ 'head'
acc. sing. ру́ку	acc. sing. го́лову
gen. sing. руки́	gen. sing. головы́
nom.-acc. pl. ру́ки	nom.-acc. pl. го́ловы
gen. pl. рук	gen. pl. голо́в
dat. pl. рука́м	dat. pl. голова́м

Similarly:

вода́ 'water'	пора́ 'time'
гора́ 'mountain'	река́ 'river'
доска́ 'board'	спина́ 'back'
душа́ 'soul'	среда́ 'Wednesday'
земля́ 'earth'	стена́ 'wall'
зима́ 'winter'	цена́ 'price'
нога́ 'foot, leg'	щека́ 'cheek'
борода́ 'beard'	полоса́ 'stripe'
борозда́ 'furrow'	сторона́ 'side'
борона́ 'harrow'	сковорода́ 'frying-pan'
железа́ 'gland'	

Note the final stress in gen. pl. of земля́: земе́ль.

In this group the acc. sing. may adopt sometimes a final stress, as in group (2).

III. SECOND DECLENSION

Unlike the first declension, the second declension contains a number of deviations, parallel types of case-ending, and abnormal forms. Their presence is attributable to the fusion of several old types of declension and to the influences of analogy resulting therefrom.

As in the first declension, the stems of second declension nouns may end in either hard or soft consonants. This twofold aspect of the stem gives rise to a double series of endings, orthographically distinct but phonetically identical:

а/я, у/ю, ы/и, ó/ё, (and о/е),

exactly as in the first declension.

The second declension comprises two subdivisions, masculine and neuter.

1. Masculine

I. EXAMPLE

Masculines of the second declension include all masculine nouns ending in a hard consonant and all masculine nouns save one (путь 'way', see p. 67) ending in a soft consonant.

The nom. sing. is characterized by a zero-ending and is reduced to the bare stem. Examples: закóн 'law' (hard type), вождь 'chief, leader' (soft type).

	Singular			*Plural*	
N.	закóн	вождь	N.	закóны	вождú
A.	закóн	вождя́	A.	закóны	вождéй
	(= N.)	(= G.)		(= N.)	(= G.)
G.	закóна	вождя́	G.	закóнов	вождéй
D.	закóну	вождю́	D.	закóнам	вождя́м
L.	закóне	вождé	L.	закóнах	вождя́х
I.	закóном	вождём	I.	закóнами	вождя́ми

2. OBSERVATIONS

The soft type is not modelled on the hard type as closely as is the case in the first declension: in the gen. pl. it takes the ending -ей as against the -ов of the hard type.

This ending in -ей is also standard for nouns in -ж and -ш. Thus,

> нож 'knife', gen. pl. ножéй
> карандáш 'pencil', gen. pl. карандашéй

On the other hand, nouns in *yod* (-й) form their gen. pl. in -ев. Thus,

> слýчай 'case', gen. pl. слýчаев
> герóй 'hero', gen. pl. герóев

As in the first declension, nouns with an -и- before the *yod* take an orthographical -и instead of -е in the loc. sing. Thus,

> Григóрий 'Gregory', loc. sing. Григóрии

3. ACCUSATIVE SINGULAR AND PLURAL

In the first declension the accusative has no special form of its own in the plural. In the second declension it has no special form in either the singular or the plural; in both numbers the accusative is identical with the nominative or with the genitive according as the noun denotes an inanimate or an animate object. Thus

> мы увúдели дом (nom.-acc. of дом) и áиста (gen.-acc. of áист) на крýше 'we saw the house and the stork on the roof'.

4. MOBILE VOWEL

As in the first declension, the mobile vowel, when it occurs, does so in the case with zero-ending, which, in the second declension, is the nom. sing. The mobile vowel may be -о- or -е-, and its function is the same as in the first declension:

> сон 'dream', gen. сна

но́готь 'fingernail', gen. но́гтя
день 'day', gen. дня
орёл 'eagle', gen. орла́
заём (*zajóm*) 'loan', gen. за́йма (*zájmə*)
бое́ц (*bajéc*) 'fighting-man', gen. бойца́ (*bajcá*)
воробе́й (*vərab'éj*) 'sparrow', gen. воробья́ (*vərab'já*)
руче́й (*ruč'éj*) 'stream', gen. ручья́ (*ruč'já*)

In one word the mobile -e- is represented orthographically
by -я-:

за́яц (záic) 'hare', gen. за́йца (zájcə)

The fact that the mobile vowel occurs in the nom. sing.
involves a certain inconvenience, since the representative
form of the noun, the nom. sing., may thereby have a
different structure from the rest of the declension. Moreover, *it is often impossible to tell* a priori *whether an -o- or an
-e- in the final syllable is mobile or not*: it is mobile in плато́к
'handkerchief' (gen. платка́), but it is not in знато́к 'con-
noisseur' (gen. знатока́).

5. STRESS

The stress of the masculine noun may be fixed or mobile.

(a) Fixed stress

The fixed stress may be either initial or final. If it falls
on a middle syllable the word naturally belongs to the
general type of words with fixed stress indicated on p. 38
and will not be examined here.

The nom. sing., being a form with zero-ending, is
incapable of indicating whether the word has a final stress
or not:

пото́к 'torrent', gen. пото́ка has the stress on the middle
syllable, whereas игро́к 'gambler', gen. игрока́ has a final
stress.

(1) The non-final fixed stress falls throughout the
declension on the same syllable as in the nom. sing.

Almost all recent borrowings in which a suffix is no longer felt, belong to this type (they form more than half of all Russian monosyllables), as for example:

банк 'bank'
газ 'gas'
душ 'shower-bath'
жест 'gesture'
клуб 'club'
лифт 'lift'

нерв 'nerve'
план 'plan'
торт 'cake'
флаг 'flag'
штраф 'fine'

ананас 'pine-apple'
билет 'ticket'
велосипед 'bicycle'
галстук 'tie'
журнал 'periodical'
идеал 'ideal'

конверт 'envelope'
лозунг 'slogan'
продукт 'product'
факел 'torch'
фонтан 'fountain'
циркуль 'compasses'

This type includes some non-suffixal nouns; both words of Russian origin and assimilated borrowings:

брак 'marriage'
брод 'ford'
вид 'view'
внук 'grandson'
знак 'sign'
нрав 'temper'
рак 'crawfish'
спор 'discussion'

груз 'cargo'
дед 'grandfather'
дух 'ghost'
звук 'sound'
храм 'temple'
шум 'noise'
яд 'poison'

верблюд 'camel'
ворон 'raven'
канат 'rope'
карман 'pocket'
ландыш 'lily of the valley'

молот 'hammer'
нахал 'insolent fellow'
товар 'goods'
ужин 'supper'
улей 'hive'
цыган 'gipsy'

The numerous and productive class of non-suffixal

nouns formed from compound verbs (see p. 72) belongs to this type of accentuation:

вопро́с 'question'	проли́в 'straits'
запа́с 'stock'	раство́р 'solution'
до́вод 'argument'·	сове́т 'advice'
наро́д 'people'	сосе́д 'neighbour'
о́пыт 'experience'	сою́з 'union'
покло́н 'bow'	уку́с 'bite'

The nouns заём 'loan' and наём 'hire, renting', which have the stress on the mobile -ё- in the nom.-acc. sing., have it on the prefix in the rest of the declension: gen. за́йма, на́йма, &c.

Suffixal nouns with unstressed suffixes follow the same pattern:

жи́тель 'inhabitant'	слу́чай 'case'
лётчик 'airman'	сто́лик 'small table'
па́харь 'ploughman'	ча́йник 'tea-pot'

as well as certain nouns with stressed suffixes, i.e.

-а́н (велика́н 'giant')
-и́н (грузи́н 'Georgian')
-тя́й (лентя́й 'lazy person')

(2) The final fixed stress moves from the last syllable of the nom. sing. onto the ending, where it remains throughout the declension: бык 'bull', gen. sing. быка́, &c. This is an essentially Russian type and includes only a few recent borrowings:

враг 'enemy'	кот 'tom-cat'	рубль 'rouble'
врач 'physician'	крест 'cross'	след 'trace'
грех 'sin'	луч 'ray'	стол 'table'
гриб 'fungus'	меч 'sword'	суд 'law-court'
двор 'court'	мяч 'ball'	царь 'tsar'
дождь 'rain'	плащ 'cloak'	шут 'fool'
зонт 'umbrella'	плод 'fruit'	щит 'shield'

багáж 'luggage'
башмáк 'shoe'
живóт 'stomach'
кирпи́ч 'brick'
кабáн 'wild-boar'
ковёр 'carpet'
комáр 'mosquito'
котёл 'boiler'
овёс 'oats'
огóнь 'fire'
палáч 'hangman'

ручéй 'brook'
рычáг 'lever'
сапóг 'boot'
соловéй 'nightingale'
сундýк 'trunk'
топóр 'axe'
утю́г 'flat-iron'
чулóк 'stocking'
язы́к 'tongue'
этáж 'storey'

The nouns ýгол 'corner, angle', ýзел 'knot', and ýгорь 'eel', which belong to this group, have the stress in the nom. sing., exceptionally, not on the last but on the first syllable.

The final fixed stress is normal in nouns with the following stressed suffixes:

-áк/-я́к	дурáк 'fool', моря́к 'sailor', пустя́к 'trifle'
-ня́к	дубня́к 'oak-wood'
-и́к	стари́к 'old man', тупи́к 'blind alley'
-ни́к	двойни́к 'the double', дневни́к 'diary'
-ови́к	грузови́к 'lorry'
-щи́к	поставщи́к 'supplier', гробовщи́к 'undertaker'
-óк	ходóк 'walker', желтóк 'yolk'
-ёж/-éж	чертёж 'draft', рубéж 'boundary'
-éнь	плетéнь 'hurdle'
-ýн	лгун 'liar', горбýн 'hunchback'
-áрь	главáрь 'ringleader', словáрь 'dictionary'
-я́р	столя́р 'joiner'
-áч	богáч 'rich man', скрипáч 'violinist'
-и́ч	москви́ч 'native of Moscow', Фоми́ч 'son of Thomas' (patronymic)
-áш	торгáш 'huckster'
-ы́ш	крепы́ш 'sturdy child'
-éц	мудрéц 'sage', дворéц 'palace'

(b) Mobile stress

The mobility of the stress may, as in the first declension, be of three types; but, whatever the type of mobility, the genitive, dative, locative, and instrumental plural take the stress on the ending.

(1) The most numerous, and the only living, type is that of nouns in which the stress differs in the singular and in the plural. But, unlike the first declension, the final stress occurs in the plural, while in the singular the stress falls on the first, or at any rate on some other syllable than the final. This type includes a certain number of monosyllables, such as

> нос 'nose', gen. sing. нóса, nom. pl. носы́, gen. pl. носóв

Similarly:

бал 'ball'	дуб 'oak'	пруд 'pond'
бой 'battle'	круг 'circle'	ряд 'row'
верх 'top'	мир 'world'	сад 'garden'
воз 'cart'	мост 'bridge'	шаг 'step'
гроб 'coffin'	пир 'feast'	шар 'ball, sphere'
долг 'duty, debt'	пол 'floor'	шкап 'cupboard'

All these nouns have a loc. sing. in -ý (see p. 52), which is normal for words of this stress-pattern. Some nouns of this type have, however, only a loc. sing. in -e, as, for example:

дар 'gift'	пуд 'pud'	сыр 'cheese'
жир 'fat'	суп 'soup'	ус 'moustache'
квас 'kvas'		

In addition, all masculine nouns which form their plural in -á/-я́ belong to this type, as, for example, гóлос 'voice', pl. голосá (see p. 53).

(2) The stress, initial in singular and in nom. pl., falls on the final syllable in the oblique cases of the plural:

гость 'guest', gen. sing. го́стя, nom. pl. го́сти, gen. pl.
гостéй

This type comprises for the most part nouns ending in a soft consonant:

го́лубь 'pigeon'	ко́готь 'claw'	па́рень 'lad, chap'
гусь 'goose'	ле́бедь 'swan'	пе́рстень 'ring'
зверь 'animal'	лось 'elk'	со́боль 'sable'
ка́мень 'stone'	но́готь 'fingernail'	сте́бель 'stalk'
ко́зырь 'trump'	о́кунь 'perch'	у́голь 'coal, charcoal'

The hard type is poorly represented:

бог 'god'	гром 'thunder'	клуб 'puff'
волк 'wolf'	зуб 'tooth'	слог 'syllable'
во́лос 'hair'		

(3) The stress is final throughout, except in the nom.-acc. sing. and pl.:

конь 'horse', gen. sing. коня́, nom. pl. ко́ни, gen. pl.
конéй

Similarly with the following two words:

червь 'worm'   гвоздь 'nail'

Types (2) and (3) are not numerous, while (3) in particular is an archaic type which is approaching extinction.

6. DOUBLE ENDINGS

Certain cases may possess not one, but two endings. In the singular this occurs in the genitive and the locative.

(a) Genitive singular

All masculine nouns of the second declension have in the gen. sing. the ending -a/-я. *In addition*, certain nouns may have the ending -y/-ю. This occurs in two types of nouns:

(1) With nouns denoting a substance, a number of objects or a collective unit, the genitive in -y/-ю has *partitive* value, for example:

> цвет песка́ 'the colour of the sand', but то́нна песку́ 'a ton of sand';
> цена́ ча́я 'the price of tea', but ча́шка ча́ю 'a cup of tea';
> во́ля наро́да 'the will of the people', but мно́го наро́ду 'many people';
> разведе́ние табака́ 'the cultivation of tobacco', but нет табаку́ 'there is no tobacco'.

(2) In certain phrases of a more or less adverbial character the genitive in -y/-ю is merely a morphological survival and has no special force, for example:

> без сро́ку 'without time-limit'
> для ви́ду 'for form's sake'
> и́з дому 'from home'
> со стра́ху 'out of fear'
> с гла́зу на глаз 'tête-à-tête'
> ни ра́зу 'not once'

The genitive in -y/-ю does not occur in nouns denoting persons or animals.

(*b*) *Locative singular*

All masculines of the second declension (apart from nouns ending in a *yod* preceded by -и-) have in the loc. sing. the ending -e. *In addition*, certain nouns, normally words with a non-final stress in the singular (see p. 50), may have the ending -у́/-ю́, which is *always stressed*. This may occur only after the prepositions в 'in' and на 'on' in a strictly local sense:

в лесу́ 'in the forest'	на балу́ 'at the ball'
в кругу́ 'in the circle'	на ветру́ 'on the wind'
в бою́ 'in battle'	на краю́ 'on the edge'

With other prepositions the same words form their locative in -e; о ле́се 'about the forest', &c. Only the word полк 'regiment' has a locative полку́ with all prepositions.

This locative form, like the genitive in -у/-ю, may have a certain adverbial character:

> на дому́ 'at home' = Fr. 'à domicile' (на до́ме 'on the house')
>
> в цвету́ 'in bloom' (в цве́те 'in the colour')

(c) *Nominative plural*

In the plural, unlike the singular, the irregular endings do not occur *parallel with* the normal endings of the declension but *in place of* them. The only cases involved are the nominative and the genitive.

A large number of nouns have in the nom. pl., instead of the ending -ы/-и, the ending -а́/-я́, which is *always stressed*.

This ending occurs only in nouns with a mobile stress— initial in the singular, final in the plural, so that the nom. pl. in stressed -а́/-я́ is *always* distinct from the gen. sing. in unstressed -а/-я:

> бок 'side', gen. sing. бо́ка, nom. pl. бока́
>
> ве́чер 'evening', gen. sing. ве́чера, nom. pl. вечера́

The monosyllables of this type are not numerous:

век 'century, age'	лес 'wood'	стог 'rick'
глаз 'eye'	луг 'meadow'	том 'volume'
год 'year'	рог 'horn'	тон 'tone'
дом 'house'	снег 'snow'	шёлк 'silk'
край 'edge, region'	сорт 'sort'	

Most of the nouns of this type are disyllabic:

бе́рег 'bank, shore'	о́стров 'island'	по́греб 'cellar'
го́лос 'voice'	па́рус 'sail'	по́езд 'train'
го́род 'town'	пе́карь 'baker'	по́яс 'belt'
ма́стер 'master'	пи́сарь 'clerk'	че́реп 'skull'
о́круг 'region'	по́вар 'cook'	я́корь 'anchor'

Some of these nouns are trisyllabic, and then the differ-ence of stress between the singular and the plural is all the more striking:

о́корок 'gammon', pl. окорока́

ко́локол 'bell', pl. колокола́

This form of the plural is steadily extending. It is par-ticularly frequent in recent borrowings; for those of them which end in -ель it is the only plural possible:

ве́нзель 'monogram'	фли́гель 'wing' (of a house)
ве́ксель 'bill of exchange'	ште́мпель 'stamp, post-mark'
ди́зель 'Diesel engine'	

Similarly:

а́дрес 'address'	па́спорт 'passport'
апте́карь 'chemist'	профе́ссор 'professor'
бу́фер 'buffer'	ре́ктор 'rector'
дире́ктор 'director'	то́рмоз 'brake'
до́ктор 'doctor'	фе́льдшер 'surgeon's assis-tant
ку́чер 'coachman'	
ла́герь 'camp'	флю́гер 'weathercock'
но́мер 'number'	ю́нкер 'military cadet'

Some of these words admit in the singular the stress on the interior syllable (апте́карь, дире́ктор, профе́ссор).

Attention is drawn to certain homonyms of this type, the most important of which are the following:

мех	(1)	'fur', pl. меха́
	(2)	'leather vessel', pl. мехи́ 'bellows'
о́браз	(1)	'ikon', pl. образа́
	(2)	'image', pl. о́бразы
о́рден	(1)	'decoration', pl. ордена́
	(2)	'order' (monastic or architectural), pl. о́р-дены
про́вод	(1)	'electric wire', pl. провода́
	(2)	'farewell': про́воды (no singular)
хлеб	(1)	'corn', pl. хлеба́ 'crops'
	(2)	'bread', pl. хле́бы 'loaves of bread'

цвет   (1) 'colour', pl. цветá
         (2) 'flowers': цветы́ (sing. 'a flower': цветóк)

Two nouns with final stress in the singular form their plural in -á:

рукáв, pl. рукавá 'sleeve'
обшлáг, pl. обшлагá 'turned-back cuff' (of a coat)

(d) Genitive plural

In certain nouns ending in a hard consonant the gen. pl. instead of the ending -ов, has a zero-ending and is thereby reduced (as in the first declension) to the bare stem. It is therefore identical in form with the nom. sing. This identity of forms does not give rise to confusion, since the zero-ending occurs only in nouns which normally are employed in the gen. pl. only with words of numerical or quantitative force (numerals, adverbs of quantity, &c.):

раз 'time' (семь раз 'seven times')
человéк 'man' (only with numerals; otherwise людéй, see p. 65)
аршúн 'arshin' (measure of length)
сапóг 'boot' (пáра сапóг 'a pair of boots')
чулóк 'stocking'
глаз 'eye'

It is the stress which distinguishes the gen. pl. волóс from the nom. sing. вóлос 'hair'.

A characteristic group is that which consists of nouns indicating various types of military:

солдáт 'soldier'	сапёр 'sapper'
драгýн 'dragoon'	гренадéр 'grenadier'
гусáр 'hussar'	кирасúр 'cuirassier'
улáн 'lancer'	кадéт 'cadet'

гардемарúн 'naval cadet' (but юнкерóв from юнкер 'military cadet', матрóсов from матрóс 'sailor')

To this class belong also:

     тýрок 'Turk'   цыгáн 'gipsy'

7. SUPPLETIVE PLURALS

(a) *Nouns of hard type in singular forming plurals of soft type*

There are two such nouns:

> чорт 'devil', pl. че́рти
> сосе́д 'neighbour', pl. сосе́ди

(b) *Plural in* -ья

A number of masculine nouns of the hard type add to their stem in the plural a *yod* which does not occur in the singular and which causes the plural to belong to the soft type with nom. in -ья (-*jə*) unstressed, gen. -ьев (-*jəv*), dat. -ьям (-*jəm*), &c. Example: брат 'brother'.

	Singular		*Plural*
N.	брат	N.	бра́тья
A.	бра́та (= G.)	A.	бра́тьев (= G.)
G.	бра́та	G.	бра́тьев
D.	бра́ту	D.	бра́тьям
L.	бра́те	L.	бра́тьях
I.	бра́том	I.	бра́тьями

To the same type belong:

брус 'beam', pl. бру́сья
кли́н 'wedge', pl. кли́нья
кол 'stake', pl. ко́лья
ком 'lump', pl. ко́мья
прут 'switch' (stick), pl. пру́тья
стул 'chair', pl. сту́лья
клок 'tuft', pl. кло́чья

крюк 'hook', pl. крю́чья
сук 'branch', pl. су́чья
ко́лос 'ear of corn', pl. коло́сья
о́бод 'felloe', pl. обо́дья
по́лоз 'runner' (of sledge), pl. поло́зья
лоску́т 'rag', pl. лоску́тья

Two nouns of the soft type form a plural in -ья, in addition to a much more usual form in -и:

> ка́мень 'stone', pl. ка́мни and каме́нья
> у́голь 'coal', pl. у́гли and у́голья

Four nouns employ the plural in -ья to mark the difference of meaning between homonyms:

лист   (1) 'sheet' (of paper, of metal), pl. листы́
           (2) 'leaf' (of plant), pl. ли́стья

зуб   (1) 'tooth' (in proper sense of word), pl. зу́бы
           (2) 'tooth' (in figurative sense: tooth of a machine, a rake, &c.), pl. зу́бья

ко́рень   (1) 'root', pl. ко́рни
           (2) 'spices', коре́нья (no singular)

по́вод   (1) 'occasion, motive', pl. по́воды
           (2) 'bridle, rein', pl. пово́дья

Three nouns form their plural in *yod*, but with stressed final syllable and genitive in -е́й:

> муж 'husband', pl. мужья́, gen. муже́й, dat. мужья́м, &c.
>
> князь 'prince', pl. князья́
>
> друг 'friend', pl. друзья́ (with the alternation *g/z*, unique in the declension of nouns, see p. 25)

Two nouns form their plural in *yod*, with the addition of the suffix -ов- (gen. pl. in -е́й):

> сын 'son', pl. сыновья́, gen. сынове́й, dat. сыновья́м, &c.
>
> кум 'gossip' (in the original sense), pl. кумовья́

(c) Plural of nouns in -ин

A number of nouns denoting persons with reference to nationality, religion, social class, &c., have a singular form in -ин, which is dropped in the plural. *All these nouns form the genitive plural with zero-ending*; the nom. pl. has various forms.

The most numerous group in this class is that of nouns in -анин, -янин. Example: англича́нин 'Englishman'.

Singular	*Plural*
N. англича́нин	N. англича́не
A. англича́нина (= G.)	A. англича́н (= G.)

	Singular		*Plural*
G.	англича́нина	G.	англича́н
D.	англича́нину	D.	англича́нам
L.	англича́нине	L.	англича́нах
I.	англича́нином	I.	англича́нами

Similarly:

славяни́н 'Slav'	мещани́н 'petit-bourgeois'
армяни́н 'Armenian'	крестья́нин 'peasant'
южа́нин 'southerner'	горожа́нин 'town-dweller'
северя́нин 'northerner'	киевля́нин 'inhabitant of
христиани́н 'Christian'	Kiev'
мусульма́нин 'Moslem'	парижа́нин 'Parisian'
дворяни́н 'nobleman'	

Most nouns of this type take the stress in the singular
either on the suffix -ин or on the preceding syllable and in
the plural on the syllable -ан-, -ян-. Exceptions are:

гражданин 'citizen', pl. гра́ждане
ри́млянин 'Roman', pl. ри́мляне
филисти́млянин 'Philistine', pl. филисти́мляне

The noun боя́рин 'boyar', pl. боя́ре, is of the same type.

The nouns ба́рин 'master, gentleman', тата́рин 'Tar-
tar', болга́рин 'Bulgarian', have in the nom. pl. the forms
ба́ры, тата́ры, болга́ры respectively.

The noun господи́н 'master, gentleman, Mr.' has nom.
pl. господа́.

The noun хозя́ин 'landlord, owner, host' has nom. pl.
хозя́ева, gen. хозя́ев, dat. хозя́евам, &c.

2. Neuter

1. EXAMPLE

Neuters of the second declension include all nouns
ending in -o (hard type) and -e (soft type), as well as the
plural of neuters in -мя, the singular of which belongs to
the third declension (see p. 68).

The masc. подмастéрье 'apprentice' follows the same declension.

The declension of neuters differs from that of masculines only in the nom.-acc. sing. and pl. and in the gen. pl. The neuters do not include any noun denoting an animate object, and their accusative is therefore always identical with the nominative. Examples: винó 'wine' (hard type), мучéнье 'torture' (soft type).

	Singular			*Plural*	
N.–A.	винó	мучéнье	N.–A.	вúна	мучéнья
G.	винá	мучéнья	G.	вин	мучéний
D.	винý	мучéнью	D.	вúнам	мучéньям
L.	винé	мучéнье	L.	вúнах	мучéньях
I.	винóм	мучéньем	I.	вúнами	мучéньями

2. OBSERVATIONS

The endings of the singular present no peculiarities. It will be noted, however, that nouns with an -и- before the final *yod* of the stem (nouns in -ие) have in the loc. sing. the ending -и instead of -е: знáние 'knowledge', loc. sing. знáнии (the same orthographical rule was observed also in masculine nouns and in the first declension).

The nom. pl. ends in -и in the following types of nouns:

(1) nouns in -ко (almost exclusively diminutives):

> колéчко 'little ring', pl. колéчки
> словéчко 'little word', pl. словéчки
> зёрнышко 'little grain', pl. зёрнышки
> окóшко 'window', pl. окóшки
> я́блоко 'apple', pl. я́блоки
> вéко 'eyelid', pl. вéки
> but the plural of óблако 'cloud' is облакá

(2) augmentatives in -ище:

> домúще 'big house', pl. домúщи

(3) the words

> плечо́ 'shoulder', pl. пле́чи
> коле́но 'knee', pl. коле́ни

The gen. pl. has the zero-ending:

> сло́во 'word', pl. слов
> со́лнце 'sun', pl. солнц
> ло́же 'couch', pl. лож
> жили́ще 'dwelling', pl. жили́щ
> бога́тство 'wealth', pl. бога́тств
> де́йствие (*d'éjstv'ijə*) 'action', pl. де́йствий (*d'éjstv'ij*)

It will be observed that neuters in -*je* form the gen. pl. in -ий, whether the nom. sing. ends in -ие or in -ье (as in the paradigm):

> волне́ние 'agitation' / волне́ний
> копьё 'spear' / ко́пий

The only noun of this type to form the gen. pl. in -ей is ружьё 'rifle', gen. pl. ру́жей.

Two nouns, мо́ре 'sea' and по́ле 'field', form the gen. pl. in -ей like masculines of the soft type: море́й, поле́й.

On the other hand, certain nouns in -ье denoting concrete things form the gen. pl. with the masculine termination -ев:

> ку́шанье 'food, dish', gen. pl. ку́шаньев
> пла́тье 'dress', gen. pl. пла́тьев
> лохмо́тья (pl.) 'rags', gen. лохмо́тьев

The only masculine in -ье, подмасте́рье 'apprentice' belongs to the same type: gen. pl. подмасте́рьев.

Similarly, о́блако 'cloud' has the gen. pl. облако́в.

3. MOBILE VOWEL

The operation of the mobile vowel is comparable to that observed in the first declension, since in both cases the zero-ending occurs in the gen. pl. Thus,

> зло 'evil', gen. pl. зол

стекло́ 'glass', gen. pl. стёкол
окно́ 'window', gen. pl. о́кон
се́рдце 'heart', gen. pl. серде́ц
весло́ 'oar', gen. pl. вёсел
письмо́ 'letter', gen. pl. пи́сем

In the word яйцо́ (*jijcó*) 'egg', the mobile vowel appears exceptionally in the form of -и-: gen. pl. яи́ц (*jiíc*).

4. STRESS

The stress system of neuter nouns is simpler than that of the other classes of nouns studied hitherto.

(a) Fixed stress

In addition to nouns which have an interior stress (as боло́то 'swamp', see p. 38) the stress is fixed in all derivative nouns in -ие, -ье (with unstressed *e*), -ство, -ище, and in a great number of other derivative nouns:

ше́ствие 'procession'   кла́дбище 'cemetery'
зна́ние 'knowledge'   ли́чико 'face' (dim.)
пе́нье 'singing'   пёрышко 'feather' (dim.)
ка́чество 'quality'   пра́вило 'rule'
божество́ 'divinity'   пла́тьице 'dress' (dim.)

Outside these types few neuters have a fixed stress, as do:

блю́до 'dish'   ры́ло 'snout'
брю́хо 'belly'   со́лнце 'sun'
ве́ко 'eyelid'   ча́до 'child'
го́рло 'throat'   чу́чело 'stuffed animal or
ду́ло '(gun-)muzzle'   bird; scarecrow'
жа́ло 'sting'   ши́ло 'awl'
кре́сло 'armchair'   я́блоко 'apple'
ло́же 'couch'

(b) Mobile stress

All other neuter nouns have a mobile stress. The mobility of the stress is simple, varying regularly from the singular to the plural. The nouns of this class constitute

the dead, non-productive, portion of the neuters and consist in their great majority of disyllabic nouns.

(1) If in the singular the stress is initial, it becomes final
in the plural. Thus,

> сло́во 'word', pl. слова́
> зе́ркало 'mirror', pl. зеркала́

Similarly:

во́йско 'army'	мо́ре 'sea'	се́рдце 'heart'
де́ло 'matter, business'	по́ле 'field'	ста́до 'herd, flock'
ме́сто 'place'	пра́во 'right'	те́ло 'body'
	кру́жево 'lace'	о́блако 'cloud'

> but о́зеро 'lake', pl. озёра
> де́рево 'tree', pl. дере́вья (see below)

(2) If in the singular the stress is final, it moves back one
syllable in the plural; in disyllabic words it thus becomes
initial, e.g.,

> окно́ 'window', pl. о́кна
> колесо́ 'wheel', pl. колёса

Similarly:

бедро́ 'hip'	клеймо́ 'mark, brand'	седло́ 'saddle'
бревно́ 'log'	копьё 'spear'	село́ 'village'
ведро́ 'bucket'	лицо́ 'face'	стекло́ 'glass'
весло́ 'oar'	письмо́ 'letter'	сукно́ 'cloth'
вино́ 'wine'	пятно́ 'spot, stain'	число́ 'number'
гнездо́ 'nest'	ребро́ 'rib'	ядро́ 'kernel'
зерно́ 'grain'	ружьё 'gun'	яйцо́ 'egg'
волокно́ 'fibre'		ремесло́ 'trade, profession'
полотно́ 'linen, canvas'		решето́ 'sieve'

and the three words with plural in -ья quoted below
(звено́, крыло́, перо́).

5. SUPPLETIVE PLURALS

(a) *Plural in* -ья

A number of nouns form the plural with the aid of *yod*,
in -ья:

звено́ 'link', pl. звéнья   дéрево 'tree', pl. дерéвья
крыло́ 'wing', pl. кры́лья   полéно 'log', pl. полéнья
перо́ 'feather', pl. пéрья   дно 'bottom', pl. до́нья (ob-
ши́ло 'awl', pl. ши́лья   serve the alternation *zero*/o)

The declension of these words is identical with those of masculines of the same type: gen. pl. пéрьев, dat. pl. пéрьям, &c. (see p. 56).

(b) Isolated Nouns

The nouns о́ко 'eye' (archaic) and у́хо 'ear' have in the plural the forms о́чи and у́ши, declined like third declension nouns (see p. 64).

The nouns нéбо 'sky' and чýдо 'miracle, wonder' add to their stem in the plural the suffix -ес-: nom. pl. небесá, чудесá, gen. pl. небéс, чудéс, &c., with final stress.

The noun судно́ 'ship' drops the -н- in the plural and forms a gen. pl. of the masculine type: nom. pl. судá, gen. pl. судо́в, dat. pl. судáм, &c.

(c) Nouns in -ёнок, -я́та

Nouns denoting young animals and certain nouns denoting children, usually with reference to their nationality, form their singular in -ёнок (with mobile -*o*-) and are declined as masculines, while they form a plural in -я́та which follows the regular neuter type. Example: телёнок 'calf':

Singular	*Plural*
N. телёнок	N. теля́та
A. телёнка (= G.)	A. теля́т (= G.)
G. телёнка	G. теля́т
D. телёнку	D. теля́там
L. телёнке	L. теля́тах
I. телёнком	I. теля́тами

Similarly:

     жеребёнок 'foal', pl. жеребя́та
     поросёнок 'young pig', pl. порося́та

медвежо́нок 'bear cub', pl. медвежа́та
слонёнок 'baby elephant', pl. слоня́та
утёнок 'duckling', pl. утя́та
орлёнок 'eaglet', pl. орля́та
ребёнок 'child', pl. ребя́та
китайчо́нок 'little Chinese', pl. китайча́та
негритёнок 'little negro', pl. негритя́та
поварёнок 'kitchen boy', pl. поваря́та

IV. THIRD DECLENSION

Almost all the nouns in this declension are feminine, but they include one masculine and ten neuters.

I. Feminine

1. EXAMPLE

The feminines end in a soft consonant or in ж, ш. Orthographically their distinguishing mark is a soft sign (ь) in the nom. sing. even after ж, ш. They include very few words denoting persons or animals.

The simple nouns of this declension are not very numerous. They are mostly monosyllables.

The numerals from 5 to 20 and 30 (пять 'five', шесть, 'six', see p. 139) also belong to the third declension.

The vast majority of feminines of this type consist of abstract nouns in -ость derived from adjectives, as мо́лодость 'youth', ста́рость 'old age', то́чность 'accuracy'.

The accusative, in both singular and plural, is identical with the nominative, except that the acc. pl. of words denoting persons and animals is identical with the gen. pl. Example: кость 'bone':

Singular	*Plural*
N. кость	N. ко́сти
A. кость (= N.)	A. ко́сти (= N.)

	Singular		*Plural*
G.	кóсти	G.	костéй
D.	кóсти	D.	костя́м
L.	кóсти	L.	костя́х
I.	кóстью	I.	костя́ми

2. OBSERVATIONS

The nouns лóшадь 'horse', лю́ди 'people', and дéти 'children' (the latter two are used only in the plural), form the instr. pl. in -ьми́: лошадьми́, людьми́, детьми́. The words дверь 'door' and плеть 'whip' may form the instr. pl. either in -ьми́ or in -я́ми.

The nouns мать 'mother' and дочь 'daughter', in all cases except the nom.-acc. sing., have the stems матер-, дочер- respectively (gen.-dat.-loc. sing. мáтери, дóчери, &c.). The instr. pl. of дочь may be either дочерьми́ or дочеря́ми.

3. MOBILE VOWEL

The mobile vowel is infrequent in this type. It occurs in the nom.-acc. sing. (zero-ending) and in the instr. sing. (case-ending beginning with *yod*) of five words; it is always -o-:

вошь 'louse', instr. вóшью, gen. вши, &c.
ложь 'lie', instr. лóжью, gen. лжи
рожь 'rye', instr. рóжью, gen. ржи
цéрковь 'church', instr. цéрковью, gen. цéркви
любóвь 'love', instr. любóвью, gen. любви́

The feminine Christian name Любóвь has no mobile -o-.

4. STRESS

(a) *Fixed stress*

(1) Apart from the words which have an interior stress (see p. 38) the non-final fixed stress occurs in nearly all derivatives in -ость, such as

рáдость 'joy' глýпость 'stupidity'

and in many other derivatives, as

боле́знь 'illness'	посте́ль 'bed'
жизнь 'life'	при́быль 'profits'
казнь 'execution'	про́пасть 'abyss'
ле́топись 'chronicle'	рукоя́ть 'handle'

The non-final fixed stress occurs likewise in a few mono-syllables and disyllables (the latter are mostly of foreign origin):

боль 'pain'	мазь 'ointment'	связь 'tie, bond'
верфь 'shipyard'	мель 'sandbank'	тварь 'creature'
грань 'verge, facet'	мысль 'thought'	ткань 'fabric,
дань 'tribute'	нить 'thread'	cloth'
ель 'fir-tree'	прядь 'lock (of hair)'	цель 'aim'
лань 'fallow-deer'	рысь 'lynx'; 'trot'	шаль 'shawl'

га́вань 'harbour'	печа́ль 'grief'
е́ресь 'heresy'	печа́ть 'seal, stamp'
крова́ть 'bed'	ступе́нь 'step, stage'
мете́ль 'snow-storm'	тетра́дь 'exercise book'

(2) The fixed final stress occurs only in the numerals from пять 'five' to де́сять 'ten', два́дцать 'twenty', три́дцать 'thirty' (gen. пяти́, &c.), and in the word любо́вь 'love', gen. любви́.

(b) Mobile stress

In the majority of simple nouns the stress is initial in the singular and in the nom.-acc. pl.; it becomes final in the oblique cases of the plural, as in the example.

Similarly:

бровь 'eyebrow'	дочь 'daughter'	речь 'speech'
весть 'news'	мать 'mother'	роль 'role'
ветвь 'branch'	мышь 'mouse'	сельдь 'herring'
вещь 'thing'	ночь 'night'	сеть 'net'
власть 'power'	ось 'axis, axle'	смерть 'death'
грудь 'breast'	печь 'stove'	соль 'salt'
дверь 'door'	плеть 'whip'	степь 'steppe'

страсть 'passion'	треть 'one third'	часть 'part'
тень 'shadow'	цепь 'chain'	щель 'chink'

ло́шадь 'horse'	по́весть 'tale'
ме́лочь 'trifle'	ска́терть 'table-cloth'
о́бласть 'region'	сте́пень 'degree'
о́чередь 'turn, queue'	це́рковь 'church'
пло́щадь 'area, square'	че́тверть 'a quarter'

A certain number of nouns in -ость have adopted this type of stress system. These are words in common use, the meaning of which has been to some extent concretized, such as но́вость 'novelty, piece of news', кре́пость 'strength, fortress', ско́рость 'speed', in the expression коро́бка скоросте́й 'gear box'.

A few monosyllables take a final stress in the loc. sing. after the prepositions в 'in' and на 'on':

на груди́ 'on the chest'	в пыли́ 'in the dust'
в грязи́ 'in the mud'	на Руси́ 'in Russia'
на двери́ 'on the door'	в связи́ 'in connexion'
в кости́ 'in the bone'	в степи́ 'in the steppe'
в крови́ 'in the blood'	в тени́ 'in the shade'
на мели́ 'on a sandbank'	на цепи́ 'chained up'
на печи́ 'on the stove'	в чести́ 'in honour'

The similarity between the stress of this locative and that of the locative in -у́/-ю́ will be observed (see p. 52).

2. Masculine

The only masculine representative of this type is the word путь 'way'. The declension of путь differs from that of the feminines only in the instr. sing., путём. The stress is final: gen. пути́, &c.

3. Neuter

For the neuters what is involved is a suppletive declension: only the singular follows the third declension, while the plural belongs to the hard type of the second declension. The neuters of this type number ten. In all of them the nom.-acc. sing. ends in -мя, while in the other cases the stem is extended by the addition of the suffix -ен-. Example: вре́мя 'time'.

	Singular		*Plural*
N.-A.	вре́мя	N.-A.	времена́
G.	вре́мени	G.	времён
D.	вре́мени	D.	времена́м
L.	вре́мени	L.	времена́х
I.	вре́менем	I.	времена́ми

The words declined like вре́мя are:

бре́мя 'burden'	пле́мя 'tribe'
вы́мя 'udder'	се́мя 'seed'
зна́мя 'banner'	стре́мя 'stirrup'
и́мя 'name'	те́мя 'crown of the
пла́мя 'flame'	head'

The gen. pl. of се́мя, стре́мя, is семя́н, стремя́н, respectively.

The stress is that of the example, except for зна́мя, which, in the plural, takes the stress on the penultimate: знамёна.

V. PLURALIA TANTUM

In view of the mixture of inflectional types in the plural, it would be impossible as well as unnecessary to try to classify in one of the three declensions those nouns which exist only in the plural form. Only the genitive, and to a less extent the nominative, can furnish any indication of the type to which these nouns belong.

Nom. -ы/-и, gen. zero:

брю́ки 'trousers'	но́жницы 'scissors'
ви́лы 'pitchfork'	по́хороны 'funeral'
крести́ны 'christening'	су́тки 'day and night' (24 hrs.)

Nom. -ы/-и, gen. -ов/-ев:

духи́ 'perfume'	помо́и 'slops'
обо́и 'wallpaper'	тиски́ 'vice, press'
очки́ 'glasses'	штаны́ 'trousers'

Nom. -а/-я, gen. zero:

воро́та 'gateway'	письмена́ 'characters'
пери́ла 'balustrade'	черни́ла 'ink'

Nom. -и, gen. -ей:

дро́жжи 'yeast'	са́ни 'sledge'
клещи́ 'pincers'	я́сли 'crêche'
ку́дри 'curls'	щи 'cabbage soup'

Nom. -а́, gen. -о́в: леса́ 'scaffolding'.
Nom. -ья, gen. -ьев: хло́пья 'flakes'.

The last two types are very rare.

VI. INDECLINABLE NOUNS

There are in Russian more than three hundred indeclinable nouns in common use, to which must be added a large number of technical terms of more restricted use, as well as proper names. Almost all these are recent borrowings from other languages.

All nouns ending in -и and -у/-ю are indeclinable, such as:

ви́ски 'whisky'	такси́ 'taxi'	я́нки 'Yankee'
жюри́ 'jury'	по́ни 'pony'	ле́ди 'lady'
пари́ 'bet'	визави́ 'vis-à-vis'	Чи́ли 'Chile'
ре́гби 'rugby'	де́нди 'dandy'	Ше́лли 'Shelley'
паспарту́ 'passe-partout'	меню́ 'menu'	кенгуру́ 'kangaroo'
табу́ 'taboo'	интервью́ 'interview'	парвеню́ 'parvenu'
рагу́ 'ragout'	зе́бу 'zebu'	Шо́у 'Shaw'
ню 'nude'	какаду́ 'cockatoo'	Пе́ру 'Peru'

Borrowings in -o and -e/-э are also indeclinable, such as:

бордо́ 'claret'	фиа́ско 'fiasco'
бюро́ 'bureau'	эмба́рго 'embargo'
кака́о 'cocoa'	флами́нго 'flamingo'
кино́ 'cinema'	импреса́рио 'impresario'
пальто́ 'overcoat'	Оте́лло 'Othello'
ра́дио 'radio'	Гла́зго 'Glasgow'
желе́ 'jelly'	шимпа́нзе 'chimpanzee'
кабаре́ 'cabaret'	атташе́ 'attaché'
кашне́ 'scarf'	рантье́ 'rentier'
кафе́ 'café'	чичеро́не 'cicerone'
ко́фе 'coffee'	Гёте 'Goethe'
шоссе́ 'highway'	Брю́гге 'Bruges'

Ukrainian surnames in -ко of the type Шевче́нко tend more and more to be indeclinable. If they are declined, they follow the first declension (in spite of their nom. sing. in -o): gen. Шевче́нки, dat. Шевче́нке.

A number of borrowings in stressed -á are indeclinable. Such are

па 'pas'	буржуа́ 'bourgeois'
боа́ 'boa'	альпага́ 'alpaca'
ура́ 'hurrah'	антраша́ 'entrechat'
амплуа́ 'role'	баккара́ 'baccara'

There are, however, borrowings in stressed -á which may be declined, as резеда́ 'mignonette', марсала́ 'marsala', канва́ 'canvas', софа́ 'sofa', &c.

All foreign proper names in stressed -á are indeclinable: Дюма́ 'Dumas', Труа́ 'Troyes'. Russo-Ukrainian proper names in -á are, on the other hand, declined: Шульга́, gen. Шульги́, &c.

The only nouns ending in a consonant which are indeclinable are those denoting women:

     мада́м 'madam'   ми́ссис 'Mrs.'

мадемуазе́ль 'mademoiselle'   фре́йлейн 'Fräulein'
ми́сс 'miss'

as well as а́льма ма́тер 'Alma Mater' and берсёз 'lullaby'.

Women's surnames ending in a consonant are never declined, even if they are of Russian or Ukrainian origin, like Волк, Го́голь.

Russian surnames ending in -ых/-их (Мелки́х), -ово́ (Дурново́), and -а́го (Мертва́го) are not declined.

The names of the musical notes (до, ре, ми, фа, соль, ля, си) and the names of the letters (а, бе, ве, ка, эль, эм, &c.) are also indeclinable, whatever be their form.

The grammatical gender of indeclinable substantives is determined by their meaning.

Nouns denoting persons are masculine (ку́ли 'coolie', пьеро́ 'pierrot', маэ́стро 'maestro') or feminine (ле́ди 'lady', инженю́ 'ingenue', мада́м 'madam') according as they refer to men or to women. Those which may refer to either are of common gender: протеже́ 'protégé(e)', визави́ 'vis-à-vis'.

Nouns denoting animals are masculine: какаду́ 'cockatoo', шимпа́нзе 'chimpanzee'.

All the rest, i.e. those denoting inanimate objects or abstract notions, are neuter. The word ко́фе can be either masculine or neuter, the words а́льма ма́тер and берсёз are feminine.

IV

Nouns: Word-Formation

I. NON-SUFFIXAL DERIVATIVES

THE most productive class of non-suffixal derivatives is that of masculine nouns of action derived from compound verbs (of the type of огород already examined, p. 35):

полёт 'flight'	отдых 'rest'
обыск 'search'	выход 'exit'
напев 'tune'	сплав 'alloy'

Other types are less frequent:
feminines in -a:

измена 'betrayal'	простуда 'cold'

feminine abstract nouns in -ь:

высь 'height'	горечь 'bitterness'

nouns of agent in -a/-я:

зайка 'stammerer'
растеря 'person who tends to lose things'

II. SUFFIXAL DERIVATIVES

1. Nouns denoting Persons

I. MASCULINE

This class includes several groups: nouns of agent, nouns of occupation, attributive nouns, and nouns of origin. The limits between them are not always perfectly distinct.

(a) *Nouns of agent, nouns of occupation, and attributive nouns*

The suffix -тель, which is extremely productive, is the suffix *par excellence* of nouns of agent formed from verbs:

мечта́тель 'dreamer'	воспита́тель 'tutor'
грабитель 'robber'	истребитель 'destroyer';
учи́тель 'teacher'	'fighter' (aircraft)

The suffix -ик, particularly in its extended forms— -чик (after д, т, з, с), -щик, -овщик, -евщик, -льщик, -ник —is frequent and productive for nouns of agent and of occupation, the suffix -ник also for attributive nouns:

лётчик 'airman'	носи́льщик 'porter'
тюре́мщик 'jailer'	сапо́жник 'cobbler'
ростовщи́к 'usurer'	колхо́зник 'collective
старьёвщик 'old-clothes	farmer'
dealer'	ро́дственник 'relation'

The suffix -ец, particularly its extended forms— -овец, -евец, -е́нец—is frequent and productive for nouns of agent and of occupation:

гребе́ц 'rower'	ле́нинец 'Leninist'
толсто́вец 'Tolstoyan'	пораже́нец 'defeatist'

The same suffix -ец serves to form nouns from adjectives: слепе́ц 'blind man'.

Among the suffixes of lesser productivity are:

-у́н in nouns of agent:

болту́н 'chatterbox'	бегу́н 'runner'

-л- in nouns of agent ending in -a:

меня́ла 'money-changer'	громи́ла 'burglar'

-а́к, -я́к, and -а́ч in attributive nouns:

проста́к 'simpleton'	чуда́к 'crank'

остря́к 'a wit'   холостя́к 'bachelor'
рифма́ч 'rhymester'   сила́ч 'athlete'

The suffix -и́ст is the only foreign suffix denoting nouns of agent which has achieved a wide extension in Russian:

шахмати́ст 'chess player'   очерки́ст 'essayist'

The other suffixes of this group are hardly or not at all productive. They include:

-арь	па́харь 'ploughman'
-о́к	знато́к 'connoisseur'
-тай	глаша́тай 'town crier'
-а́н	горла́н 'bawler'
-я́й	негодя́й 'scoundrel'
-е́й	дурале́й 'blockhead'
-ень	при́хвостень 'hanger-on'
-а́ш	торга́ш 'huckster'
-я́га	бедня́га 'poor man'
-у́га	пьянчу́га 'drunkard'
-ы́га	сквалы́га 'miser'
-а́ка	зева́ка 'idler'
-ица	у́мница 'clever person'

(b) *Nouns of origin*

The suffix -ич (for Christian names in -а/-я) and -ович/-евич (for all other Christian names) is the only suffix employed to form the patronymic (о́тчество). In conversation the endings -ович, -евич, where the -о- or -е- is not stressed, are normally abbreviated to -ыч, -ич respectively. Thus:

Ильи́ч 'son of Илья́'
Петро́вич 'son of Пётр'
Анто́нович (Анто́ныч) 'son of Анто́н'
Алексе́евич (Алексе́ич) 'son of Алексе́й'

The suffix -ич occurs also in certain nouns denoting the inhabitants of towns. Thus:

москви́ч 'native of Moscow'

The two remaining productive suffixes in nouns indicating origin in terms of country, region, or town are -ец:

> кавка́зец 'Caucasian'
> шотла́ндец 'Scotsman'
> полта́вец 'inhabitant of Poltava'

and -анин/-янин, the -ин of which disappears in the plural (see p. 57).

> датча́нин 'Dane'   парижа́нин 'Parisian'

This last suffix also denotes social class and religion

> дворяни́н 'noble'   христиани́н 'Christian'

The suffix -ёнок (pl. -я́та/-а́та) is the suffix *par excellence* used to denote young living creatures (see p. 63), both animals:

> волчёнок 'wolf-cub'   гусёнок 'gosling'

and, more rarely, people:

> октябрёнок 'child of October' (member of
>   Communist children's organization)
> турчёнок 'little Turk'

The two remaining suffixes:

> -ёныш   тигрёныш 'young tiger'
> -ыш   глупы́ш 'silly little thing'

are of limited productivity and have either an affectionate or a pejorative connotation.

2. FEMININE

The suffixes which characterize nouns denoting persons of the female sex only rarely possess independent force: for the most part they are the feminine counterparts of the corresponding masculine suffixes.

The suffix -к-, which is extremely productive, may be *added* directly to the masculine noun, sometimes in an extended form -овк-, -енк-, -анк-. Thus:

> арти́стка 'woman stage artist' (masc. арти́ст)

блонди́нка 'blonde' (masc. блонди́н)
москви́чка 'native of Moscow' (masc. москви́ч)
скрипа́чка 'woman violinist' (masc. скрипа́ч)
шве́дка 'Swedish woman' (masc. швед)
воро́вка 'thief' (masc. вор)
францу́женка 'Frenchwoman' (masc. францу́з)
служа́нка 'servant' (masc. слуга́)

It may also replace the masculine suffixes -ец:

голла́ндка 'Dutchwoman' (masc. голла́ндец)
торго́вка 'huckstress' (masc. торго́вец)

and -ин:

англича́нка 'Englishwoman' (masc. англича́нин)
крестья́нка 'peasant-woman' (masc. крестья́нин)

The same suffix, with various extensions, may possess independent force:

доя́рка 'milkmaid'   коке́тка 'coquette'
пра́чка 'laundress'   курси́стка 'girl-student'

The suffix -ица, which is less productive, furnishes, above all in the form -ница, the feminines corresponding to the nouns in -тель:

учи́тельница 'school-teacher' (masc. учи́тель)
повели́тельница 'sovereign' (masc. повели́тель)

It also replaces the suffixes

-ик перево́дчица 'translator' (masc. перево́дчик)
-ец певи́ца 'singer' (masc. певе́ц)

It is common in the names of female animals:

волчи́ца 'she-wolf' (masc. волк)
льви́ца 'lioness' (masc. лев)

Other suffixes are less frequent:

-ья лгу́нья 'liar' (masc. лгун)
-ша касси́рша 'cashier' (masc. касси́р)
     адмира́льша 'admiral's lady' (masc. адмира́л)
-иха портни́ха 'dress-maker' (masc. портно́й 'tailor')

The patronymic suffix -овна corresponds to the masc. -ович, -евна to the masc. -евич, -ична, and -инична to the masc. -ич. Thus:

> Петро́вна (masc. Петро́вич), Алексе́евна (masc. Алексе́евич), Ники́тична (masc. Ники́тич), Ильи́-нична (masc. Ильи́ч).

2. Abstract Nouns

This section includes both abstract nouns properly so called, which are derived from nouns and adjectives, and nouns of action, which are normally derived from verbs, with all their variants: pure action, result of action (often a concrete noun), occupation, profession, collective force. The suffixes are to some extent the same in both categories.

I. NOUNS OF ACTION

The extremely productive suffix -нье/-ние is the suffix *par excellence* of nouns of action. Nouns of this category were derived originally from the past participle passive:

> кра́шенье 'painting'   расписа́ние 'time-table'

The tendency now is to form them directly from the infinitive. Thus:

> гуля́нье 'walk'   жанти́льничанье 'affectation'
> стара́нье 'zeal'

The suffix -тье/-тие, corresponding to the past participle passive in -т-, no longer gives rise to new formations:

> разви́тие 'development'   взя́тие 'capture'

Certain nouns in -ье take the stress on the last syllable; these all belong to the colloquial or vulgar style:

> враньё 'lies'   мытьё 'washing'

For the suffix -ье in compound words, see p. 91.

The very productive suffix -ка is distinguished from the suffix -нье by its more colloquial, and often concrete, character:

ва́рка 'cooking'   наши́вка 'chevron'
чи́стка 'cleaning, purge'   остано́вка 'stop'

The suffix -ёж is less productive and belongs to the colloquial style:

грабёж 'looting'   платёж 'payment'

It is sometimes combined with -ка:

бомбёжка 'bombardment'   кормёжка 'feeding'

Two modern foreign suffixes have a certain degree of productivity:

-иза́ция

воениза́ция 'militarization'
озимиза́ция 'transformation of spring corn into winter corn'

-а́ж (Fr. -*age*)

инструкта́ж 'instruction'   подхалима́ж 'toadying'

Among the suffixes which are almost or entirely dead are:

-ба	стрельба́ 'shooting'	борьба́ 'struggle'
-ок	прыжо́к 'jump'	толчо́к 'push, bump'
-ня	мазня́ 'daub'	стряпня́ 'cooking'
-тва	кля́тва 'oath'	би́тва 'battle'

2. ABSTRACT NOUNS PROPER

The very productive suffix -ость is the suffix *par excellence* of abstract nouns derived from adjectives (almost all adjectives may form abstract nouns with the aid of -ость) and participles. It is the most frequent of nominal suffixes:

го́рдость 'pride'
экспанси́вность 'demonstrativeness'

терпи́мость 'toleration'
задо́лженность 'indebtedness'

The parallel suffix -есть is much less common:

све́жесть 'freshness'   живу́честь 'vitality'

The suffix -ство (-ество after ж, ш, ч, щ), also very productive, supplies nouns indicating condition (quality, occupation, profession, social status, ideological trend, &c.):

зве́рство 'ferocity'   птицево́дство 'poultry
де́тство 'childhood'   breeding'
родство́ 'kinship'   англофи́льство 'pro-
вещество́ 'substance'   English feeling'
госуда́рство 'State'   това́рищество 'company'

This suffix occurs also in the extended forms:

-овство   хвастовство́ 'boastfulness'
-ничество бродя́жничество 'vagrancy'
-енчество пораже́нчество 'defeatism'

The suffix -ина, which is unproductive in its simple form (ширина́ 'width') is extremely productive in the extended forms -щина (-чина) and -овщина to denote unfavourably a state of mind or a political, social or artistic movement or trend. Thus:

вое́нщина 'soldiery'
уголо́вщина 'criminal activity'
кружко́вщина 'coterie spirit'
чертовщи́на 'devilry'
кере́нщина 'Kerensky régime'
хлестако́вщина 'reckless boastfulness'

The borrowed suffix -и́зм has been completely nationalized:

большеви́зм 'Bolshevism'
бытови́зм 'portrayal of manners' (in literature)

Among the suffixes which are almost or quite dead are:

-ствие бе́дствие 'hardship'　сле́дствие 'investigation'
-ота́ быстрота́ 'quickness'　глухота́ 'deafness'
-ица (indicating an unfavourable condition)
　　　 безрабо́тица 'unemployment'
-изна белизна́ 'whiteness'　дороговизна 'dearness'
-знь боя́знь 'fear'　　　жизнь 'life'
-ыня горды́ня 'pride'

3. Collective and Singulative Nouns

1. COLLECTIVES

The only productive suffix is -ьё. Words formed with its help from other nouns often have a contemptuous shade of meaning. Thus:

сырьё 'raw material'	тряпьё 'rags'
бабьё 'women'	старьё 'old stuff'
дурачьё 'fools'	зверьё 'animals'

Among the suffixes which are almost or quite dead are:

-ня́　родня́ 'relations'
-ина　мешани́на 'medley'
-тва́　братва́ 'comrades'
-ник and -ня́к (in collectives formed from the names of trees): е́льник 'fir-grove'
　　　　лозня́к 'clump of young willows'

2. SINGULATIVES

A singulative noun denotes one member of a category or group. The only singulative suffix is -ина, which is often extended to -инка:

жемчу́жина 'pearl'	песчи́нка 'grain of sand'
гра́дина 'hailstone'	соло́минка 'straw'
горо́шина 'pea'	крови́нка 'drop of blood'

4. Concrete Nouns

The suffixes which serve to form nouns of concrete meaning constitute the least clear-cut category of the word-formation of nouns. The same suffix may have more than one function. Nouns derived from adjectives are the most numerous, followed by those derived from nouns and from verbs.

The suffix -ка is distinguished from the other suffixes by the manner in which it usually operates in word-formation: in a group made up of an adjective and a noun, the latter is dropped and the adjective, assuming the character of a noun, takes the suffix -ка. This phenomenon is recent and frequent:

> треуго́лка (треуго́льная шля́па) 'cocked hat'
> откры́тка (откры́тое письмо́) 'postcard'
> водя́нка (водяна́я боле́знь) 'dropsy'
> пятиле́тка (пятиле́тний план) 'five-year plan'

In the form -лка the same suffix is used to form nouns from verbs:

> ве́шалка 'rack'   гре́лка 'hot-water bottle'

Other suffixes are:

-ик   тупи́к 'blind alley', or, more usually:

-овик   грузови́к 'lorry'   чернови́к 'rough draft'

-ник   воротни́к 'collar'   сбо́рник 'collection'

-льник   буди́льник 'alarm-clock' умыва́льник 'wash-basin'   холоди́льник 'refrigerator'

-ица,   the feminine form corresponding to the preceding suffix:

> петли́ца 'button-hole'   черепи́ца 'tile'

-овица   передови́ца 'leading article'
         шелкови́ца 'mulberry tree'

-ница   ме́льница 'mill'   пе́пельница 'ash-tray'
-ок   (with mobile -o-), to denote particularly:

   (1) the product of action:
          отры́вок 'fragment'   свёрток 'parcel'

   (2) (in the form of *pluralia tantum*) refuse:
          объе́дки 'leavings'   опи́лки 'sawdust'

Four suffixes indicating place names:

-ня   каменоло́мня 'quarry'   пека́рня 'bakery'
-льня   краси́льня 'dye-works'   спа́льня 'bed-room'
-ще   пожа́рище 'site of a fire'   убе́жище 'refuge'
-ье   (with prefixes):
          подно́жье 'foot' (fig.)
          примо́рье 'coastal district'
-ина,   with different meanings:

   (1) meat or fish:
          свини́на 'pork'   теля́тина 'veal'
          лососи́на 'salmon'

   (2) names of trees or plants:
          мали́на 'raspberry'   ряби́на 'rowan'

   (3) various:
          равни́на 'plain'   разва́лина 'ruin'

Suffixes of little or no productivity:

-а́к/-я́к   пята́к 'five-copeck coin'   костя́к 'skeleton'
-а́рь   слова́рь 'dictionary'   суха́рь 'rusk'
-ень   ли́вень 'cloud-burst'   плете́нь 'hurdle'
-ец   рубе́ц 'hem; scar'   трезу́бец 'trident'
-йка, names of berries:
          клубни́ка 'strawberry'   черни́ка 'bilberry'
-ло   мы́ло 'soap'   одея́ло 'blanket'
-во   за́рево 'glow'   то́пливо 'fuel'

5. Diminutives and Augmentatives

Diminution is not the only, or indeed the essential, function of the diminutive suffixes: more often than not these suffixes indicate only an attitude—favourable (affection, good humour) or unfavourable, pejorative (depreciation, contempt)—on the part of the speaker to a person or thing, whether concrete or abstract, with no reference to size.

The same is true of the augmentative suffixes, with this difference, that they do not express affection.

A. DIMINUTIVES

Diminutives have generally an intensely expressive and familiar character. The system of diminutives is extremely rich in Russian; there are words which may have as many as half a dozen diminutives, for example, головá 'head':

голóвка	головёшка	головёнка
голóвушка	голóвонька	головёночка

Such an abundance implies a gradation in the system of diminutives; and indeed three degrees, characterized by a progressive accumulation of suffixes, may be distinguished. The base of the diminutive suffix remains the suffix -к- (more rarely -ц-); in the higher degrees the consonants -ч-, -ш-, -н- may be added. The mobile vowels play an important role in the diminutive suffixes.

I. FIRST DEGREE

The first degree is characterized by the consonant -к-, rarely -ц-. It expresses the simple diminutive, in which, along with the idea of actual diminution, that of affection (though without too pronounced a shade of familiarity) is also present and sometimes predominates. The pejorative force is very rare.

(1) The suffix -к- (with alternations к/ч, г/ж, х/ш, ц/ч in the stem). This suffix is extremely productive in the masculine and feminine, and is little used in the neuter.

Fem. -ка:

> бородка 'goatee' (борода 'beard')
> ножка (нога 'foot')
> ночка (ночь 'night')

Masc. -óк, -ёк, -ик, -чик:

> часóк (час 'hour')
> божóк (бог 'god')
> зверёк (зверь 'animal')
> нóсик (нос 'nose')
> стýльчик (стул 'chair')
> аэроплáнчик (аэроплáн 'aircraft')

Neut. -ко, -ико:

> молочкó (молокó 'milk')
> колёсико (колесó 'wheel')

(2) The suffix -ц-, which does not often occur in the masculine and feminine, is common in the neuter.

Fem. -ца, -ица:

> двéрца (дверь 'door')
> сестрúца (сестрá 'sister')

Masc. -ец:

> брáтец (брат 'brother')
> товáрец (товáр 'wares')

Neut. -цó, -ецó (stressed), and -це, -ице (unstressed):

> винцó (винó 'wine')
> ружьецó (ружьё 'rifle')
> дéльце (дéло 'business')
> плáтьице (плáтье 'dress')

2. SECOND DEGREE

Diminutives of the second degree have the compound suffixes -чк-, -шк-, -нк-. The diminutive force properly so called almost disappears and is replaced by the expressive force of the suffix, characterizing not the object or the idea themselves but the speaker's attitude to them.

(a) Suffixes of endearment

(1) The suffix -чк-. This is the suffix of the second degree in the most direct meaning of the term; it supplies the diminutive of the diminutives of the first degree:

> я́ма 'ditch'
> я́мка 'small ditch' (1st degree)
> я́мочка 'dimple' (2nd degree)

Similarly:

> кни́жечка (кни́жка—кни́га 'book')
> вещи́чка (вещи́ца—вещь 'thing')
> листо́чек (листо́к—лист 'leaf')
> голосо́чек (голосо́к—го́лос 'voice')

Masc. dim. in -ик, -чик have no second degree. In the neuter the second degree is rare:

> ведёрочко (ведёрко—ведро́ 'bucket')

(2) The suffixes -ушк- and -ышк- (unstressed). These are not normally derived from suffixes of the first degree:

> коро́вушка (коро́ва 'cow')
> дя́дюшка (дя́дя 'uncle')
> хле́бушек (хлеб 'bread')
> ко́лышек (кол 'stake')
> зёрнышко (зерно́ 'grain')

(3) The suffix -еньк- (unstressed) is limited almost entirely to the feminine and is not derived from a suffix of the first degree:

> ду́шенька (душа́ 'soul')
> ма́менька (ма́ма 'mamma')
> Бо́женька (Бог 'God')

(b) Pejorative suffixes

The pejorative suffixes of the second degree are:

(1) The suffixes -ишк- (stressed or unstressed), -у́шк- (stressed, only in fem.). The endings are -a for all feminines

and for masculines denoting persons and animals, -o for all neuters and masculines denoting objects:

> страсти́шка ('страсть 'passion')
> актёришка (актёр 'actor')
> пиджачи́шко (пиджа́к 'jacket')
> письми́шко (письмо́ 'letter')
> речу́шка (река́ 'river')

(2) The suffix -о́нк-, -ёнк- (stressed) operates only in the feminine and in a few masculine nouns denoting persons; the ending is -a:

> старушо́нка (стару́ха 'old woman')
> избёнка (изба́ 'peasant's hut')
> мужичо́нка (мужи́к 'peasant')

3. THIRD DEGREE

Diminutives of the third degree are formed by adding the diminutive suffix -к- to the pejorative forms of the second degree -у́шка, -и́шка, -о́нка. The new suffix appears as:

> -у́шечк-а, -и́шечк-а, -о́ночк-а,

and expresses always affection-with a shade of familiarity:

> комнату́шечка (комнату́шка—ко́мната 'room')
> хвастуни́шечка (хвастуни́шка—хвасту́н 'braggart')
> рубашо́ночка (рубашо́нка—руба́шка 'shirt')

4. EMANCIPATION OF DIMINUTIVES

It need hardly be said that not all the links in the chain of diminutive-formation are always represented in the language.

Moreover, certain diminutives lose their special force and take the place of the words from which they were derived; these latter acquire then an augmentative force:

> молото́к 'hammer' (мо́лот)
> буты́лка 'bottle' (буты́ль)

The diminutive may also lose its special force by being assigned a particular meaning:

чáшка 'cup' (чáша 'goblet')
мужи́к 'peasant' (муж 'man')
гóрлышко 'neck of a bottle' (гóрло 'throat')
пузырёк 'small bottle' (пузы́рь 'bubble, bladder')
булáвка 'pin' (булавá 'mace')
крыльцó 'flight of steps' (крылó 'wing')

B. AUGMENTATIVES

The system of augmentatives in Russian is much poorer than that of diminutives. The augmentative suffix never expresses affection, but is often pejorative.

(1) -ищ- is the augmentative suffix *par excellence*. In it the pejorative force is definitely subordinate to the augmentative; the endings are -a for the feminine, -e for the masculine and neuter:

собачи́ща (собáка 'dog')   сундучи́ще (сундýк 'trunk')
кни́жища (кни́га 'book')   вини́ще (винó 'wine')
урóдище (урóд 'monster, abortion')   болóтище (болóто 'swamp')

(2) The suffix -ин-a has a less definite augmentative force. It is rare with words other than masculine:

доми́на (дом 'house')   купчи́на (купéц 'merchant')

6. Diminutives of Christian Names

The system of diminutives of Christian names in Russian has certain characteristics of its own. The use made of these diminutives is very considerable: apart from the full form of the name accompanied by the patronymic (и́мя и óтчество) almost the only form of address employed in familiar relations is the diminutive of the Christian name, the force of which is purely expressive.

I. SUFFIXES OF ENDEARMENT

(a) *First degree*

The stems of these diminutives tend to be monosyllabic. Generally, they consist of the first syllable of the name.

(1) The non-suffixal diminutives end in -я, more rarely in -a:

Ва́ся (Васи́лий)	Ка́тя (Екатери́на)
Ми́тя (Дми́трий)	Стёпа (Степа́н)
На́дя (Наде́жда)	Ли́да (Ли́дия)

(2) The suffix -ша is less frequent than the non-suffixal forms:

Гри́ша (Григо́рий)	Да́ша (Да́рья)
Са́ша (Алекса́ндр)	Ната́ша (Ната́лья)

It occurs sometimes in the form -у́ша/-ю́ша:

Марфу́ша (Ма́рфа)	Андрю́ша (Андре́й)

(3) The suffix -ня is less frequent than the two preceding:

Се́ня (Семён)	Та́ня (Татья́на)
Лёня (Леони́д)	Со́ня (Со́фья)

(4) Other types are represented by a small number of examples:

Па́влик (Па́вел)	А́ся (А́нна)
Ко́ка (Никола́й)	Бо́ба (Бори́с)

(b) *Second degree*

(1) The suffix -енька may be employed with all names except those the stem of which ends in -н-; it is very rarely employed with non-suffixal diminutives of the first degree in -a:

То́ленька (То́ля—Анато́лий)
На́стенька (На́стя—Анастаси́я)
Ми́шенька (Ми́ша—Михаи́л)
Ма́шенька (Ма́ша—Ма́рья)
А́сенька (А́ся—А́нна)

(2) The suffix -очка/-ечка is obligatory with diminutives the stem of which ends in -н- and is usual with non-suffixal diminutives in -а:

Ва́нечка (Ва́ня—Ива́н)	Ле́ночка (Ле́на—Еле́на)
Кла́вочка (Кла́ва—Кла́вдия)	Ю́рочка (Ю́ра—Ю́рий)

First degree diminutives in -ша only very rarely form second degree diminutives in -ечка:

$$\text{Илю́шечка (Илю́ша—Илья́)}$$

(c) Other forms

The suffix -ушка (unstressed) may be added to the full form of the name to form diminutives of an essentially popular character:

Ива́нушка (Ива́н)	А́ннушка (А́нна)
Его́рушка (Его́р)	Праско́вьюшка (Праско́вья)

2. PEJORATIVE SUFFIX

The pejorative suffix is -ка, which replaces the final -а/-я of the form of the first degree:

Воло́дька (Воло́дя—Влади́мир)
Ва́рька (Ва́ря—Варва́ра)
Ду́нька (Ду́ня—Авдо́тья/Евдоки́я)
Зи́нка (Зи́на—Зинаи́да)
Па́шка (Па́ша—Па́вел)
Петру́шка (Петру́ша—Пётр)
Се́нька (Се́ня—Семён)

III. COMPOUND NOUNS

Russian compound nouns are extremely numerous and constitute a continuously expanding category.

Compounds resulting from the mere juxtaposition of two words, such as occur frequently in other European languages (Eng. *windmill*, Fr. *timbre-poste*, Ger. *Luftwaffe*) do not occur in Russian. In Russian the component elements are dovetailed together and the resultant compound noun has a specific form of its own. An important part is played by suffixes.

1. Compounds with Connecting Vowel

These form the most important group in respect both of number and of productivity. The first element, of substantival or adjectival origin, is connected with the second by the vowel -o- (-e- after a soft consonant).

I. COMPOUNDS WITH SECOND ELEMENT OF VERBAL ORIGIN

The first term serves as determinant to the second. Most frequently it is a noun.

(*a*) *Non-suffixal compounds*

These consist to a great extent of nouns of agent and of instrument:

водола́з 'diver'	водопа́д 'waterfall'
людое́д 'cannibal'	парохо́д 'steamer'
пивова́р 'brewer'	пулемёт 'machine-gun'
старожи́л 'old resident'	пылесо́с 'vacuum cleaner'
языкове́д 'philologist'	самолёт 'aeroplane'

(*b*) *Suffixal compounds*

(1) *Nouns of agent and of instrument:*

богомо́лец 'pilgrim'	рукомо́йник 'wash-basin'
законода́тель 'legislator'	самоу́чка 'self-educated person'
очеви́дец 'eye-witness'	зубочи́стка 'tooth-pick'
бронено́сец 'iron-clad'	мышело́вка 'mouse-trap'

(2) *Abstract nouns:*

земледе́лие 'agriculture'	богомо́лье 'pilgrimage'
плодоро́дие 'fertility'	единобо́рство 'single combat'
честолю́бие 'ambition'	головоло́мка 'puzzle'

(3) Words belonging to other groups are few:

лесопи́льня 'sawmill'   во́доросль 'waterweed'

(c) Compounds with an independent word as second element

  (1) Nouns of agent and of instrument:

золотоиска́тель 'gold prospector'
судовладе́лец 'ship-owner'
человеконенави́стник 'misanthrope'
огнетуши́тель 'fire-extinguisher'

  (2) Nouns of action:

землетрясе́ние 'earthquake'
рукопожа́тие 'handshake'
судопроизво́дство 'legal procedure'
общежи́тие 'social life, hostel'
нововведе́ние 'innovation'
самозащи́та 'self-defence'

2. COMPOUNDS WITH SECOND ELEMENT OF SUBSTANTIVAL ORIGIN

(a) Non-suffixal compounds

Compounds of this type are very few:

чернозём 'black earth'
толстосу́м 'money-bag' (rich man)

(b) Suffixal compounds

Compounds of this type are very common. Almost all are of the type adjective (determinant) + noun (determinate). The most usual suffix is -ье/-ие (collective and abstract nouns):

новолу́нье 'new moon' (но́вая луна́)
мелково́дье 'low water'
плоского́рье 'plateau'
средневеко́вье 'Middle Ages'
доброду́шие 'good nature'
своеобра́зие 'originality, peculiarity'

гололе́дица 'ice-covered ground'
Черного́рия 'Montenegro'
красноарме́ец 'Red Army man'
фальшивомоне́тчик 'coiner'

(c) Compounds with an independent word as second element

This type is infrequent. It is confined to the literary language and to technical terminology:

светоте́нь 'chiaroscuro'
лесопромы́шленник 'timber merchant'
углекислота́ 'carbonic acid'
носоро́г 'rhinoceros'
частоко́л 'palissade'

2. Other Types of Compounds

1. COMPOUNDS WITH A NUMERAL AS FIRST ELEMENT

In these compounds the first element is a genitive or at least a form which is felt as such. The second element may be either suffixal or non-suffixal:

двусмы́слица 'ambiguity'   пятикни́жие 'Pentateuch'
трёхсотле́тие 'tricentenary'   полубо́г 'demigod'

This type is infrequent and literary. It will be observed that such words as

пятиле́тка 'five-year plan ' (see p. 81)
трено́жник 'tripod'

are not compound nouns but suffixal nouns formed from compound adjectives.

2. COMPOUNDS WITH AN INVARIABLE FIRST ELEMENT

(a) With a prefix as first element

These compounds are formed by the substantivization of a syntactical group consisting of preposition + noun:

безры́бье 'lack of fish' (from без ры́бы 'without fish')

The prefix без- 'without' is the most productive of the prefixes employed in the formation of denominative compounds:

> бездоро́жье 'lack, or bad condition, of roads'
> безде́лье 'inactivity'
> бессмы́слица 'absurdity'

The other prefixes are less productive:

Заво́лжье 'the trans-Volga region'	пра́дед 'great-grandfather'
	предчу́вствие 'presentiment'
наме́стник 'governor'	пристра́стие 'partiality'
переми́рие 'armistice'	противоя́дие 'antidote'
побере́жье 'coast'	сверхчелове́к 'superman'
подотде́л 'subsection'	сожи́тель 'room-mate'

(b) With a negative particle as first element

This type is not numerous:

непра́вда 'untruth'   неудово́льствие 'dissatisfaction'

(c) With a foreign word as first element

Compounds of this type are frequently created in modern Russian:

> авиапо́чта 'airmail'
> автозаво́д 'motor works'
> кинопромы́шленность 'motion picture industry'
> контрразве́дка 'counter-espionage'
> псевдонау́ка 'pseudo-science'
> электросе́ть 'electricity network'

3. Compounds formed by Abbreviation

Russian may form new compounds from fragments, whether entire syllables or mere initials, of existing words. These compounds are not found before the twentieth century.

(1) The commonest type is also the most recent (since

1917): a determinant reduced to one or, rarely, two syllables is prefixed, as first element of the compound, to an entire word. For example:

> ветврáч 'veterinary surgeon' (ветеринáрный врач)
> гостеáтр 'State theatre' (госудáрственный теáтр)
> нарсýд 'people's court' (нарóдный суд)
> политбюрó 'political bureau' (политúческое бюрó)
> сберкáсса 'savings bank' (сберегáтельная кáсса)
> физкультýра 'physical training' (физúческая культýра)

The other types of compounds formed by abbreviation are much less frequent and are limited to technical terms:

(2) Both elements are reduced to syllables:

> колхóз 'collective farm' (коллектúвное хозя́йство)
> линкóр 'battleship' (линéйный корáбль)
> медфáк 'medical faculty' (медицúнский факультéт)

(3) The compound is made up of the initials alone. This type is very rare in common nouns:

> вуз = вы́сшее учéбное заведéние 'institute of higher education'
> рик = райóнный исполнúтельный комитéт 'district executive committee'

Such compounds are virtually limited to names denoting the new institutions of the régime, such as:

ВОКС = Всесоюзное Óбщество Культýрной Свя́зи с заграницей 'All-Union Society for Cultural Relations'

ТАСС = Телегрáфное Áгентство Совéтского Союза 'Soviet Union Telegraph Agency'

They are frequently ephemeral, as

СТО = Совéт Трудá и Оборóны 'Council of Labour and Defence'

V

Adjectives

I. DECLENSION

1. General Characteristics

The declension of adjectives is less varied than that of nouns. The vast majority of adjectives follow a single type of declension which may be termed *normal*. This declension is also that of the participles.

Descriptive adjectives and passive participles possess, in addition to this normal declension, a form known as the *short form*, limited to the nominative case and serving only as predicate. The endings of this short form are identical with those of nouns of the first (fem.) and second (masc. and neut.) declensions.

Certain groups of adjectives, notably possessive and certain relative adjectives, have a mixed type of declension which combines the short form in the nom.-acc. with the normal forms in the oblique cases.

Surnames in -ов and -ин, which were originally possessive adjectives, also present a mixture of short (substantival) and normal (adjectival) forms.

The stress is fixed in the normal and in the mixed declension of adjectives. In the short form it may be mobile and may vary from one gender to another.

Substantivized adjectives form a very rich category. Their syntactical use is that of nouns, but their declension differs in no way from that of adjectives proper.

2. Normal Declension

Adjectives have only one declension, which comprises, as in the case of nouns, a hard and a soft type, with the same orthographical variations in the endings: а/я, у/ю, о/е, ы/и.

I. EXAMPLE

The singular possesses three series of inflexion, one for each gender; the neuter differs from the masculine only in the nom.-acc. The plural possesses only one, with no distinction of gender.

Hard type: но́вый 'new'

	Singular Masc.	Neut.	Fem.	Plural
N.	но́вый	но́вое	но́вая	N. но́вые
A.	N. or G.	но́вое	но́вую	A. N. or G.
G.	но́вого		но́вой	G. но́вых
D.	но́вому		но́вой	D. но́вым
L.	но́вом		но́вой	L. но́вых
I.	но́вым		но́вой	I. но́выми

Soft type: ве́рхний 'upper'

	Singular Masc.	Neut.	Fem.	Plural
N.	ве́рхний	ве́рхнее	ве́рхняя	N. ве́рхние
A.	N. or G.	ве́рхнее	ве́рхнюю	A. N. or G.
G.	ве́рхнего		ве́рхней	G. ве́рхних
D.	ве́рхнему		ве́рхней	D. ве́рхним
L.	ве́рхнем		ве́рхней	L. ве́рхних
I.	ве́рхним		ве́рхней	I. ве́рхними

2. OBSERVATIONS

Adjectives of the hard type which take the stress on the

final syllable have in the nom. sing. masc. the ending -о́й

молодо́й 'young'　　　　слепо́й 'blind'

The ending of the gen. sing. masc. and neut. is -ovo/-evo. By an orthographical archaism the sound v is represented by the letter г.

The pronunciation of the final syllable of the nom. sing. masc. of the hard type may be either orthographical (*-yj, -ij*: recent pronunciation) or identical with that of the gen.-dat.-loc.-instr. fem. (*-əj*: traditional pronunciation). For example:

но́вый (*nóvyj* or *nóvəj*)　ло́вкий (*lófk'ij* or *lófkəj*)

As with nouns of the first declension, the instr. sing. fem. may have, in addition to the normal ending -ой, -ей, the literary ending -ою, -ею.

3. STRESS

The stress of adjectives of the normal declension is always fixed. It may fall either on the stem or on the ending; in the latter case it falls on the first syllable of the ending (слепо́й, gen. слепо́го, fem. слепа́я, &c.). In other words, the stress is always that of the nom. sing. Adjectives of the soft type never take the stress on the ending.

3. Short Form

I. GENERAL OBSERVATIONS

A large number of adjectives and all passive participles have in the nominative of both numbers, in addition to the normal (long or compound) form, another (short or simple) form:

masc. нов, neut. но́во, fem. нова́, pl. но́вы

The endings of this short form, it will be observed, are those of nouns of the second and first declensions.

The short form exists alongside the normal long form

only for descriptive adjectives and passive participles. Adjectives other than descriptive, in particular all adjectives in -ск-, have only the long form, as:

серебряный 'of silver'   майский 'of May'
комнатный 'of a room'   городской 'urban'

As adjectives of the soft type are never descriptive they do not occur in the short form. The two exceptions are синий 'blue' (синь) and искренний 'sincere' (искренен, with *hard* н).

On the other hand, there are only two adjectives which occur only in the short form: рад 'pleased' and the colloquial горазд 'good at'.

2. THE FORCE OF THE SHORT FORM

The long form may serve either as epithet (regular use) or as predicate. The short form occurs in normal usage only as predicate:

холодный день 'a cold day'
день холоден 'the day is cold'

The short form occurs as epithet only in popular or dialectal expressions.

In the oblique cases, which are formed in accordance with the declension of nouns of the first and second declensions, the short form has survived only in a few phrases of an adverbial character such as:

среди бела дня 'in broad daylight'
на босу ногу 'without stockings'

In addition, it has given rise to a large number of adverbs, such as:

снова 'again' (see p. 149)

But even as predicate the short form is a living category only in the case of past participles passive. There its use is obligatory, and it is employed for all verbs, even the most recent. Thus:

простенографи́рован 'taken down in shorthand'

With adjectives proper the long form is frequently used predicatively instead of the short form (see p. 286).

3. MOBILE VOWEL

A mobile vowel may occur in the short form only in the masculine, which is a form with zero-ending:

кре́пок 'strong' кре́пко, крепка́, кре́пки
хо́лоден 'cold' хо́лодно, холодна́, хо́лодны

4. STRESS

Unlike the long form, the short form of the adjective may have either a fixed or a mobile stress.

(1) The fixed stress may fall on any syllable:

(*a*) other than final: краси́в 'beautiful', краси́во, краси́ва, краси́вы;

(*b*) final: хоро́ш 'good', хорошо́, хороша́, хоро́ши.

The second type is commoner than the first.

(2) The mobile stress is of a single type: final in the feminine, non-final in the other forms:

ве́сел 'gay' ве́село, весела́, ве́селы

The majority of primary adjectives (without suffixes or prefixes) which are monosyllabic in the masculine belong to this type:

горд 'proud', го́рдо, горда́, го́рды
прав 'right', пра́во, права́, пра́вы
чист 'clean', чи́сто, чиста́, чи́сты

This mobility of stress is not always rigorously observed and the neuter, and still more the plural, constantly waver between the initial stress and the final stress, under the influence of the feminine.

The stress of the short form has no fixed place in relation to that of the long form. Usually the stress of the masculine is the same in the two forms. Sometimes it moves back by one syllable in the short form, especially in adjectives with -оро-, -оло- in the stem:

дорогóй/дóрог 'dear'	весёлый/вéсел 'gay'
голóдный/гóлоден 'hungry'	дешёвый/дёшев 'cheap'
молодóй/мóлод 'young'	зелёный/зéлен 'green'
холóдный/хóлоден 'cold'	больнóй/бóлен 'ill'
холостóй/хóлост 'bachelor'	

More rarely it moves forward:

óстрый/остёр 'sharp'	сúльный/силён 'strong'
ýмный/умён 'intelligent'	хúтрый/хитёр 'sly'

4. Adjectives of Mixed Declension

Two groups of adjectives are of mixed declension: the nom.-acc. of both numbers has the short form, while the rest of the declension has the long form.

1. RELATIVE ADJECTIVES IN *yod*

Most of this group consists of adjectives derived from the names of animals, as:

лúсий 'fox's'	рýбий 'fish's'
корóвий 'cow's'	собáчий 'dog's'

it includes also a few derived from nouns denoting persons, as:

охóтничий 'hunter's'   вдóвий 'widow's'

and also:

Бóжий 'God's'   трéтий 'third'

Example: во́лчий 'wolf's':

	Singular			*Plural*
	Masc.	*Neut.*	*Fem.*	
N.	во́лчий	во́лчье	во́лчья	N. во́лчьи
A.	N. or G.	во́лчье	во́лчью	A. N. or G.
G.		во́лчьего	во́лчьей	G. во́лчьих
D.		во́лчьему	во́лчьей	D. во́лчьим
L.		во́лчьем	во́лчьей	L. во́лчьих
I.		во́лчьим	во́лчьей	I. во́лчьими

It will be observed that the nom. sing. masc. has, instead of a mobile -e-, a mobile -и-.

2. POSSESSIVE ADJECTIVES IN -ИН AND -ОВ

Adjectives in -ин (see p. 116) are derived from nouns in -a/-я denoting persons and consisting almost exclusively of words indicating kinship, such as:

ма́мин 'mamma's'   тётин 'aunt's'

and of the diminutives of Christian names, such as:

Ко́лин 'Kolya's'   Ната́шин 'Natasha's'

Example: дя́дин 'uncle's':

	Singular			*Plural*
	Masc.	*Neut.*	*Fem.*	
N.	дя́дин	дя́дино	дя́дина	N. дя́дины
A.	N. or G.	дя́дино	дя́дину	A. N. or G.
G.		дя́диного	дя́диной	G. дя́диных
D.		дя́диному	дя́диной	D. дя́диным
L.		дя́дином	дя́диной	L. дя́диных
I.		дя́диным	дя́диной	I. дя́диными

Possessive adjectives in -ов/-ев, derived from nouns of the second declension and parallel to those in -ин (отцо́в from оте́ц 'father') are now archaisms which tend to be avoided in normal language (see p. 116). Adjectives in -ов/-ев still occur in a few fixed phrases such as чо́ртова дю́жина 'baker's dozen' (lit. 'devil's dozen'), цвет во́ронова крыла́ 'the colour of a raven's wing'. The same is true of the short forms of the oblique cases of adjectives in -ин: Татья́нин день, 'St. Tatiana's Day', gen. Татья́нина дня, dat. Татья́нину дню, &c.

5. Surnames in -ов/-ев and -ин

Surnames in -ов/-ев and -ин were originally possessive adjectives of the short type. Their declension nowadays presents a mixture of short and long forms, i.e. of substantival and adjectival endings. Russian surnames occur in three forms: masculine, feminine, and plural. Example:

	Singular			*Plural*	
	Masc.	*Fem.*			
N.	Во́лков	Во́лкова	N.	Во́лковы	
A.	Во́лкова	Во́лкову	A.	*Во́лковых	
G.	Во́лкова	*Во́лковой	G.	*Во́лковых	
D.	Во́лкову	*Во́лковой	D.	*Во́лковым	
L.	Во́лкове	*Во́лковой	L.	*Во́лковых	
I.	*Во́лковым	*Во́лковой	I.	*Во́лковыми	

The adjectival forms are marked with an asterisk.

It is to be observed that the archaic ending -ою/-ею does not occur in the instr. sing. fem.

Surnames in -ин (Пу́шкин) follow the same type of inflexion.

Surnames in -ов/-ев always have a fixed stress, which falls on the same syllable as in the nom. sing. masc.

Surnames in -ин also have a fixed stress, except that if in the nom. sing. masc. the stress falls on the syllable -ин, it passes to the final syllable in the other cases: Фоми́н, Фомина́, Фомину́, pl. Фомины́, &c.

6. Substantivized Adjectives

Russian possesses a large number of substantivized adjectives. These are inflected like adjectives but employed syntactically like nouns.

As the substantivization of adjectives is a living phenomenon in Russian, it may be observed at all the stages between the adjective and the noun:

(1) adjectives used occasionally as nouns:

> бородáтый 'the bearded man'

(2) words which exist both as adjectives and as nouns:

> больнóй 'ill' and 'the patient'
> рабóчий 'of work' and 'the worker'
> столóвая 'of the table' and 'dining-room'
> живóтное 'animal' and 'the animal'
> морóженое 'frozen' and 'ice-cream'

(3) words which are nouns only:

> портнóй 'tailor'   вселéнная 'the universe'
> прохóжий 'passer-by'   насекóмое 'insect'
> гóрничная 'maid'   пирóжное 'cake'

The greater the degree of substantivization of the adjective, the less is its faculty of possessing the three genders. Nouns of the third category have only one gender; but even in the second category a similar tendency is to be observed: if, alongside больнóй 'the patient' and слепóй 'the blind man', the feminines больнáя, слепáя also occur, the only feminine corresponding to рабóчий 'worker' is рабóтница.

The regular correspondence of masculine and feminine forms in substantivized adjectives occurs only in the names of persons. It is obligatory in surnames of adjectival form:

> Толстóй—Толстáя   Никóльский—Никóльская

In the case of animals and inanimate objects, substantivization affects only one of the three genders.

Masculine substantivized adjectives indicate persons of the male sex. There are a few rare exceptions, in particular certain names of coins:

> золото́й 'gold piece'
> целко́вый 'rouble'
> двугри́венный 'twenty-copeck piece'
> пятиалты́нный 'fifteen-copeck piece'

A masculine substantivized adjective in -ский may often designate, elliptically, a language, but only in the cases other than the nominative:

> он хорошо́ зна́ет ру́сский 'he knows Russian well'
> перево́д с англи́йского 'translation from English'

Cf. also such expressions as the following, which are still felt as elliptical:

> Не́вский (проспе́кт) 'the Nevsky Prospect'
> пассажи́рский (по́езд) 'passenger train'

A large number of substantivized adjectives are used only in the plural:

> командиро́вочные 'expense allowance'
> членистоно́гие 'arthropoda'

II. DEGREES OF COMPARISON

1. Comparative

Russian has two types of comparative: an analytical and a suffixal type.

I. THE ANALYTICAL COMPARATIVE

The analytical comparative is formed, similarly to the corresponding type of comparative in English, by the use of the adverb бо́лее 'more' followed by the adjective:

> бо́лее си́льный 'stronger'
> бо́лее драмати́ческий 'more dramatic'

All adjectives may form their comparatives in this manner. Moreover, it offers a convenient parallel both with the comparative of inferiority formed with the aid of ме́нее 'less' (ме́нее си́льный 'less strong') and with the superlative (see p. 108). From this fact it derives wide diffusion and great vitality.

2. THE SUFFIXAL COMPARATIVE

This comparative is a synthetic form. It is invariable, being without distinction of gender, case or number.

Only descriptive adjectives (those which possess a short form) may form suffixal comparatives.

There are several suffixes of comparison.

(1) the suffix -ee, which occurs also in the form -ей, is the only one of them which is productive:

> но́вый: нове́е 'new'
> лири́чный: лири́чнее 'lyrical'
> обма́нчивый: обма́нчивее 'deceptive'
> леси́стый: леси́стее 'wooded'

The position of the stress is the same as in the feminine of the short form.

(2) The suffix -e, limited to some very common adjectives, either primary with stems ending in velars and dentals, or with the suffix -к-. This is an archaic type, which presents a mutation of the stem-consonant, as may be seen in the following list:

> к : ч   вя́зкий : вя́зче 'viscous'
>   ги́бкий : ги́бче 'flexible'
>   го́рький : го́рче 'bitter'
>   гро́мкий : гро́мче 'loud'
>   жа́ркий : жа́рче 'hot'
>   жёсткий : жёстче 'hard, stiff'
>   кре́пкий : кре́пче 'strong'
>   лёгкий : ле́гче 'light'

	ме́лкий : ме́льче 'shallow, small, fine'
	мя́гкий : мя́гче 'soft'
	пры́ткий : пры́тче 'quick'
	ре́зкий : ре́зче 'harsh, sharp'
	я́ркий : я́рче 'bright'
г : ж	дорого́й : доро́же 'dear'
	стро́гий : стро́же 'severe'
	туго́й : ту́же 'tight'
х : ш	глухо́й : глу́ше 'deaf'
	сухо́й : су́ше 'dry'
	ти́хий : ти́ше 'calm, slow'
д : ж	молодо́й : моло́же 'young'
	твёрдый : твёрже 'hard'
т : ч	бога́тый : бога́че 'rich'
	круто́й : кру́че 'steep'
ст : щ	густо́й : гу́ще 'thick'
	просто́й : про́ще 'simple'
	то́лстый : то́лще 'fat'
	ча́стый : ча́ще 'frequent, thick'
	чи́стый : чи́ще 'clean'
в : вл	дешёвый : деше́вле 'cheap'

Some adjectives with the suffixes -к- and -ок- form their comparatives in -e direct from the stem, omitting the suffix. They present a mutation of the stem-consonant:

д : ж	га́дкий : га́же 'nasty'
	гла́дкий : гла́же 'smooth'
	жи́дкий : жи́же 'liquid, thin'
	ре́дкий : ре́же 'rare, sparse'
т : ч	коро́ткий : коро́че 'short'
з : ж	бли́зкий : бли́же 'near'
	ни́зкий : ни́же 'low'
	у́зкий : у́же 'narrow'
р	широ́кий : ши́ре 'broad'

(3) Different suffixes, sometimes with softening of the

preceding consonant, and limited to a few isolated adjectives:

-ше	далёкий : да́льше 'far, distant'
	до́лгий : до́льше 'long-lasting'
	ста́рый : ста́рше 'old'
	то́нкий : то́ньше 'thin, delicate'
-ще	сла́дкий : сла́ще 'sweet' (with an
	irregular alternation д : щ)
-же	глубо́кий : глу́бже 'deep'

Finally, there are a few suppletive or irregular forms:

большо́й 'big, great' : бо́льше 'bigger, greater'
ма́лый, ма́ленький 'small' : ме́ньше 'smaller'
хоро́ший 'good' : лу́чше 'better'
плохо́й 'bad' : ху́же 'worse'

A few declinable forms of the suffixal comparative survive in Russian. Their meaning is frequently more specific
than that of the positive forms. They may be divided into
four pairs:

бо́льший 'greater' : ме́ньший 'less'

These are the only true comparatives of this group. They
occur in the literary language, in phrases involving abstract
nouns, as for example: с бо́льшим внима́нием 'with
greater attention';

лу́чший 'better, best' : ху́дший 'worse, worst'
вы́сший 'superior, supreme' : ни́зший 'inferior'

These are normally superlatives, but may occasionally be
used as comparatives;

ста́рший 'elder, eldest, senior' : мла́дший 'younger,
youngest, junior'

3. USE OF THE COMPARATIVE

The analytical form may occur either as epithet or as

predicate. The second term of comparison is in the nominative preceded by the conjunction чем (rarely нѐжели):

> я не отказываюсь от работы более тяжёлой чем вчерашняя 'I do not refuse harder work than yesterday's'

The suffixal form, which, while indeclinable, is not an adverb, is used above all predicatively:

> наша улица чище 'our street is cleaner'

As epithet it is used only as subject or direct object, i.e. in the nom., acc., and (with negative) gen.:

> видали мы представления веселее 'we have seen more amusing shows'
> нет у вас материи светлее? 'have you no lighter material?'

With the suffixal form the second term of comparison may be either in the genitive (this is the usual construction) or, as with the analytical form, in the nominative preceded by чем or нѐжели. Thus:

> лицо белее бумаги or лицо белее чем бумага 'a face whiter than paper'

Needless to say, such forms as чище, веселее, &c., may also be adverbs:

> одеваться чище 'to dress more cleanly'
> смотреть веселее 'to look more cheerfully'

In this case, however, they are associated, not with the adjectives чистый, весёлый, but with the adverbs чисто, весело (see p. 148).

2. Superlative

The superlative has an essentially analytical form, consisting of the positive form of the adjective preceded by самый (neut. -ое, fem. -ая, pl. -ые):

> самый светлый 'the lightest'

This form reveals a convenient parallelism with the analytical comparative.

In addition to this analytical superlative, there is also a declinable suffixal form in -ейший (-айший after ж, ш, ч, щ). It may be formed only from those adjectives which admit the suffixal comparative. This form has only rarely true superlative force:

> величайший из современников 'the greatest of our contemporaries'

More frequently this form expresses only the absolute superlative, the quality in the highest degree, without any comparative force:

> честнейший человек 'a most honourable man'
> интереснейший вопрос 'a most interesting question'

This form may be preceded by the prefix наи-, which, besides intensifying its meaning, gives it a literary character:

> наивернейшее средство 'a completely reliable means'

The second term of comparison goes into the gen. pl. preceded by the preposition из 'of':

> самая бедная из стран 'the poorest of countries'

III. WORD-FORMATION
A. *SUFFIXAL DERIVATIVES*

Fewer suffixes are employed in the formation of adjectives than in that of nouns. On the other hand, the productivity of the living adjectival suffixes is much greater; it may be said that there are no nouns from which an adjective may not be formed with the aid of one of the three commonest suffixes: -н-, -ск-, or -ов-.

1. Adjectives with the Suffix -н-

I. DENOMINATIVE ADJECTIVES

The all-purpose suffix -н- is the principal suffix for the formation of adjectives from nouns. Its productivity is very great: about half of all the adjectives in Russian have the suffix -н-. Nouns denoting living creatures, however, with few exceptions, do not make use of this suffix.

From nouns denoting inanimate things the suffix -н- is employed to form both relative and descriptive adjectives, as:

ва́жный 'important'	ме́дный 'of copper'
вку́сный 'tasty'	не́жный 'tender'
жи́рный 'fat'	сме́ртный 'mortal'
кра́сный 'red'	таба́чный 'of tobacco'
лесно́й 'forest' (adj.)	трамва́йный 'of trams'

The same suffix occurs also in extended forms:

-енн-: жи́зненный 'vital'   обще́ственный 'public'
      ли́ственный 'deci-   уби́йственный 'murderous'
      duous'

-онн-, for foreign borrowings in -ия:
      традицио́нный 'traditional'
      эмиссио́нный 'of emission'

-ичн-: годи́чный 'annual'
      втори́чный 'second, secondary'

-овн-/-евн-, unproductive:
      духо́вный 'spiritual'   душе́вный 'sincere'

-ебн-, unproductive:
      враждéбный 'hostile'   целéбный 'salubrious'

2. DEVERBAL ADJECTIVES

The suffix -н- in its pure form is used to form descriptive adjectives, usually passive in meaning; the stress falls on the penultimate syllable:

      поддéльный 'counterfeit'   досту́пный 'accessible'

Such adjectives often exist only in a negative form:

небре́жный 'careless'   неусы́пный 'vigilant'

Two extended forms of this suffix are to be noticed:

-льн-, productive:

точи́льный 'sharpening'   копирова́льный 'copying'

-тельн-, also productive:

оборони́тельный 'defensive'
подозри́тельный 'suspect'
дыха́тельный 'respiratory'
замеча́тельный 'remarkable'

3. RUSSIFICATION OF FOREIGN ADJECTIVES

Foreign adjectives are Russianized most frequently by means of the same universal suffix -н-:

легенда́рный 'legendary'   продукти́вный 'productive'
либера́льный 'liberal'   серьёзный 'serious'

2. Relative Adjectives

1. SUFFIXES WITH GENERAL VALUE: -СК- AND -ОВ-

(1) The suffix -ск- comes, in respect of productivity, immediately after the suffix -н-. Unlike the latter, it is used to form adjectives also from nouns denoting persons:

мужско́й 'masculine'   а́дский 'infernal'
генера́льский 'of a general'   ло́ндонский 'London'

In some adjectives formed from nouns in -а́к, -я́к, -и́к this suffix may occur in the form -цк-:

дура́цкий 'stupid'   мужи́цкий 'of a muzhik'

The same suffix occurs also in extended forms:

-овск-: воровско́й 'of a thief'   ма́ртовский 'of March'
-ческ-, rare: рыбово́дческий 'of pisciculture'

-тельск-, rare (not to be confounded with the suffix -ск- added to nouns in -тель, like учи́тельский 'teacher's'):

издева́тельский 'mocking'

The same suffix is used to Russianize certain types of foreign adjectives, under the forms

-ическ-: биологи́ческий 'biological'
социалисти́ческий 'socialist'
-анск-: италья́нский 'Italian'
картезиа́нский 'Cartesian'

(2) The suffix -ов- is not employed to form adjectives from nouns denoting persons:

боково́й 'lateral, side' свинцо́вый 'leaden'
почто́вый 'of the post' тигро́вый 'tiger's'

It is common with names of trees:

берёзовый 'of birch' дубо́вый 'of oak'

This suffix is used also to Russianize foreign adjectives of colour:

фиоле́товый 'violet' бе́жевый 'beige'

2. SUFFIXES WITH SPECIAL VALUE

(1) The relative suffix -j-. The suffix -j- does not occur in the nom. sing. masc.:

ли́сий 'fox's' (neut. ли́сье, fem. ли́сья) (see p. 100)

Adjectives of this type are formed principally from nouns denoting animals, and show a certain degree of productivity. They are also formed from nouns denoting persons:

ко́зий 'goat's' павли́ний 'peacock's'
верблю́жий 'camel's' разбо́йничий 'brigand's'
теля́чий 'calf's' каза́чий 'Cossack's'

(2) The relative suffix -ин- is used to form adjectives

from nouns denoting animals, more particularly birds and
insects:

ослѝный 'ass's'	воробьѝный 'sparrow's'
змеѝный 'snake's'	пчелѝный 'bee's'
гусѝный 'goose's'	муравьѝный 'ant's'

(3) The suffix -ян- (-ан-), indicating material, is fairly
productive:

глѝняный 'of clay'	шерстянóй 'woollen'
кровянóй 'of blood'	кóжаный 'of leather'

(4) The suffix soft -н- (whence the endings -ний, -нее,
-няя, -ние) is used to form adjectives of place and time
from nouns and adverbs. It is unproductive:

лéтний 'of summer'	крáйний 'extreme'
прéжний 'previous'	сосéдний 'neighbouring'

The same suffix occurs also in the extended form -шн-:

всегдáшний 'perpetual'   внéшний 'external'

3. Descriptive Adjectives

I. DENOMINATIVE ADJECTIVES

The denominative adjectives express various degrees of
quality. Some of these suffixes are employed also with
verbal roots.

(1) The suffix -ив-, of neutral force, is unproductive in
its pure form:

плешѝвый 'bald'   правдѝвый 'truthful'

But is still living in two extended forms:

-лив- (used also in the formation of adjectives from
verbal roots):

привéтливый 'affable'   терпелѝвый 'patient'

-чив- (used also in the formation of adjectives with active meaning from verbal roots). The stress falls on the syllable before the suffix:

обма́нчивый 'deceptive'   заду́мчивый 'pensive'

(2) The suffix -а́в- (-я́в-), is quite dead:

крова́вый 'bloody'   дыря́вый 'full of holes'

(3) The suffix -и́т- is dead in its pure form (знамени́тый 'famous') but retains a slight degree of productivity in the extended form -ови́т- (-еви́т-):

домови́тый 'thrifty'   глянцеви́тый 'glossy'

(4) The suffix -ист- is highly productive. It usually indicates plenitude of the particular quality:

бархати́стый 'velvety'   желе́зистый 'ferruginous'
волни́стый 'wavy'   леси́стый 'wooded'

(5) The suffix -а́т- is only slightly productive in its pure form:

крыла́тый 'winged'   полоса́тый 'striped'

It is more productive in the extended forms:

-чат-:   гребе́нчатый 'serrated'
          сво́дчатый 'vaulted'
-ова́т-:   узлова́тый 'knotty'
          замыслова́тый 'complicated'

usually with attenuating force:

зеленова́тый 'greenish'
простова́тый 'somewhat simple-minded'

(6) The suffix -а́ст- is productive and has the same functions as the suffix -ист- but is at once more expressive and more colloquial:

глаза́стый 'with big eyes'   груда́стый 'big-bosomed'
горла́стый 'bawling'   очка́стый 'wearing glasses'

2. DEVERBAL ADJECTIVES

(a) Suffixes of participial origin

A large number of adjectives are of participial origin:

> теку́щий счёт 'current account'
> люби́мое блю́до 'favourite dish'
> па́дший а́нгел 'fallen angel'
> вита́я ле́стница 'winding staircase'

Morphologically, such forms have not ceased to be participles. There also exist, however, suffixes of participial origin which serve to form true verbal adjectives.

(1) The suffixes -я́ч- (-а́ч-) and -ю́ч- (-у́ч-) were once popular suffixes of the present participle active. Both are unproductive; the latter is the more frequent:

стоя́чий 'standing, stagnant'	летучий 'flying'
бродя́чий 'strolling, vagabond'	паху́чий 'fragrant'
могу́чий 'mighty'	скрипу́чий 'creaking'

(2) The suffixes -а́щ- (-я́щ-) derive from the present participle active, with a familiar shade of meaning:

> пропа́щий 'ruined, incorrigible'　　завал я́щий 'trashy'

(3) The suffixes -им- and -а́ем-, derived from the present participle passive, are used almost exclusively with negatives. They are common but not especially productive. They correspond to the English suffixes *-ible, -able*.

The suffix -им- is used to form adjectives from transitive verbs, in the great majority perfectives with prefix:

> невыноси́мый 'unbearable'
> недостижи́мый 'unattainable'
> ненаруши́мый 'inviolable'
> непримири́мый 'irreconcilable'

The suffix -а́ем- is used to form adjectives from imperfective verbs, both transitive and intransitive:

> незабыва́емый 'unforgettable'

неподража́емый 'inimitable'
несгора́емый 'fire-proof'
непромока́емый 'water-proof'

(4) The suffix -л-, the old suffix of the past participle active, has almost lost its productivity. It operates mostly with intransitive verbs:

спе́лый 'ripe'	окамене́лый 'petrified'
хри́плый 'hoarse'	жило́й 'habitable, lived-in'
отста́лый 'backward'	было́й 'past, erstwhile'

(b) The suffix -к-

This suffix, of a low degree of productivity, is added to the consonantal stem of imperfective verbs to indicate the possibility of undergoing or of performing some action:

вя́зкий 'viscous'	ско́льзкий 'slippery'
ло́мкий 'fragile'	е́дкий 'corrosive'

It also occurs in many primary adjectives:

у́зкий 'narrow'   коро́ткий 'short'

4. Possessive Adjectives

I. ADJECTIVES IN -ОВ AND -ИН

(1) Possessive adjectives in -ов (with short form) derived from masculine and feminine nouns, are completely dead in Russian and occur only in certain fixed phrases (see also p. 101):

Петро́в день 'St. Peter's Day'
чо́ртова ги́бель 'an enormous quantity'

(2) Possessive adjectives in -ин (with short form in nom.-acc.) are frequent, although restricted to nouns of

endearment in -а, -я, whether Christian names or nouns denoting kinship:

(*a*) nouns of kinship and related nouns (almost exclusively words created by or for children):

сестрин 'sister's'   дядин 'uncle's'
папин 'daddy's'   бабушкин 'grandma's'
мамин 'mummy's'   нянин 'nurse's'

(*b*) diminutives of Christian names (see p. 88). In this class the suffix -ин is productive:

Сашин   Володин   Шурин
Сашенькин   Олин   Аннушкин

Apart from these categories, the suffix -ин occurs only in certain fixed phrases (see also p. 102):

Троицын день 'Whitsun' (Trinity Day)
сукин сын 'son of a bitch'

2. SURNAMES IN -ов/-ев AND -ин

These two suffixes, originally possessives, are the suffixes *par excellence* of surnames:

Павлов   Петухов   Никитин   Калинин

Of these only the suffix -ов/-ев is productive. It, and not -ин, is found, for example, in the new names formed from nouns in -а (Розов from роза 'rose'), from oriental names in -а (Ходжаев) and -и (Алиев) and from adjectives (Чернов from чёрный 'black').

5. Diminutive and Augmentative Adjectives

1. DIMINUTIVES

The diminutive suffix is -еньк- (-оньк- after a velar):

худенький (худой 'thin')
беленький (белый 'white')
полосатенький (полосатый 'striped')
тихонький (тихий 'quiet')

The diminutive adjective has a purely affective force which applies less to the adjective itself than to the noun it qualifies. Only descriptive adjectives may take a diminutive form.

2. AUGMENTATIVES

The augmentative suffixes -ющ-, -ущ-, -éнн- are of literary origin but are employed in popular speech. They are colloquial in tone. They are not numerous:

злющий 'spiteful'   здоровéнный 'great big'
большущий 'huge'   толстéнный 'great fat'

B. *COMPOUND ADJECTIVES*

The rules governing the formation of compound adjectives are the same as for nouns.

1. Compound Adjectives with Connecting Vowel

I. COMPOUND ADJECTIVES WITH SECOND ELEMENT OF VERBAL ORIGIN

Non-suffixal compound adjectives are extremely rare:

чернома́зый 'swarthy'

The commonest suffix is -н-:

плодоро́дный 'fertile'
гостеприи́мный 'hospitable'
миролюби́вый 'pacific'

Compounds with a complete word as their second element are limited almost entirely to those formed from participles:

главнокома́ндующий 'commander-in-chief'
новоприбы́вший 'newly arrived'
мертворождённый 'still-born'
скороспе́лый 'precocious'

2. COMPOUND ADJECTIVES WITH SECOND ELEMENT OF SUBSTANTIVAL or ADJECTIVAL ORIGIN

Non-suffixal compound adjectives are more common than nouns of the same type, although they are limited to nouns indicating parts of the body:

> длиннору́кий 'with long arms'
> голубогла́зый 'blue-eyed'
> смуглоли́цый 'swarthy'
> черногри́вый 'with black mane'

Suffixal compound adjectives are as common as the same class of nouns. They usually have the suffix -н-:

> пресново́дный 'of fresh water' (from
> · пре́сная вода́, 'fresh water')
> разноцве́тный 'variegated'
> шарови́дный 'spherical'

Unlike compound nouns, compound adjectives quite frequently have a complete word as their second element:

> синезелёный 'blue-green'
> малогра́мотный 'semi-literate'
> глухонемо́й 'deaf-mute'
> кислосла́дкий 'bitter-sweet'

2. Other Types of Compound Adjectives

1. COMPOUND ADJECTIVES WITH A NUMERAL AS FIRST ELEMENT

These adjectives are formed in the same way as the nouns of the corresponding category, and are more numerous:

> односторо́нний 'unilateral'
> двугри́венный 'twenty-copeck piece'
> двухэта́жный 'of two storeys'
> четырёхкла́ссный 'of four classes'

> шестидесятилѐтний 'sixty-year old'
> полуофициа́льный 'semi-official'

2. COMPOUND ADJECTIVES WITH AN INVARIABLE FIRST ELEMENT

(a) With a preposition or a prefix as first element

These adjectives are a good deal more common than the nouns of the same type:

> бесконѐчный 'infinite'
> внеочереднóй 'extraordinary'
> внутрипартѝйный 'taking place
>   within the party'
> допотóпный 'antediluvian'
> закулѝсный 'behind the scenes'
> междунарóдный 'international'
> накóжный 'cutaneous'
> надгрóбный 'funerary'
> поштýчный 'by the piece'
> подзѐмный 'subterranean'
> послевоѐнный 'post-war'
> праславя́нский 'proto-Slavonic'
> предóбрый 'very kind'
> предвы́борный 'pre-election'
> примóрский 'maritime'
> противозакóнный 'illegal'
> сверхштáтный 'supernumerary'
> совремѐнный 'contemporary'

(b) With a negative particle as first element

The adjectives of this type also are much more frequent than the corresponding nouns:

> неземнóй 'unearthly'
> неимýщий 'indigent'
> некрасѝвый 'ugly'
> небезупрѐчный 'not irreproachable'

(c) With a foreign prefix as first element

антинау́чный 'antiscientific'
архизаня́той 'extremely busy'
просове́тский 'pro-Soviet'
псевдонаро́дный 'pseudo-traditional'
ультрапра́вый 'extreme right-wing'

Pronouns

RUSSIAN grammar gives to the term *pronoun* a more extended sense than it possesses in English. In Russian the pronouns include not only words which are employed syntactically in the same manner as nouns but also words which in English grammar would be classed as adjectives. This is explained by the fact that the majority of Russian pronouns possess a special type of declension which distinguishes them from adjectives.

As in English, personal pronouns are to be distinguished from non-personal.

I. PERSONAL PRONOUNS

As in many languages, the personal pronouns possess certain forms which fit into no system of declension. This applies only to the pronouns of the first and second person and to the reflexive pronoun. The pronoun of the third person is an old demonstrative, and its declension is that of non-personal pronouns.

1. Pronouns of the First and Second Persons and the Reflexive Pronoun

	'I'	'thou'	reflexive	'we'	'you'
N.	я	ты	—	мы	вы
G.–A.	меня́	тебя́	себя́	нас	вас
D.	мне	тебе́	себе́	нам	вам
L.	мне	тебе́	себе́	нас	вас
I.	мной	тобо́й	собо́й	на́ми	ва́ми

The instr. sing. of я, ты, and the reflexive pronoun has also a literary form in -óю: мнóю, тобóю, собóю.

The reflexive себя́ *is used for both numbers and all three persons. It always refers back to the agent of the action of the verb*:

> я зна́ю себя́ 'I know myself'
> возьми́те с собо́й еду́ 'take food with you'
> мать не забо́тится о себе́ 'the mother takes
> no care of herself'
> я посове́товал ему́ купи́ть себе́ велосипе́д 'I
> advised him to buy himself a bicycle'
> мо́жно ли мне захвати́ть с собо́й бра́та? 'May
> I take my brother with me?'

The instrumental собо́й used in conjunction with a noun or an adjective means 'in his (her) person':

> она́ хороша́ собо́й 'she is good-looking'

The pronoun ты, like the corresponding pronoun in most other European languages, is used only in addressing children and close friends. Вы is the form of polite address. In texts intended to be read by the person addressed as вы (letters, requests, &c.), the pronoun is written with a capital letter.

2. The Pronoun of the Third Person

The pronoun of the third person belongs to the pronominal declension proper, which will be examined later. Its declension is given here only to maintain the unity of the personal pronouns:

	Singular				*Plural*	
	Masc.	*Neut.*	*Fem.*			
N.	он	онó	онá	N.	они́	
G.–A.	егó		её	G.–A.	их	
D.	ему́		ей	D.	им	
L.	нём		ней	L.	них	
I.	им		е́ю	I.	и́ми	

In the nominative the stem is он- (an old demonstrative); in the oblique cases the stem is a bare *yod* (*j*, likewise an old demonstrative).

While it belongs to the pronominal declension proper, the pronoun of the third person has two features which are characteristic of personal pronouns:

(1) diversity of stem between the nominative and the other cases;
(2) identity between the genitive and the accusative, even in the neuter and the feminine genders.

The pronoun of the third person takes a prefixed н- when it is preceded by a preposition:

> gen. без него́ 'without him'
> dat. к ней 'towards her'
> loc. при них 'in their presence'
> instr. с ни́ми 'with them'

The locative, never being employed without a preposition, does not possess the forms without н-.

It is to be observed that in the feminine declension the form ней, besides the dat. and loc. sing., may represent:

(1) the gen. sing., but only with the preposition у: у ней (parallel with у неё);
(2) the instr. sing., with all prepositions: с ней (parallel with с не́ю) 'with her'.

When used without a preposition, the gen. and instr. sing. fem. may occur only in the forms её and е́ю respectively.

When used as a possessive pronoun, the gen. его́, её, их never takes the prefixed н-. Thus:

> от него́ 'from him'
> от его́ сы́на 'from his son' (see p. 126)

II. NON-PERSONAL PRONOUNS

1. Classification

Non-personal pronouns include a few which are employed syntactically in the same manner as nouns. The larger number may be assimilated, syntactically, to the adjectives; but, like adjectives, they may on occasion assume the character of nouns.

All the non-personal pronouns, except кто 'who', что 'what', and друг дрýга 'one another', distinguish both numbers and all three genders (the latter only in the singular, like adjectives).

In respect of declension, non-personal pronouns may be divided into two groups:

(1) Those the declension of which is peculiar to pronouns;
(2) Those which are declined in the same way as adjectives.

From the semantic point of view, the pronouns may be divided into several groups.

I. POSSESSIVE PRONOUNS

The possessive pronouns are:

> мой, моя́, моё 'my, mine'
> твой, твоя́, твоё 'thy, thine'
> свой, своя́, своё possessive from
>   the reflexive себя́
> наш, нáша, нáше 'our, ours'
> ваш, вáша, вáше 'your, yours'
> чей, чья, чьё 'whose'
> ничéй, ничья́, ничьё 'nobody's'

The possessive свой is a true reflexive and normally refers to the subject of the clause, whether this be in the first, second, or third person. With subjects in the third person its use is obligatory, and it then has the meaning 'his, her, hers, their, theirs', as:

> врач остановился у своего дома 'the doctor stopped at his (own) house'

It is virtually obligatory also with subjects in the second person singular:

> ты сказа́л своё (not твоё) мне́ние 'you have expressed your opinion'

But with subjects in the 1st pers. sing. and pl. and 2nd pers. pl. the use of мой, наш, ваш is no less frequent than that of свой:

> мы забы́ли свой долг
> *or* мы забы́ли наш долг 'we have forgotten our duty'

свой is always used when it is desired to emphasize the notion of ownership:

> своего́ автомоби́ля у меня́ не́ было 'I had no car of my own'

In this case свой has the same force as со́бственный 'own'.

In certain fixed phrases свой loses all idea of person:

> я свой челове́к в э́том до́ме 'I am like one of the family in this house'

All these pronouns follow the pronominal declension.

The possessive pronoun of the third person, when it does not refer to the subject of the clause, is rendered by the genitive of the personal pronoun; these forms are, obviously, indeclinable:

> его́ 'his': его́ бороды́ 'of his beard'
> её 'her': в её рука́х 'in her hands'
> их 'their': их забо́той 'by their care'

These indeclinable forms have the disadvantage that they cannot be used absolutely (in the manner of the English possessive pronouns), a drawback which is particularly noticeable when it is desired to employ the possessive pronoun of the third person after a comparative.

2. DEMONSTRATIVE PRONOUNS

The demonstrative pronouns are:

> э́тот, э́та, э́то 'this'
> тот, та, то 'that'
> сей, сия́, сие́ 'this'

This last pronoun is obsolete and is employed only for archaistic effect, except in a number of adverbial phrases in everyday use:

сейча́с 'immediately'	до сих поρ 'hitherto'
сию́ мину́ту 'immediately'	от сих поρ 'henceforth'
сего́дня 'today'	

These three pronouns follow the pronominal declension.

3. DETERMINATIVE PRONOUNS

Determinative pronouns with pronominal declension:

> весь, вся, всё 'all'
> сам, сама́, само́ '-self'
> оди́н, одна́, одно́ 'only, alone'
> то́т же, та́ же, то́ же 'the same'

—with adjectival declension:

> са́мый 'same, the most'
> таково́й (archaic) and тако́й 'such, so'
> таково́й же (archaic) and тако́й же 'of the same type'
> ка́ждый 'every, everyone'
> вся́кий 'every, every kind of'
> друго́й and ино́й 'other'
> мно́гие 'many' (only in plural)
> сто́лько 'so much, so many'
> сто́лько-же 'as much, as many'

This group also includes one compound pronoun declined like a noun:

друг дру́га 'each other, one another'

which is more commonly applied to persons than to things.

4. INTERROGATIVE-RELATIVE PRONOUNS

Interrogative-relative pronouns with pronominal declension:

кто 'who'
что 'which, what'
ко́его, fem. ко́ей 'whose' (gen.: no nom. sing.)
чей 'whose'

—with adjectival declension:

каково́й (archaic) and како́й 'what, of what sort'
кото́рый 'what, who'
ско́лько 'how many'

The pronouns кто and что do not vary according to gender. They are used, although they have no plural form, to refer both to the singular and to the plural. The pronoun кто is used for persons, while что is used for inanimate things. Where the reference is to animals, sometimes кто, sometimes что is used: the higher the type of animal, the greater the tendency to use кто. For example:

кто там ла́ет? 'what's that barking there?'
    (speaking of a dog)
что там лета́ет? 'what's flying about there?'
    (speaking of an insect)

The interrogative pronoun кто always takes its verb in the singular, even if it refers to a number of persons: кто э́то ви́дел? In the past tense the verb has the masculine form, even if it refers to a woman: кто из сестёр догада́лся? 'which of the sisters guessed the answer?'

As a relative pronoun кто may take its verb either in the singular or in the plural, the latter only if the antecedent of кто is a plural pronoun: все, кто э́то ви́дел or все, кто э́то ви́дели 'all those who saw this'.

5. NEGATIVE PRONOUNS

Negative pronouns with pronominal declension:

> никто́ 'nobody'
> ничто́ 'nothing'
> ниче́й, ничья́, ничьё 'nobody's'

To these may be added не́кого, не́чего (gen.), pronouns which have no nominative and which are equivalent to нет кого́, нет чего́ respectively, for example:

> не́кому пожа́ловаться 'there is nobody to whom
> one can complain'

They are not to be confused with the indefinites не́кто, не́что, which exist only in the nominative (see below).

Mention must also be made of the following two phrases:

> нико́им о́бразом 'by no means'
> ни в ко́ем слу́чае 'under no circumstances'

The pronoun in question is not found outside of these very common phrases.

—with adjectival declension: никако́й 'no, none'

6. INDEFINITE PRONOUNS

The indefinite pronouns are formed from the interrogative-relative pronouns by means of various particles prefixed or postfixed.

The prefixed particles are:

не- (stressed):

> не́кто 'someone, a certain' (Lat. *quidam*)
> не́что 'something' (Lat. *quiddam*)
>   both employed only in the nominative;
> не́кий 'a certain'
> не́который 'some'

кое- (unstressed in the oblique cases, sometimes stressed in the nom. sing.):

кое-кто́ 'some people or other, somebody'
кое-что́ 'something or other'
кое-како́й 'some'

The postfixed particles are -то, -нибудь, -либо. They may be attached to кто, что, чей, какой, and the last two to кото́рый also, for example:

кто́-то 'someone' (Lat. *aliquis*)
кто́-нибудь 'someone, anyone' (Lat. *quilibet*)
кто́-либо 'someone, anyone' (Lat. *quivis*)

The particle -то indicates an existing but unidentified person or object, while the particles -нибудь and -либо indicate a person or an object the very existence of which is not certain. Thus, on returning home, I ask my wife:

звони́л кто́-нибудь? 'Did anyone ring up?'

(a person whose existence is only possible); my wife replies:

да, кто́-то звони́л 'Yes, someone rang'

(an existing but unidentified person).

2. Declension

Only pronominal declension proper will be examined in this chapter. For the adjectival declension of pronouns, see the chapter on adjectives.

Pronominal declension has many affinities with that of adjectives. It is of two types. The consonantal element of the endings is the same in both groups. The difference lies only in the vowel in the ending of the instr. sing. masc. and neut. and throughout the plural.

As with nouns and adjectives, the case-ending of the instr. sing. fem. may have the literary form -ою, -ею, parallel with the normal form -ой, -ей.

1. FIRST DECLENSION

In this declension the vowel -e- occurs in the instr. sing. masc. and neut. and throughout the plural. In the singular there are two types, hard and soft; in the plural there is a single declension of the soft type.

(a) Hard type

Example: тот 'that', кто 'who'.

	Singular				*Plural*		
	Masc.	*Neut.*	*Fem.*				
N.	тот	то	та	N.	те	N.	кто
A.	= N. or G.	то	ту	A.	= N. or G.	A.	кого
G.	того		той	G.	тех	G.	кого
D.	тому		той	D.	тем	D.	кому
L.	том		той	L.	тех	L.	ком
I.	тем		той	I.	теми	I.	кем

Apart from the pronouns of the example, this type includes only compounds of кто:

> никто 'nobody'
> кто-то, кто-нибудь, кто-либо 'someone, anyone'
> кое-кто 'some people or other, somebody'
> некто 'a certain' (*quidam*), used only in the nominative
> некого, used only in the oblique cases (see p. 129)

The particle which enters into the formation of these compounds remains indeclinable.

If the pronouns никто, некого, and кое-кто are employed with a preposition, the preposition is inserted between the particle and the pronoun proper, and the three elements are then written separately:

> ни от кого 'from nobody'
> ни с кем 'with nobody'
> не от кого 'there is nobody from whom'
> не с кем 'there is nobody with whom'
> кое с кем 'with some people or other'

When, however, никто́ and ничто́ (see below) are used not in their literal sense, but with the meanings 'a nobody', 'a mere nothing', respectively, the above rule does not apply and the preposition precedes ни-:

> нас за никого́ счита́ет 'she regards us as nobodies' (Griboedov, Го́ре от ума́)
>
> мно́го шу́ма из ничего́ 'much ado about nothing'

(b) *Soft type*

Example: весь 'all', что 'what, which'.

	Singular				*Plural*			
	Masc.	*Neut.*	*Fem.*					
N.	весь	всё	вся	N.	все	N.	что	
A. =	N. or G.	всё	всю	A. =	N. or G.	A.	что	
G.	всего́		всей	G.	всех	G.	чего́	
D.	всему́		всей	D.	всем	D.	чему́	
L.	всём		всей	L.	всех	L.	чём	
I.	всем		всей	I.	все́ми	I.	чем	

The same declension is followed only by the compounds of что, which are absolutely parallel to those of кто:

> ничто́ 'nothing'
> что́-то, что́-нибудь, что́-либо 'something, anything'
> кое-что́ 'something or other'
> не́что 'something' (*quiddam*), used only in the nominative and accusative
> не́чего, used only in the oblique cases (see p. 129)

The construction of ничто́, не́чего, and кое-что́ with a preposition is identical with that of никто́, не́кого, and кое-кто́.

In all pronouns of the *first declension* the stem is reduced to one or two consonants (т-, к-, ч-, вс-); as the nom. sing. masc. has a zero-ending it requires the support of a syllabic element (-от, -то, mobile *e*). The stress falls on the final syllable in the gen. and dat. masc. and neut.

2. SECOND DECLENSION

In this declension the vowel -и- occurs in the instr. sing. masc. and neut. and throughout the plural. In the singular there are two types, hard and soft; in the plural there is a single declension of the soft type.

(a) *Hard type*

Example: э́тот 'this'.

	Singular				Plural
	Masc.	*Neut.*	*Fem.*		
N.	э́тот	э́то	э́та	N.	э́ти
A. =	N. or G.	э́то	э́ту	A. =	N. or G.
G.	э́того		э́той	G.	э́тих
D.	э́тому		э́той	D.	э́тим
L.	э́том		э́той	L.	э́тих
I.	э́тим		э́той	I.	э́тими

Other words which follow the same declension are:

> сам, само́, сама́, са́ми '-self'
> оди́н, одно́, одна́, одни́ 'alone, only'

The nom. sing. masc. of э́тот, like тот, is formed with the syllable -от.

The pronoun оди́н has in the nom. sing. masc. a mobile -и-:

> neut. одно́, fem. одна́, gen. sing. masc. одного́, &c.

The fem. сама́ has two forms of the acc. sing.:

> саму́ (usual form) and самоё (slightly archaic)

The pronoun э́тот takes the stress on the first syllable; сам (neut. само́, fem. сама́, gen. sing. masc. самого́, &c.) and оди́н take it on the last syllable, except in the nom. pl. са́ми.

(b) Soft type

Example: мой 'my, mine'

	Singular			*Plural*	
	Masc.	*Neut.*	*Fem.*		
N.	мой	моё	моя́	N.	мои́
A. =	N. or G.	моё	мою́	A. =	N. or G.
G.	моего́		моéй	G.	мои́х
D.	моему́		моéй	D.	мои́м
L.	моём		моéй	L.	мои́х
I.	мои́м		моéй	I.	мои́ми

The same declension is followed by all the possessives:

> твой, твоё, твоя́, твои́ 'thy, thine'
> свой, своё, своя́, свои́, possessive from reflexive себя́
> наш, на́ше, на́ша, на́ши 'our, ours'
> ваш, ва́ше, ва́ша, ва́ши 'your, yours'
> чей, чьё, чья, чьи 'whose', with its compounds
> ниче́й, ничьё, ничья́, ничьи́ 'nobody's'
> сей, сиé, сия́, сии 'this'
> ко́его, ко́ей 'whose' (occurs only in the oblique cases
> in the singular; pl. ко́и, ко́их)

The personal pronoun of the third person also belongs to this type of declension (see p. 123).

The pronoun чей has a mobile -e- in the nom. sing. masc. The rest of the declension is based on the stem *čj-* :

> neut. чьё, fem. чья, gen. sing. masc. чьего́, pl. чьи, &c.

The pronoun сей has the nom. sing. neut. сиé, fem. сия́, acc. sing. fem. сию́, nom. pl. сии. The rest of the declension is regular, with c- as the stem (gen. sing. masc. ceró, fem. сей, &c.).

The pronouns наш, ваш, and ко́его take the stress on the first syllable, all the others on the final syllable.

The majority of the pronouns of the *second declension* have stems which include a vocalic element: эт-, сам-, одн-, мо-, наш-, ваш-, &c.

The stem of чей, however, is reduced to the consonants *čj-* (чьё, чьего́, &c.), while that of сей occurs under the two forms с- and си-.

3. PRONOUNS WITH ABNORMAL DECLENSION

(1) The pronoun друг дру́га 'each other, one another', is the only pronoun declined like a noun. Only the second element is declined:

> gen. друг дру́га, dat. друг дру́гу, &c.

Where a preposition is used, it is inserted between the two elements: друг с дру́гом 'one with another'.

(2) The pronouns of quantity ско́лько 'how much', сто́лько 'so much', сто́лько же 'as much', не́сколько 'a few' have a nominative of the same type as neuter nouns of the hard declension, while their oblique cases follow the adjectival plural declension. After the form in -o the dependent noun (or pronoun) goes into the genitive; in the oblique cases, pronoun of quantity and noun agree in case in the normal way:

> nom. сто́лько зада́ч 'so many problems'
> gen. сто́льких зада́ч
> dat. сто́льким зада́чам, &c.

The pronoun мно́гие 'many', which has a complete plural declension, has also a form in -o, мно́го (only nom. and acc.), which takes the genitive.

VII

Numerals

NUMERALS in Russian do not constitute a regular morphological group: they were originally either nouns, adjectives, or pronouns, and their declension is extremely heterogeneous. At the same time, the numerous interactions and parallel trends which exist between them, above all in the field of syntax, while they have not completely unified them, have marked them off from the other parts of speech to a sufficient extent to justify their examination in a special chapter.

I. CARDINALS

1 оди́н, одно́, одна́	16 шестна́дцать
2 два, две	17 семна́дцать
3 три	18 восемна́дцать
4 четы́ре	19 девятна́дцать
5 пять	20 два́дцать
6 шесть	21 два́дцать оди́н
7 семь	22 два́дцать два
8 во́семь	30 три́дцать
9 де́вять	40 со́рок
10 де́сять	50 пятьдеся́т
11 оди́ннадцать	60 шестьдеся́т
12 двена́дцать	70 се́мьдесят
13 трина́дцать	80 во́семьдесят
14 четы́рнадцать	90 девяно́сто
15 пятна́дцать	100 сто

200 двести	600 шестьсот
300 триста	700 семьсот
400 четыреста	800 восемьсот
500 пятьсот	900 девятьсот

1,000 тысяча
2,000 две тысячи
5,000 пять тысяч
100,000 сто тысяч
1,000,000 миллион
1½ один с половиной or полтора
150 сто пятьдесят or полтораста
1,500 тысяча пятьсот or полторы
тысячи
'both' оба, обе

I. DECLENSION

(a) *General observations*

The cardinal numerals have no unity of declension. Their system presents the following four characteristics:

(1) absence of the category of number;
(2) absence of the category of gender;
(3) disparity between the nominative and the rest of the declension;
(4) a tendency to abandon declension.

These characteristics do not apply to the number один 'one', which is a pure pronoun (see p. 133) and of which the true meaning is 'alone'. It is used to mean 'one' only when the notion of unity is emphasized. Normally Russian does not express the notion of unity at all:

проспать час 'to sleep for one hour'
опоздать на день 'to be one day late'
цена рубль 'price one rouble'

They also do not apply to the numbers 'a thousand' and

above (тысяча, миллион, миллиард, &c.), which are true nouns.

The other numerals are declined either as singulars or as plurals; they can never have both declensions. In other words, the category of number does not apply to them. As to the category of gender, only оба, обе 'both' maintains the distinction between the masc.-neut. and the feminine in all the cases, while два, две shows it only in the nominative. The distinction of gender between the masc.-neut. полтора and the fem. полторы 'one and a half' is also to be observed.

(b) The numerals два, три, четыре, and оба

These numerals follow a declension which resembles that of plural pronouns:

	Masc.-neut.	Fem.			Masc.-neut.	Fem.
N.	два	две	три	четыре	оба	обе
A.	= N. or G.		= N. or G.	= N. or G.	= N. or G.	
G.	двух		трёх	четырёх	обоих	обеих
D.	двум		трём	четырём	обоим	обеим
L.	двух		трёх	четырёх	обоих	обеих
I.	двумя		тремя	четырьмя	обоими	обеими

The unusual vocalism of два, три, четыре, and their peculiar endings in the instrumental case are to be observed.

The numeral оба distinguishes gender in the plural. It is the only anomaly of this type, not merely in the declension of the numerals, but in Russian declension in general.

The numeral два, две, likewise varies as between the masc.-neut. and the fem., but it does so only in the nominative. Since, in this case, it takes the genitive *singular* of the noun (see p. 141), this cannot be regarded as a distinction of genders in the plural.

(c) Other numerals

The numerals from 5 to 20, and 30, are declined like feminines of the third declension (кость), with the peculiarity that the numerals 5 to 10, 20 and 30 take the stress on the final syllable in the oblique cases:

> nom.-acc. де́вять
> gen.-dat.-loc. девяти́
> instr. девятью́

This stress does not occur in nouns of this type (see p. 66). The number во́семь 'eight' has a mobile -e- in the nominative and instrumental (gen.-dat.-loc. восьми́, instr. восемью́).

The numerals 50 to 80 decline both parts:

> nom.-acc. пятьдеся́т
> gen.-dat.-loc. пяти́десяти
> instr. пятью́десятью

It will be noted that the second element is declined like де́сять although the nom.-acc. ends in a hard consonant.

The numerals denoting the hundreds from 200 to 900 also decline both elements, the second (сто) in the plural.

> nom. две́сти, пятьсо́т
> gen. двухсо́т, пятисо́т
> dat. двумста́м, пятиста́м
> loc. двухста́х, пятиста́х
> instr. двумяста́ми, пятьюста́ми

It will be noted that the first elements of три́ста and четы́реста have in gen., dat., and loc. the vowel -ё-, although it is unstressed or only very slightly stressed:

> gen. трёхсо́т, четырёхсо́т
> dat. трёмста́м, четырёмста́м
> loc. трёхста́х, четырёхста́х
> instr. тремяста́ми, четырмяста́ми

The same occurs with compound nouns and adjectives formed with трёх, четырёх (see pp. 92, 119).

The numerals сорок 'forty', девяносто 'ninety', and сто 'a hundred' have each a single form in -a for all the oblique cases: сорока, девяноста, ста. Phonetically, therefore, девяносто is not declined, unstressed final -o and -a having the same pronunciation (ə).

полтора (fem. полторы) 'one and a half' and полтораста 'a hundred and fifty' also have only one form for the oblique cases:

> полутора (masc.-neut.)
> полуторы (fem.)
> полутораста

The numerals

> тысяча 'a thousand'
> миллион 'a million'
> миллиард 'a milliard'

are true nouns; they retain substantival declension both in the singular and in the plural. However, тысяча shows the influence of the other numerals, in that it forms its instr. sing. in -ью (тысячью) after the pattern of the numerals from 5 to 80.

Compound numerals have practically the same structure as in English. Their elements are linked together in diminishing order without conjunction (unlike English, Russian does not insert the conjunction before the final element where this is less than 100), for example:

> две тысячи четыреста пятьдесят восемь 'two thousand, four hundred and fifty-eight'

Each element is declined separately:

> gen. двух тысяч четырёхсот пятидесяти восьми
> dat. двум тысячам четырёмстам пятидесяти восьми,
> &c.

2. USE OF THE CARDINAL NUMERALS

The numeral один agrees like an adjective in gender and case with the noun to which it refers:

один год 'one year', gen. одного года
одна подпись 'one signature', instr. одной подписью,
  &c.

The other cardinals are treated in the nominative (and
in the accusative, if it is identical with the nominative)
like nouns and in the oblique cases like adjectives.

In the nominative the numbers 2, 3, 4 and оба, обе,
take the gen. sing.; numbers from 5 on, the gen. plur.:

> два брата 'two brothers'
> три дороги 'three roads'
> четыре лошади 'four horses'
> пять братьев 'five brothers'
> семь дорог 'seven roads'
> шестьдесят лошадей 'sixty horses'

In the oblique cases all the numerals take the case of the
noun to which they refer (always in plural):

> N.–A.   два рубля 'two roubles'
>   шесть рублей 'six roubles'
>
> G.   двух ⎱ рублей
>   шести ⎰
>
> D.   двум ⎱ рублям
>   шести ⎰
>
> L.   двух ⎱ рублях
>   шести ⎰
>
> I.   двумя ⎱ рублями
>   шестью ⎰

With the numbers два, три, четыре, оба, обе the stress
of the dependent noun may sometimes differ from that of
the normal gen. sing.:

> два ряда 'two rows' (gen. sing. ряда)
> три шага 'three paces' (gen. sing. шага)

This phenomenon is particularly frequent with the fem.

óбе, to such an extent that with this numeral Russian tends to use the gen. sing. and the nom. pl. indifferently. Thus, óбе руки́ and óбе ру́ки 'both hands', óбе сестры́ and óбе сёстры 'both sisters', and even only óбе сто́роны 'both sides' (gen. sing. стороны́). This confusion is doubtless to be explained by the very numerous cases in which identity of stress makes the gen. sing. and the nom. pl. coincide, as in óбе ло́жки 'both spoons'.

With compound numerals the syntactical construction is determined by the last number:

> два́дцать оди́н офице́р 'twenty-one officers'
> сто со́рок три солда́та 'a hundred and forty-three soldiers'

The numerals ты́сяча, миллио́н, and миллиа́рд behave like nouns in all cases, i.e. they take a gen. pl. of the dependent noun:

> dat. ты́сяче до́лларов
> loc. в миллио́не до́лларов
> instr. pl. миллиа́рдами до́лларов

If the noun depending on два, три, четы́ре, óба, óбе in the nominative is accompanied by an adjective, the latter goes either into the gen. pl. or into the nom. pl. The gen. pl. is almost obligatory with masculines and neuters:

> три молоды́х (rarely молоды́е)
> петуха́ 'three young cocks'

With feminine nouns, particularly those which have the same stress in gen. sing. and nom. pl., the gen. pl. and the nom. pl. of the adjective are used indifferently:

> две спе́лых гру́ши or две спе́лые гру́ши
> 'two ripe pears'

In the oblique cases the adjective agrees with the noun:

> dat. трём молоды́м петуха́м
> instr. двумя́ спе́лыми гру́шами

The gen. pl. is obligatory with masculine and neuter substantivized adjectives:

четы́ре пожа́рных 'four firemen'
два пиро́жных 'two cakes'

With feminines, on the other hand, the tendency is to use the nom. pl.:

две столо́вые 'two dining-rooms'
три го́рничные 'three housemaids'

II. COLLECTIVES

1. DECLENSION

Collective numerals exist only for the numbers from 2 to 10. Their declension is mixed: while the nominative has the form of a neut. sing., the oblique cases have a plural declension.

N.	дво́е 'two'	че́тверо 'four'
A.	= N. or G.	= N. or G.
G.	двои́х	четверы́х
D.	двои́м	четверы́м
L.	двои́х	четверы́х
I.	двои́ми	четверы́ми

тро́е 'three' is declined like дво́е; пя́теро 'five', ше́стеро 'six', се́меро 'seven', во́сьмеро 'eight', де́вятеро 'nine', and де́сятеро 'ten' are declined like че́тверо.

The collectives display most of the characteristics of the cardinals (see p. 137): absence of the categories of number and gender, disparity between the nominative and the rest of the declension.

2. USE OF THE COLLECTIVES

Collective numerals were associated with certain collective nouns, now obsolete, and they too now show symptoms of decay.

The *obligatory* use of the collectives is limited to the nom.-acc. of двóе, трóе, чéтверо with the *pluralia tantum*, for the simple reason that the latter, having no gen. sing., cannot be employed with the cardinals два, три, четы́ре:

> двóе детéй 'two children'
> трóе ворóт 'three gates'
> чéтверо су́ток 'four days and four nights'
> (four times twenty-four hours)

In the oblique cases, however, modern usage, encountering no morphological obstacle, normally makes use of the cardinals, that of the collectives remaining optional for nouns denoting persons:

> gen. двух детéй or двои́х детéй
> dat. трём ворóтам
> instr. четырьмя́ су́тками

The same applies to the numbers above 4, in all cases: пять су́ток.

Apart from this special category, the collectives are employed, normally in the nominative, with personal pronouns in such phrases as:

> мы все трóе 'all three of us'
> вас двóе 'there are two of you'
> их бы́ло чéтверо 'there were four of them'
> нам трои́м 'to the three of us'

These collectives may always, however, be replaced by other turns of expression: их бы́ло четы́ре человéка, and so on.

Finally, the collectives *may* be employed with nouns denoting persons of the male sex (feminine nouns are excluded from this usage) and children:

> двóе игрокóв 'two gamblers'
> трóе слу́жащих 'three clerks'
> чéтверо ребя́т 'four children'

But in this case the use of the cardinals is always possible: два игрока́, три слу́жащих, четы́ре ребёнка.

To sum up: only the collectives дво́е, тро́е, че́тверо retain a certain vitality; the use of пя́теро, ше́стеро, се́меро is steadily on the wane; во́сьмеро, де́вятеро, де́сятеро do not nowadays occur except in more or less fixed phrases, such as есть за десятеры́х 'to eat enough for ten'.

From the numeral о́ба is derived a form обо́и which, being used only with the *pluralia tantum* in the nominative (обо́и са́ни 'both sledges'), may therefore be assimilated to the collectives.

Two other forms of the old singular of the same word have been preserved in the administrative language:

<blockquote>
обо́его по́ла (gen.) 'of both sexes'
обо́ему по́лу (dat.) 'to both sexes'
</blockquote>

III. ORDINALS

The ordinals are true adjectives and are declined in accordance with the hard type, except тре́тий 'third', which follows the mixed declension of во́лчий (see p. 101).

All the ordinals, with the exception of пе́рвый 'first' and второ́й 'second', are derived from the corresponding cardinals, either with the aid of suffixes:

тре́тий 'third'	сороково́й 'fortieth'
четвёртый 'fourth'	ты́сячный 'thousandth'

or without suffixes:

пя́тый 'fifth'	двадца́тый 'twentieth'
восьмо́й 'eighth'	девяно́стый 'ninetieth'
трина́дцатый 'thirteenth'	со́тый 'hundredth'

The ordinal седьмо́й 'seventh' presents a modified stem.

As in English, only the final element of compound ordinal numerals has the characteristic ordinal ending:

> пять тысяч семьсо́т шестьдеся́т второ́й 'the five thousand, seven hundred and sixty-second'

The following characteristics of compound ordinal numerals are also to be noted:

(1) the first element of ordinals formed from cardinals ending in -деся́т (50–80) or in сто in one of its forms (200–900) has the form of the genitive case:

> пятидеся́тый 'fiftieth'
> трёхсо́тый 'three hundredth'

(2) compound ordinals formed from numerals ending in ты́сяча, миллио́н, or миллиа́рд take everything preceding those numbers (with the exception of девяно́сто and сто) in the genitive; the ordinals thus formed are written as a single word:

> четырёхты́сячный 'four thousandth'
> стосорока́семиты́сячный 'hundred and forty-seven thousandth'
> пяти́десятидву́хмиллио́нный 'fifty-two millionth'

These therefore are compound adjectives of the type examined on p. 119.

VIII

Adverbs

THE adverbs may be regarded as a separate part of speech
only because of the uniformity of their use and their precise semantic value. From the morphological point of view
they present no unity, apart from the lack of all inflexion.
They are defined rather by the relationship in which they
stand to other parts of speech.

The variety of their origins divides adverbs into well-
defined morphological groups but at the same time blurs
the distinction between them and the other parts of speech.
Between adverbs on the one hand and nouns, gerunds, prepositions, conjunctions, and the different particles on the
other there exist zones of transition. Between adverbs and
adjectives, however, the line of demarcation is clearly drawn.

Within the category of adverbs two major groups may
be distinguished:

(1) a productive group consisting of adverbs formed by
    means of suffixes or prefixes;
(2) an unproductive group made up of fossilized forms.

I. PRODUCTIVE TYPES

All the productive types of adverbs are formed from
adjectives.

1. ADVERBS IN -o/-e

Adverbs in -o/-e may be formed from any descriptive
adjective:

высоко́ 'high' (высо́кий)

крѐпко 'firmly' (крѐпкий)
хорошо́ 'well' (хоро́ший)
и́скренне 'sincerely' (и́скренний)

Morphologically, the adverb in -о/-е is identical with the nom. sing. neut. of the short form of the adjective. No confusion is possible between the two in the matter of function; the stress, moreover, is often different in the two classes:

adv. о́стро 'wittily': adj. остро́
adv. ма́ло 'little': adj. мало́

These adverbs may have a comparative, which coincides, in form but not in use, with that of the corresponding adjectives:

вы́ше, крѐпче, лу́чше, и́скреннее

Adverbs in -е may be formed from present participles active in -щий:

угнета́юще 'oppressively'
вызыва́юще 'provocatively'
подкупа́юще 'seductively'

2. ADVERBS IN -и

Adjectives in -ский, -цкий form adverbs in -и:

дьѧ́вольски 'devilishly'   техни́чески 'technically'

These adverbs may be combined with the prefix по-, indicating conformity to the norm, to custom:

преда́тельски 'treacherously'
по-преда́тельски 'in the manner of a traitor'

Adverbs derived from adjectives of nationality or origin occur only with по-:

по-кита́йски 'in the Chinese manner, in Chinese'
по-сове́тски 'in the Soviet way'
по-моско́вски 'in the Moscow fashion'

Relative adjectives in -ий form adverbs in -ьи, exclusively with по-:

по-птичьи 'like a bird'   по-казачьи 'like a Cossack'

3. ADVERBS FORMED FROM ПО- + DATIVE

Adjectives other than those in -ский, -цкий, and pronouns, may form adverbs from the dat. sing. masc.-neut. preceded by по:

по-настоящему 'really'
по-другому 'in a different way'
по-моему 'in my own way, in my opinion'

II. UNPRODUCTIVE TYPES

1. Fossilized Noun and Verb Forms

1. SUBSTANTIVIZED ADJECTIVE WITH PREPOSITION

The adjectives are almost exclusively masc.-neut. sing. of the short form. The fossilized case-form may be:

(1) accusative:

налево 'to the left'   засветло 'before dark'

(2) genitive:

слегка 'slightly'   добела 'white-hot'

(3) dative:

попросту 'without ceremony'
понемногу 'little by little, a little'

(4) locative:

вскоре 'soon'   навеселе 'in one's cups'

The feminine is represented only by the accusative of the long form with the preposition в, as:

вслепую 'blindly'   врукопашную 'hand-to-hand'

2. NOUN WITH PREPOSITION

The noun is normally in the singular, much more rarely in the plural. The case-form may be:

(1) accusative, particularly with the prepositions на 'onto' and в 'into':

> на́спех 'hastily'
> вслух 'aloud'
> подча́с 'from time to time'
> вво́лю 'to one's heart's content'
> наизна́нку 'inside out'

(2) locative, with на 'on' and в 'in':

> наверху́ 'on top, upstairs'
> внизу́ 'below, downstairs'
> накану́не 'on the eve'
> вме́сте 'together'

(3) genitive:

> сра́зу 'immediately, at once'
> и́здали 'from a distance'
> отча́сти 'to some extent'
> спросо́нок 'half awake'

(4) dative:

> кста́ти 'apropos'
> попола́м 'in two, half-and-half'

(5) instrumental (infrequent):

> сли́шком 'too'
> совре́менем 'in the course of time'

3. NOUN WITHOUT PREPOSITION

What is involved is almost exclusively a fossilized instrumental singular. Examples are numerous:

> пешко́м 'on foot'　　　ры́сью 'at a trot'
> целико́м 'entirely'　　украдкой 'by stealth'

The instrumental of time is used only for the different parts of the day:

> у́тром 'in the morning'
> ве́чером 'in the evening'
> днём 'in the day, in the afternoon'
> но́чью 'in the night'

and for the four seasons:

> весно́й 'in the spring'   ле́том 'in the summer'
> о́сенью 'in the autumn'   зимо́й 'in the winter'

Cf. also:

> сего́дня (gen. sing.) 'today'
> то́тчас (acc. sing.) 'immediately'

In addition, a few colloquial adverbs of intensification are furnished by the nominative, as:

> страх (lit. 'fear') ⎫
> у́жас (lit. 'horror') ⎬ 'awfully, terribly'
> смерть (lit. 'death') ⎭

These adverbs occur usually in combination with как:

> у́жас как интере́сно 'awfully interesting'
> ему́ смерть хо́чется пойти́ 'he wants terribly
>   much to go'

4. REPETITION OF THE SAME NOUN IN DIFFERENT CASES

The nouns are linked by a preposition:

> рука́ о́б руку 'hand in hand'
> лицо́м к лицу́ 'face to face'
> вре́мя от вре́мени 'from time to time'
> день за днём 'day after day'
> с гла́зу на глаз 'tête-à-tête'

5. NUMERALS

Numeral adverbs are either case-forms, particularly of collectives, with prepositions:

> вдвое 'doubly'
> втроём 'three together'
> во пéрвых 'first' (in enumeration);

or multiplicatives formed with the suffix -жды:

однáжды 'once'	трúжды 'three times' .
двáжды 'twice'	четы́режды 'four times'

6. THE GERUND

Certain present gerunds become adverbs through the loss of their verbal features (tense, aspect, completion). This evolution is sometimes marked by a change of stress:

> стóя 'standing' (ger. стоя́)
> си́дя 'sitting' (ger. сидя́)
> мóлча 'silently' (ger. молчá)
> шутя́ 'jokingly'

The adverbialized gerund is frequently combined with a negative particle:

> нéхотя 'unwillingly'   немéдля 'without delay'

Gerunds in -ая, -яя normally do not assume adverbial character.

Gerunds in -чи do furnish adverbs:

> припевáючи 'in clover'
> крáдучись 'furtively'

In several cases a compound adverb is formed by a gerund with direct object:

> спустя́ рукавá 'in a slack manner' (lit. with sleeves down)
> очертя́ гóлову 'headlong'

7. GENERAL OBSERVATIONS

This entire type II is unproductive in the sense that one cannot at will make an adverb out of a substantival case-form in the same way as one can form adverbs from adjectives. At the same time, type II is not actually closed; it is continually being enriched by substantival case-forms and gerunds to which current usage tends to give an adverbial character. In other words, there is at any time a considerable number of substantival or verbal phrases which are, so to speak, half-way between the noun and the adverb or the verb and the adverb. Reference has already been made to this intermediary zone. It includes, for example, such phrases as:

> на дому́ 'at home'
> во всеору́жии 'fully equipped'
> на ско́рую ру́ку 'hastily'
> доро́гой 'on the way'

2. Primary Adverbs

There are a certain number of adverbs which cannot be attached to a noun or verb form, usually because the principle of their formation is no longer clear. This very fact renders them a completely dead group, which, unlike the preceding groups, receives no fresh contributions. On the other hand, it includes the adverbs in commonest use. They may be divided into several groups.

I. ADVERBS OF TIME

The adverbs of time are:

когда́ 'when'
тогда́ 'then'
всегда́ 'always'
иногда́ 'sometimes'
никогда́ 'never'
не́когда 'there is no time to'
не́когда 'at one time' (archaic)

тепе́рь 'now'
ны́не 'now' (archaic)
опя́ть 'again'
уже́ 'already'
по́сле 'after'
пре́жде 'before'

Indefinite adverbs may be formed from the adverb когда́ by means of the same particles as the indefinite pronouns (see p. 130):

когда́-то 'once'
когда́-нибудь and когда́-либо 'at some time or other, some day'
кое-когда́ 'from time to time'

2. ADVERBS OF PLACE

Adverbs of place may indicate:

(1) position:

где 'where'	нигде́ 'nowhere'
здесь and тут 'here'	не́где 'there is no room to'
там 'there'	вне 'outside'
везде́ and всю́ду 'everywhere'	

The following indefinite adverbs are formed from где:

где́-то, где́-нибудь, где́-либо, кое-где́

(2) motion towards:

куда́ 'where'	никуда́ 'nowhere' (with verbs
вон 'out'	of motion)
сюда́ 'here'	не́куда 'there is no room to'
туда́ 'there'	(with verbs of motion)

The following indefinite adverbs are formed from куда́:

куда́-то, куда́-нибудь, куда́-либо, кое-куда́

(3) motion from:

отку́да 'from where'	ниотку́да 'from nowhere'
отсю́да 'from here'	не́откуда 'there is no place
отту́да 'from there'	from which'
отовсю́ду 'from everywhere'	

The following indefinite adverbs are formed from отку́да:

отку́да-то, отку́да-нибудь

3. ADVERBS OF MANNER

The adverbs of manner are:

как 'how'	э́так 'thus, so' (colloquial)
так 'thus, so'	и так и сяк 'this way and that'
ника́к 'in no way'	ни так ни сяк 'neither this way nor that'

The following indefinite adverbs are formed from как:

ка́к-то 'in some way, somehow'
ка́к-нибудь and ка́к-либо 'somehow or other'
кое-ка́к 'somehow or other, anyhow'

4. ADVERBS OF QUANTITY

The adverbs of quantity are:

ско́лько 'how much'	почти́ 'almost'
сто́лько 'so much'	едва́ 'hardly'
ниско́лько 'not at all'	е́ле-е́ле 'only just'
не́сколько 'some'	чуть-чу́ть 'a very little'
о́чень and весьма́ 'very'	

The indefinite adverb ско́лько-нибудь is formed from ско́лько. The adverbs ско́лько, сто́лько and не́сколько are not to be confused with the pronouns which have the same form in the nominative (see p. 135).

III. USE OF THE ADVERBS

All the adverbs are employed with verbs; this is their normal function.

They may be employed also with adjectives and adverbs, and even, in certain cases, with nouns.

The living categories are employed only with verbs,

adjectives, and adverbs. Except for the type по- + -ски they are not employed with nouns:

шни́цель по-ве́нски 'Wiener Schnitzel'

Adverbs which consist of a case-form, with or without preposition, are used very rarely with adjectives and adverbs, but quite frequently with nouns:

вход да́ром 'entrance free'
геро́й понево́ле 'a hero in spite of himself'
любо́вь наве́к 'love undying'
грудь колесо́м 'puffed-out chest' (lit. 'like a wheel')

In these cases the adverb always follows the noun.

Adverbs formed from gerunds are employed only with verbs. They may, exceptionally, occur with the short form of the adjective (because of its character of predicate):

он груб мо́лча 'he is silently rude'

Finally, adverbs of quantity are employed not only with verbs but with adverbs, adjectives, and, more rarely, nouns:

о́чень не дура́к 'not at all stupid'
пое́здка в Москву́ далеко́ не пустя́к 'a journey to Moscow is far from being a trifle'

Note that the adverb так 'so' is used only with an adverb or a short adjective, while a long adjective requires the adjectival pronoun тако́й:

здесь так хо́лодно 'it is so cold here'
он так мо́лод ⎱
он тако́й молодо́й ⎰ 'he is so young'

If the number of adverbs is continuously being increased by the adverbialization of nouns and gerunds, there is a simultaneous contrary process by which adverbs are assimilated to other parts of speech or at least form hybrid categories and zones of transition. There is a tendency for adverbs to become

(*a*) prepositions (see p. 275):

вокру́г 'around'   несмотря́ на 'in spite of'

(*b*) conjunctions (see p. 277):

то́чно 'as if'   пока́ 'while'

(*c*) particles and modal words of all types (see p. 279):

положи́тельно 'definitely'   то́чно 'just so'

IX

Values of the Cases

I. GENERAL OBSERVATIONS

THE Russian case-forms may occur either alone or with prepositions. In both categories their value remains, generally speaking, the same. However, as the use of prepositional constructions extends (as it is doing) in Russian, the real values of the cases tend to lose in precision. In prepositional constructions today either the semantic weight falls on the preposition or the entire construction becomes a syntactical idiom. For this reason prepositional constructions will be examined in the chapter devoted to prepositions.

There are certain grammatical cases the general values of which remain distinct and are obvious, so to speak, at a glance: the *nominative*, the *accusative*, and the *dative*. In the *instrumental* this value, while still discernible, is already considerably weakened. The *genitive*, because of its complex origin, presents shades of meaning which it would be difficult, and certainly unhelpful, to class under a single heading. In all the cases the secondary, non-productive, values are tending to disappear.

The case-forms normally depend on the verbs. Often the value of the case is so indistinct that all that can be said is that such-and-such a verb takes such-and-such a case, no explanation being possible.

It is unusual for nouns to be followed by other nouns in a case other than the genitive. The dependence of a noun in the genitive on another noun is normal and frequent.

2. NOMINATIVE

The nominative is the only case which is completely autonomous and which cannot depend on any other word. Its syntactical functions are those of subject (see p. 281) and complement (see p. 285) and of the words in apposition to these. It also performs functions which in some languages belong to the vocative.

3. ACCUSATIVE

The accusative indicates the object which, in its totality, endures the action of the verb.

(1) With transitive verbs it serves as direct object:

старик взял ключ 'the old man took the key'
женщина, собирающая клубнику 'woman picking strawberries'

(2) With transitive and intransitive verbs it indicates the time or space entirely covered by the action of the verb:

танцовать целую ночь 'to dance all night'
пройти пять миль 'to walk five miles'

In this second use, the accusative is moving towards the domain of fixed idioms. It has already reached it in the construction with стоить 'to cost' (стоить сто фунтов 'to cost a hundred pounds') and in tautological expressions like шутки шутить 'to joke' (cognate accusative).

The accusative is so closely associated with action that it can never depend on a noun, even a verbal noun; the direct object in such cases passes into the genitive:

взять город 'to capture a town'
взятие города 'the capture of the town'

4. DATIVE

The dative indicates the remoter object to which the action of the verb applies, though less completely than in the case of the accusative. It is in the first instance the case of the person or thing interested in the action of the verb:

кухáрка готóвит нам обéд 'the cook is preparing dinner for us'

покáзывать дéтям картѝнки 'to show pictures to the children'

улыбáться наѝвности 'to smile at naïveté'

учѝться механике 'to learn mechanics'

мне хóчется 'I feel like' (see p. 249)

The dative is also frequent with adjectives:

вéрный обещáниям 'faithful to the promises'

достýпный нарóду 'accessible to the people'

The construction with nouns appears to be only an extension of verbal and adjectival constructions:

подáрок родѝтелям 'a present for the parents'

прéданность идéям 'devotion to ideas'

Similarly with such constructions as:

привéт друзьям 'greetings to my friends' (cf. послáть привéт друзьям)

конéц весéлью 'an end to the merriment' (cf. положѝть конéц весéлью)

5. INSTRUMENTAL

The main value of the instrumental is that of instrument, agent or means:

рéзать нóжницами 'to cut with scissors'

мост испрáвлен рабóчими 'the bridge has been repaired by the workmen'

судьбá игрáет человéком 'man is the plaything of destiny'

управлять бáнком 'to manage a bank'

писáть цветѝстым слóгом 'to write in a flowery style'

The same value of instrument or means is still present,

though less distinct, in the use of the instrumental of function, which is still current:

> работать слéсарем 'to work as a locksmith'

Finally, the predicative instrumental constitutes a special category in which the idea of instrumentality is no longer perceptible:

> мы все бы́ли детьми́ 'we have all been children' (for the details, see p. 287)

In its other uses, which have to a large extent lost the idea of instrumentality, the instrumental, losing its productivity, assumes more and more the character of an adverb. This is the case with the instrumental of respect:

> упáсть дýхом 'to lose heart'

of cause:

> болéть кóрью 'to have the measles'

of comparison:

> выть вóлком 'to howl like a wolf'

of 'way by which':

> итти́ пóлем 'to walk through the field'

The instrumental of time has completely attained adverbial quality:

> éхать нóчью 'to travel by night'

It is, therefore, not surprising that, of all the cases employed without prepositions, the instrumental is almost the only one which furnishes any considerable contingent to the category of adverbs (see p. 150).

The only nouns which are followed by the instrumental are those derived from verbs. In such cases, the instrumental is transferred from the verbal construction:

> удáр кулакóм 'a blow with the fist'
> поéздка парохóдом 'a journey by ship'
> заня́тия спóртом 'sporting activities'

The use of the instrumental with adjectives is restricted almost entirely to the relatively unproductive category of the instrumental of respect:

обильный рыбой 'abounding in fish'

The instrumental of respect may also occur with nouns, but only when these are used predicatively:

он монах душой 'he is a monk at heart'

6. GENITIVE

The genitive indicates that the object participates only partially if at all in the action of the verb; the genitive thus expresses limitation or definition. This formula, however, embraces too many varieties of usage to be of much practical value. These varieties of usage are the following:

(a) *With verbs*

With verbs the force of the genitive may be

(1) partitive:

отрежь ветчины 'cut off some ham'
поддать жару 'to add fuel to the flames'

(2) indicative of non-participation in the action, viz:

negation of the verb-direct object relationship:

не слышать музыки 'not to hear the music' (see also p. 295)

separation:

лишить пищи 'to deprive of food'

goal:

просить отсрочки 'to ask for a postponement'

The genitive of time is now only an isolated idiom limited to dates:

второго августа 'on the second of August'

(b) With nouns

(1) With nouns and the pronoun что, as with verbs, the genitive may have partitive force:

> кусóк дéрева 'a piece of wood'
> что нóвого 'what news'

(2) The genitive is the only case which may depend on a noun of other than verbal or adjectival origin. It therefore comes to assume a large number of functions:

objective genitive, dependent on a noun of verbal origin:

> открытие выставки 'the opening of
>   an exhibition'

genitive of possession:

> нóги лóшади 'the legs of the horse'
> долг человéка 'the duty of man'

genitive of quality:

> человéк дóлга 'a man who is strict
>   in performing his duty'
> врéмя óтдыха 'rest time'
> вагóн трéтьего клáсса 'a third-class carriage'

genitive of relation:

> начáльник стáнции 'station-master'

(c) With adjectives

The genitive dependent upon an adjective is rare:

> пóлный воды 'full of water'

It is normal only with the comparative. It may then be assimilated to the genitive of separation:

> любóвь сильнéе смéрти 'love is
>   stronger than death'

(d) With numerals

When it depends upon a numeral the noun goes into the genitive case—singular with 'two, three, four', plural with numbers above 'four':

три окнá 'three windows'

дéсять óкон 'ten windows'

(for details, see p. 141)

The same construction applies also to adverbs of quantity:

мнóго пескý 'much sand'

мáло людéй 'few people'

7. LOCATIVE

The locative is employed only with prepositions. Its specific value is limited accordingly. Constructions with the locative will be examined in the chapter devoted to prepositions.

X

Verbs: Forms

I. GENERAL OBSERVATIONS

THE verb is the most original and the most difficult part of Russian morphology. The Russian verbal forms taken as a whole constitute a system which differs widely from the English verb system.

The tense system is poor and amounts to three tenses in all: present, past, and future. Moreover, half of the verbs in Russian have no present tense. Furthermore, the personal forms of the Russian verb are of extreme simplicity. On the other hand, the system of verbal adjectives and adverbs is rich: four participles and two gerunds. The verbal forms are derived from one another by a simple system of personal endings and suffixes.

Differences of mood are expressed principally by particles which are not incorporated into the verbal form proper. The expression of mood acquires thereby a great degree of flexibility.

The entire Russian verb system—and herein lies its originality—is permeated by the notion of *aspect*, i.e. the contrast between the *uncompleted action* (*imperfective verbs*) and the *completed action* (*perfective verbs*). Differences of aspect are expressed in Russian by elements employed in word-formation—suffixes and prefixes.

It is necessary, for the purposes of a grammar, to examine separately the different elements of which the Russian

verb system is made up: verbal forms and their classification, aspect, tense, mood, &c. It should not, however, be
forgotten that all these elements interpenetrate and condition one another to the point of constituting an indissoluble whole. Frequent cross-references will draw attention to this fact.

The entire system of forms of any Russian verb rests
upon two principles: inflexion and word-formation. These
two principles are associated much more closely in the
verb than in the noun and adjective. Thus, the Russian
past tense is entirely a product of word-formation; for
which reason it has no personal endings but, on the other
hand, varies according to gender and number. Similarly,
the system of aspects is based entirely on word-formation.

For the purposes both of inflexion and of word-formation, all the forms of a Russian verb are derived from two
stems which are commonly known as the *present stem* and
the *infinitive stem* respectively.

The verb forms are distributed between the two stems
in accordance with the following table. The verb звать 'to
call' may serve as example:

Present stem: зов-

Present: зову́, зовёшь

Present participles:

    (*a*) *active*: зову́щий

    (*b*) *passive*: зово́мый

Present gerund: зовя́

Imperative: зови́

Infinitive stem: зва-

Infinitive: звать

Past: звал

Past participles:

    (*a*) *active*: зва́вший

    (*b*) *passive*: зва́нный

Past gerund: (по)звав,
(по)зва́вши

The *compound future* (бу́ду звать) belongs to the group of
the infinitive stem.

The two stems may be either identical or different, and
in the latter case their relations may be somewhat com-
plicated. Within each of the two groups, however, inflexion and word-formation are of great simplicity and
regularity.

This chapter indicates only the general principles of the formation of the various verbal categories. For details, see the following chapter on 'Classification of Verbs'.

II. PRESENT GROUP

Any form derived from the present stem contains this stem plus an ending. If the ending is vocalic it is added directly to the stem. This occurs in the 1st pers. sing. and 3rd pers. pl. of the present tense, the present participles, the gerund, and the imperative. If, on the other hand, the ending is consonantal, a *connecting vowel* is inserted between it and the stem. This occurs in the 2nd and 3rd pers. sing. and the 1st and 2nd pers. pl. of the present tense. In other words, the present stem is always followed by a vowel, except in the imperative, when it may be followed by a *yod* or by no ending at all.

1. PRESENT

(a) *Forms*

The conjugation of the present is extremely simple because the endings are always the same; only three verbs are irregular in this respect (see p. 204).

The consonantal endings (i.e. all except those of the 1st pers. sing. and the 3rd pers. pl.) are connected with the stem by means of a vowel. This vowel may be either -e- or -и-. In other words, Russian has only two types of conjugation, of which the following are the examples:

несу́ 'I carry'   говорю́ 'I speak'

де́лаю 'I make'   сто́ю 'I cost'

Singular

1. нес-у́	де́ла-ю	говор-ю́	сто́-ю
2. нес-ё-шь	де́ла-е-шь	говор-и́-шь	сто́-и-шь
3. нес-ё-т	де́ла-е-т	говор-и́-т	сто́-и-т

Plural

1. нес-ё-м	де́ла-е-м	говор-и́-м	сто́-и-м
2. нес-ё-те	де́ла-е-те	говор-и́-те	сто́-и-те
3. нес-у́т	де́ла-ют	говор-я́т	сто́-ят

Verbs with the connecting vowel -e- have in the 3rd pers. pl. the ending -ут, -ют; those with the connecting vowel -и- have the ending -ят (-ат after ж, ш, ч, щ).

Each of the two types has two variants, according as the stem ends in a consonant or in a vowel. In the latter case a *yod* naturally occurs between the vowel of the stem and the connecting vowel or the vowel of the ending. In the present tense with the connecting vowel -и- the *yod* disappears before the -и-.

The difference between the two types appears only when the stress falls on the connecting vowel. If that vowel is unstressed, the difference disappears in pronunciation:

де́лаешь (*d'élaiš*)　　　сто́ишь (*stóiš*)

In the 3rd pers. pl. the confusion of the two types in pronunciation is due not to phonology but to analogy:

де́лают (*d'élajut*)　　　сто́ят (pronounced *stójut*)

There is, however, a tendency to restore the difference in the 3rd pers. pl. under the influence of the spelling.

The use of the personal pronoun, while normal, is not obligatory (see p. 281).

The present is the only verbal category in which true conjugation occurs.

(b) Stress

In the inflexion of verbs the stress plays a far less important role than in that of nouns. In the verb mobility of stress is felt as an anomaly.

The stress is always fixed in the present of verbs with a vocalic stem. It may fall upon any syllable:

де́лаю 'I do'

умѐю 'I know how to'
стою̀ 'I stand'

In verbs with a consonantal stem the stress may be either fixed or mobile. If it is fixed it may fall upon any syllable:

рѐжу 'I cut'   несу̀ 'I carry'

If it is mobile, its mobility is always of the same type: the stress falls upon the final syllable in the 1st pers. sing. and moves back one syllable in the rest of the conjugation:

пишу̀ 'I write'	пѝшем
пѝшешь	пѝшете
пѝшет	пѝшут

In these verbs, the stress of the 1st pers. sing. coincides always with the stress of the infinitive.

2. PRESENT PARTICIPLE ACTIVE

The present participle active is characterized by the suffix -ущ-/-ющ- for verbs of the -е- type, and -ящ-/-ащ- for those of the -и- type. A convenient way of forming this participle is by replacing the final -т of the 3rd pers. pl. by the ending -щий:

несу̀т:	несу̀щий (masc.), -щая (fem.), -щее (neut.)
дѐлают:	дѐлающий — —
говоря̀т:	говоря̀щий — —
стоя̀т:	стоя̀щий — —

As with the 3rd pers. pl., the difference in pronunciation between participles of the two types exists only under the stress (стоя̀щий is commonly pronounced *stójuš'š'ij*).

Несу̀щий is equivalent to the Lat. *ferens*. Its use is accordingly wider than that of the English present participle (*carrying*).

In verbs with fixed stress the present participle retains the verbal stress. In verbs with mobile stress it generally has the same stress as the personal forms other than the

1st pers. sing.: пи́шущий. There are, however, a few exceptions.

Only imperfective verbs form a present participle active.

3. PRESENT PARTICIPLE PASSIVE

The present participle passive is characterized by the suffix -м- which is added to the stem by means of the connecting vowel -e- or -и-, according to the conjugation. If the connecting vowel -e- is stressed (-ё-), it becomes -o- without softening of the preceding consonant. A convenient way of forming this participle is by adding the adjectival ending -ый to the 1st pers. pl., taking care to replace -ё- by -o-:

несём: несо́мый (masc.), -мая (fem.), -мое (neut.)
де́лаем: де́лаемый — —
говори́м: говори́мый — —

This participle has also a short form:

несо́м, несо́мо, несо́ма, несо́мы

The present participle passive is a very literary form and is hardly used in colloquial Russian. It is normally used only from verbs with a vocalic stem. A number of verbs with consonantal stems do not possess this participle at all.

English has no equivalent to this form; несо́мый corresponds to the Greek participle φερόμενος 'being carried'.

In verbs with fixed stress this participle retains the verbal stress. In verbs with mobile stress it generally has the same stress as the 1st pers. sing.:

люби́мый (from люблю́, лю́бишь 'love')

Only transitive imperfective verbs form a present participle passive.

4. PRESENT GERUND

The present gerund is formed by the addition of the final syllable -я to the stem. If the stem ends in a consonant, this is softened; if it ends in a vowel, a *yod* is inserted between the stem and the ending; orthographically the ending is -я (or -a after ж, ш, ч, щ):

> неся́, де́лая, говоря́, сто́я
> дрожа́ (from дрожа́ть 'to tremble')

The gerund неся́ means 'carrying' (Fr. *en portant*).

In verbs with fixed stress the gerund retains the verbal stress. In verbs with mobile stress it has the same stress as the 1st pers. sing.:

> любя́ 'loving'

There exists also a present gerund in -учи, -ючи. Except for the verb быть 'to be', the present gerund of which is regularly бу́дучи (see p. 205), this form is either archaic or non-literary. Some gerunds of this type survive only as adverbs (see p. 152).

Normally the present gerund is limited to imperfective verbs; however, numerous perfective verbs of the first and fourth classes may also possess this form; it then has the force of a past gerund (see pp. 179, 208).

5. IMPERATIVE

The imp. sing. has three endings:

(1) The ending -и. This occurs only in three types of verbs with consonantal stems:

(*a*) verbs with final stress (the -й then takes the stress):

> неси́ 'carry'   говори́ 'speak'

(*b*) the same verbs with the stressed prefix вы́-:

> вы́неси 'carry out; endure'
> вы́говори 'pronounce'

(*c*) verbs with stem ending in two consonants:

> ко́нчи 'end'   кри́кни 'shout'

(2) Softening of the final consonant of the stem (expressed orthographically by -ь). This occurs in all other verbs with consonantal stems:

будь 'be'   брось 'throw'

(3) *Yod* (expressed orthographically by -й). This occurs in all verbs with vocalic stem:

де́лай 'do'   мой 'wash'

This form of the imperative is that of the 2nd pers. sing., but may also serve for the 3rd pers. sing. and pl.

From this basic form a 2nd pers. pl. form is derived by the addition of the ending -те:

неси́те	вы́несите	ко́нчите	кри́кните
бу́дьте	бро́сьте	де́лайте	мо́йте

For the inclusive form of the imperative and for the various modal values of the basic form, see the chapter on moods (pp. 236–9).

The stress of the imperative is regularly that of the 1st pers. sing. The only exception is constituted by verbs with vocalic stem and final stress, which necessarily shift the stress back by one syllable: стой 'stop' (стою́).

III. INFINITIVE GROUP

All verbal forms based on the infinitive stem derive not from inflexion but from word-formation.

The infinitive stem may end either in a consonant or in a vowel. The endings always begin with a consonant. The contact between the final consonant of the stem and the initial consonant of the ending may occasion phonetic changes which in some cases obscure the derivation.

Certain verbs have in the infinitive a stem which is slightly lengthened in comparison with that of the past tense and the participles.

I. INFINITIVE

The usual infinitive ending is -ть:

де́лать, говори́ть, сто́ить

In certain verbs with consonantal stem the ending is -ти́, which is always stressed:

нести́ 'to carry'; ползти́ 'to crawl'

However, when such verbs take the stressed prefix вы́-, the ending -ти then loses the stress:

вы́нести 'to carry out; to endure'
вы́ползти 'to crawl out'

The parallel with the imperative in this respect is complete.

If the stem ends in -т, -д, these consonants become -с- before the infinitive ending:

плести́ 'to plait', вести́ 'to lead' (pres. плету́, веду́, past part. act. плётший, ве́дший)

By analogy, -б undergoes the same change:

грести́ 'to row', скрести́ 'to scratch' (pres. гребу́, скребу́, past tense грёб, скрёб)

If the stem ends in a velar (-к or -г), this combines with the -т- of the infinitive to form -ч-:

печь 'to bake', мочь 'to be able' (pres. пеку́, могу́, past tense пёк, мог)

In verbs with mobile stress, the stress of the infinitive coincides always with that of the 1st pers. sing. of the present.

2. PAST TENSE

(a) Forms

The past tense is formed by the addition of the suffix -л to the infinitive stem. In the majority of cases it is sufficient to replace the -ть (or -ти́) of the infinitive by -л.

This form was originally a past participle active, which was employed in conjunction with an auxiliary, the present of the verb 'to be', the combination having the value of a past tense. The auxiliary having disappeared, only the participle remains, with the function of the past tense. This is the reason why in Russian the past tense has no verbal inflexion. It has two forms, corresponding to singular and plural. This fact renders obligatory the use of the personal pronoun. Within the singular, the past tense distinguishes three genders:

Singular

1. я дéлал (masc.), дéлала (fem.), дéлало (neut.)
2. ты дéлал, дéлала, дéлало
3. он дéлал, онá дéлала, онó дéлало

Plural

1. мы дéлали
2. вы дéлали
3. онú дéлали

The forms of the past tense, it will have been observed, are comparable to those of the predicative adjective:

я вéсел 'I am gay'; ты веселá, он вéсел, мы вéселы

When the infinitive stem ends in a consonant, the combination of this consonant with the -л- of the past tense is always simplified:

(i) If the consonant is -т- or -д- it disappears in all the forms of the past tense:

stem плет- (inf. плестú 'to plait'): плёл, плелá, плелó, плелú

stem вед- (inf. вестú 'to lead'): вёл, велá, велó, велú

(ii) If the consonant is one other than -т- or -д-, it is the -л- which disappears, but only in the final position, i.e. in the masculine:

нёс, неслá, неслó, неслú (нестú 'to carry')

мог, могла́ (мочь 'to be able')
скрёб, скребла́ (скрести́ 'to scratch')
у́мер, умерла́ (умере́ть 'to die')
зача́х, зача́хла (зача́хнуть 'to waste away')

(b) Stress

The stress of the past tense is normally fixed and identical with that of the infinitive. This occurs always in verbs the stems of which are not monosyllables (no account being taken, naturally, of verbal prefixes):

говори́л, говори́ла, говори́ло, говори́ли

Verbs with an infinitive in -ти́ or -чь also have a fixed stress, which in this case is final:

ползти́ 'to crawl': полз, ползла́, ползли́
печь 'to bake': пёк, пекла́, пекли́

The stress is mobile only in a certain number of primary verbs the stems of which are both monosyllabic and vocalic. The mobility of the stress is of only one type: in the feminine the stress moves onto the final syllable:

жить 'to live': жил, жила́, жи́ло, жи́ли
спать 'to sleep': спал, спала́, спа́ло, спа́ли

Similarly in the verbs:

брать 'to take'	вить 'to twist'	пить 'to drink'
быть 'to be'	дать 'to give'	плыть 'to swim'
взять 'to take'	лить 'to pour'	снять 'to take off'
слыть 'to have the reputation of'		

In some of these verbs the stress moves onto the prefix, except in the feminine, where it remains final:

нажи́ть 'to acquire': на́жил, нажила́, на́жило, на́жили

Similarly in the following verbs when they take a prefix:

быть 'to be'	(на)ча́ть 'to begin'
дать 'to give'	*ять 'to take' (see pp. 185–6)

клясть 'to curse'   мерéть 'to die'
лить 'to pour'   перéть 'to push'
пить 'to drink'

In verbs of this type the usage in this respect is not definitely established, because of numerous analogies.

It will be seen that the entire system of the mobile stress in the past tense, including the absence of a definite rule in one type, recalls that of the short form of the adjective, the syntactical function of which (predicate) is, moreover, similar to that of the past tense (see p. 99).

3. PAST PARTICIPLE ACTIVE

This participle is characterized by the suffixes -вш- (if the stem is vocalic) and -ш- (if the stem is consonantal):

дéлать: дéлавший (masc.), -шая (fem.), -шее (neut.)
говори́ть: говори́вший   —   —
нести́:   нёсший   —   —
вести́:   вéдший   —   —

The participle дéлавший means 'who has done, who was doing'.

The stress of this participle is identical with that of the infinitive. In the case of infinitives with the stress on -ти́, the stress necessarily moves back one syllable in the past participle active:

ползти́ 'to crawl': пóлзший

4. PAST PARTICIPLE PASSIVE

This participle, which is equivalent to the past participle in English, is characterized by two suffixes: -нн- and -т-.

(a) The suffix -нн-

This suffix is by far the commoner and alone survives as a living form. It is added directly to the vocalic stem:

сдéлать 'to make': сдéланный, -ое, -ая

and by means of the vowel -e- to the consonantal stem:

> принести́ 'to bring': принесённый

Verbs in -ить of the fourth class are treated like verbs with consonantal stems: they insert an -e- between the stem (minus -и-) and the -нн- of the participle:

> вы́говорить 'to pronounce': вы́говоренный

Moreover, the same consonantal alternation is observed as in the 1st pers. sing. of the present tense (see p. 199):

> бро́сить 'to throw': бро́шенный
> купи́ть 'to buy': ку́пленный

According to the modern rule, this participle is spelt with a double -н-. Some people however still follow the rule according to which one wrote -н- with simple verbs and -нн- with compound verbs: де́ланый, but сде́ланный.

The stress corresponds generally to that of the infinitive in the verbs with fixed stress:

> привести́ 'to bring': приведённый
> переде́лать 'to transform': переде́ланный
> запрети́ть 'to forbid': запрещённый

The stress moves generally one syllable back in verbs with mobile stress:

> описа́ть 'to describe': опи́санный
> заплати́ть 'to pay': запла́ченный

and in some verbs in -а́ть with fixed final stress:

> собра́ть 'to collect': со́бранный
> прочита́ть 'to read': прочи́танный
> изда́ть 'to publish': и́зданный

(b) The suffix -т-

Only certain groups of verbs form their past participle passive in -т-, namely:

(1) *all* verbs ending in:

> -уть   согну́ть 'to bend': со́гнутый

-ыть открыть 'to open': открытый
-оть смолоть 'to grind': смолотый
-ереть запереть 'to lock': запертый

(2) verbs with *monosyllabic* stems ending in:

-ить побрить 'to shave': побритый
-еть согреть 'to warm': согретый
-ять занять 'to occupy': занятый
-ать after ж, ш, ч, щ: начать 'to begin': начатый

The participle in -тый occurs only in unproductive classes.

The stress corresponds generally to that of the past tense:

убить 'to kill', убил: убитый
понять 'to understand', понял: понятый

In the verbs in -нуть with stressed -у́-, and in verbs in -олоть, -ороть (see p. 187), the stress moves back one syllable as compared with the past tense and the infinitive:

сомкнуть 'to close', сомкнул: сомкнутый
проколоть 'to pierce', проколол: проколотый

The past participle passive is the most frequent of all the participles. It occurs necessarily in the short form when employed predicatively, above all with the function of the passive voice (see pp. 98, 246): сделан, принесён, открыт. It is formed almost exclusively from perfective verbs. When formed from imperfective verbs it nearly always has adjectival force. When it is employed as an adjective, it is never written with the double -н-:

раненый солдат 'a wounded soldier' (adj.)
солдат, раненный в голову 'a soldier wounded in the head' (part.)

5. PAST GERUND

The past gerund is formed in the same way as the past participle active.

If the stem ends in a vowel, the gerund ending is -в or -вши (the latter is rather less frequent than the former):

> сде́лав, сде́лавши 'having done'
> поговори́в, поговори́вши 'having spoken'

Reflexive verbs have only the form in -вши:

> сде́лавшись 'having become'

If the stem ends in a consonant, the gerund ending is -ши:

> принёсши 'having brought'
> сберёгши 'having saved'

There is a tendency to avoid gerunds of the last type by replacing them, wherever possible, by the present gerund form of the perfective verb:

> приведя́ 'having brought' (rather than приве́дши)

The past gerund expresses prior action.

Like that of the past participle active, the stress of the past gerund corresponds exactly to that of the infinitive; in the case of verbs in -ти́, it moves back by one syllable.

The past gerund is limited to perfective verbs. The only imperfective verbs which normally form a past gerund are those which have no present gerund; in such cases it expresses, like the latter, simultaneous action (in the past):

> гнув 'bending', from гнуть (the pres. gerund *гня does not exist)
> пив 'drinking' from пить (the pres. gerund *пья does not exist)

6. COMPOUND FUTURE

In the perfective verbs the present form has usually the force of the future (see p. 207).

Only imperfective verbs have a special form to express

the future. It is obtained by the conjunction of the infinitive with the present-future of the verb 'to be' (see p. 205):

Singular 1. я бу́ду де́лать 'I shall do'
2. ты бу́дешь де́лать
3. он, она́, оно́ бу́дет де́лать

Plural 1. мы бу́дем де́лать
2. вы бу́дете де́лать
3. они́ бу́дут де́лать

No perfective verb may form a compound future.

XI

Verbs: Classification

I. GENERAL OBSERVATIONS

THE forms within each of the two groups—of the present stem and of the infinitive stem—present a simple and coherent system with very few irregularities.

On the other hand, relations between the two stems may be both varied and complex.

In a large number of verbs the two stems are identical.

Frequently, however, the two stems are different. The difference may show itself in various ways:

(1) by suffixion: either the infinitive stem or (rarely) the present stem may be extended by the addition of a suffix;

(2) by the different structure of the roots of the two stems;

(3) by a combination of the two preceding features.

As a general rule, it is not sufficient to know the present stem in order to be able to form the infinitive stem, and conversely; it is necessary to know both. Thus any system of classification of Russian verbs must aim at establishing groups which present a constant relationship between the two stems.

The system of classification adopted in this grammar is based upon the differences arising in the form of the present. The subdivisions within each class are based upon differences in the infinitive stem. In spite of some drawbacks, it brings out adequately enough the main lines of the Russian verb system.

The form of the present which constitutes the basis of the classification is characterized by the connecting vowel. As this vowel does not occur in the 1st pers. sing., reference will regularly be made to the 3rd pers. sing.

The nature of the connecting vowel divides Russian verbs naturally into two conjugations: verbs in -e- and verbs in -и-. It is more convenient, however, in view of the vast number of verbs in -e-, to divide them into three separate classes according to the form assumed by the stem before the connecting vowel -e-. This gives four classes in all.

The system followed in this grammar differs from the traditional system only in one respect: verbs of the third class with consonantal stem are incorporated in the first class (groups I A 8, 9 and I B 3).

The order in which the classes are presented here is traditional and does not, unfortunately, correspond to the degree of vitality, and consequently the importance, of each. A better order would be: III, IV, II, I.

II. FIRST CLASS: VERBS IN -E- WITH CONSONANTAL STEM

In most verbs of this class the final consonant of the stem is hard.

This class is entirely unproductive. Moreover, in many verbs of this class the structure of the root of the present differs more or less widely from that of the root of the infinitive; the only explanation of these differences is historical. This class, therefore, consists of primary, strong, archaic verbs which at the same time are extremely frequent in use. That makes it necessary to give a nearly exhaustive list of such verbs.

A. *INFINITIVE STEM WITHOUT SUFFIX*

The stem, which is always consonantal in the present, is usually so in the infinitive also. The simplifications arising from the contact of two consonants in the infinitive (see p. 173) and the past tense (see p. 174) occur in this subdivision A of the first class.

1. PRESENT AND INFINITIVE STEMS IDENTICAL IN STRUCTURE

The conjugation of this type may be illustrated by the verb везти́ 'to carry in a vehicle':

Singular 1. вез-у́   *Plural* 1. вез-ё-м
         2. вез-ё-шь   2. вез-ё-те
         3. вез-ё-т   3. вез-у́т

Like везти́ are conjugated verbs the stems of which end in:

-с-   нести́ 'to carry' (несу́, несёт)
      пасти́ 'to pasture' (пасу́, пасёт)
      трясти́ 'to shake' (трясу́, трясёт)
-з-   ползти́ 'to crawl' (ползу́, ползёт)
      лезть 'to climb' (ле́зу, ле́зет)
-т-   гнести́ 'to oppress' (гнету́, гнетёт)
      мести́ 'to sweep' (мету́, метёт)
      обрести́ 'to find' (обрету́, обретёт)
      плести́ 'to plait' (плету́, плетёт)
      цвести́ 'to bloom' (цвету́, цветёт)
-д-   блюсти́ 'to observe' (блюду́, блюдёт)
      брести́ 'to wander' (бреду́, бредёт)
      вести́ 'to lead' (веду́, ведёт)
      класть 'to put' (кладу́, кладёт)
      красть 'to steal' (краду́, крадёт)
      пасть 'to fall' (паду́, падёт)
      прясть 'to spin' (пряду́, прядёт)

The last four verbs form their past participle active
in -вший and their past gerund in -в, -вши, as
though their stems were vocalic:

клáвший   крáвший   пáвший   прáвший
наклáв   укрáв   пáвши   напрáвши

-б- грести 'to row' (гребу́, гребёт)
     скрести 'to scrape' (скребу́, скребёт)

Verbs with stems ending in -к- or -г- change к to ч and
г to ж before the connecting vowel -е-, i.e. in the 2nd and
3rd pers. sing. and 1st and 2nd pers. pl.:

-к- течь 'to flow' (теку́, течёшь, течёт, течём, течёте,
     теку́т)
     влечь 'to drag' (влеку́, влечёт)
     печь 'to bake' (пеку́, печёт)
     сечь 'to cut, thrash' (секу́, сечёт)

-г- стричь 'to shear' (стригу́, стрижёшь, стрижёт,
     стрижём, стрижёте, стригу́т)
     бере́чь 'to guard' (берегу́, бережёт)
     мочь 'to be able' (могу́, мóжет)
     стере́чь 'to watch' (стерегу́, стережёт)
     запря́чь 'to harness, to yoke' (запрягу́, запряжёт);
     the stressed я is pronounced in this verb like -é-
     (before a soft consonant) or like -ё- (before a
     hard consonant)

2. PRESENT AND INFINITIVE STEMS OF DIFFERENT STRUCTURE

The difference appears in:

(1) the vowel of the root:

     сесть 'to sit down' (ся́ду, ся́дет)
     лечь 'to lie down' (ля́гу, ля́жет)

The verb сесть forms the past participle active сéвший
and the past gerund сев, сéвши. The verb лечь forms an

imperative ending in a hard consonant (ляг), the only one of its kind;

(2) a mobile vowel -e- in the infinitive stem:

> жечь 'to burn' (жгу, жжёт)
> прочéсть 'to read' (прочтý, прочтёт)

(3) a supplementary vowel -o- in the infinitive stem:

> толóчь 'to pound' (толкý, толчёт)

(4) a supplementary consonant in the present:

т	ростú 'to grow' (ростý, ростёт, past tense рос, рослá; past part. act. рóсший)
в	жить 'to live' (живý, живёт)
	плыть 'to swim' (плывý, плывёт)
	слыть 'to have the reputation of' (слывý, слывёт)

(5) the two stems as a whole. The verbs of this group are those with a nasal in the present:

н	жать 'to reap' (жну, жнёт)
	мять 'to crumple' (мну, мнёт)
	начáть 'to begin' (начнý, начнёт)
	распя́ть 'to crucify' (распнý, распнёт)
	клясть 'to curse' (клянý, клянёт, past part. act. кля́вший, pass. кля́тый, past tense клял)
м	жать 'to press' (жму, жмёт)
	the numerous compounds of the old verb *ять 'to take' (the present stem shows the root -ьм-, йм-, or -им-):
-ьм-	взять 'to take' (возьмý, возьмёт)
-йм-	заня́ть 'to occupy, borrow' (займý, займёт)
	наня́ть 'to hire' (наймý, наймёт)
	поня́ть 'to understand' (поймý, поймёт)
	уня́ть 'to calm' (уймý, уймёт)

-им- обня́ть 'to embrace' (обниму́, обни́мет)
отня́ть 'to take away' (отниму́, отни́мет)
подня́ть 'to raise' (подниму́, подни́мет)
приня́ть 'to receive' (приму́, при́мет)
разня́ть 'to take to pieces' (разниму́, разни́мет)
снять 'to take off, photograph' (сниму́, сни́мет)

(6) the existence of three stems, the infinitive group having two distinct stems. The verbs of this group are those of which the present stem ends in -р-, the infinitive in -ере- and the other forms of the infinitive stem in -ер-:

терéть 'to rub' (pres. тру, трёт; past tense тёр, тёрла; past part. act. тёрший, pass. тёртый)

мерéть 'to die', which normally occurs in combination with prefixes, as умерéть 'to die' (умру́, умрёт, у́мер)

перéть 'to push', normally in combination with prefixes, as заперéть 'to lock' (запру́, запрёт, за́пер), отперéть 'to unlock'

(7) the verb итти́ 'to go'. In this verb the present stem ид- (иду́, идёт) differs from that of the infinitive ит- (итти́) and from that of the past tense and the past participle active шед- (past tense шёл, шла, шло, шли, with mobile vowel; past part. act. шéдший). In compounds these stems are respectively:

-йд- (пройду́, пройдёт)
-й- (пройти́ 'to pass')
-шед- (прошёл, прошéдший)

It is to be observed that in the past part. pass. the stem is the same as in the present: пройдённый;

(8) five verbs in which a *yod* in the present corresponds to an -и- in the infinitive:

бить 'to beat' (бью = *b'ju*, бьёшь = *b'još*, бьёт, бьём, бьёте, бьют)
вить 'to twist' (вью, вьёт)

лить 'to pour' (a liquid) (лью, льёт)
пить 'to drink' (пью, пьёт)
шить 'to sew' (шью, шьёт)

(9) five verbs in which the present stem ends in *soft* -л-
or -р-, and the infinitive stem in -ло- or -ро-:

колоть 'to split, prick' (колю, колешь, колет, колем,
     колете, колют)
бороться 'to struggle' (борюсь, борется)
полоть 'to weed' (полю, полет)
пороть 'to unstitch, thrash' (порю, порет)
молоть 'to grind' (мелю, мелет)

In the last verb, the root-vowel -о- of the infinitive is
replaced by -е- in the present.

3. STRESS

The verbs of subdivision A normally have a fixed final
stress. The following verbs have a fixed initial stress:

лезть 'to climb' (лезу, лезет)
лечь 'to lie down' (лягу, ляжет)
сесть 'to sit down' (сяду, сядет)

The following verbs have a mobile stress (see p. 169):

мочь 'to be able' (могу, может);
compounds of the verb *-ять which have the stem
     -им- in the present (see p. 186), as принять 'to
     receive' (приму, примет);
the колоть group in (9), above.

The imperative is in -и, except for the verbs лезть, лечь,
сесть, where it ends in a consonant (лезь, ляг, сядь), and
the бить group in (8), where it ends in -ей (бей, &c.).

B. *INFINITIVE STEM WITH SUFFIX* -A-

1. PRESENT AND INFINITIVE STEMS IDENTICAL IN STRUCTURE

The only difference therefore lies in the presence of the suffix -a- in the infinitive:

> вр-а-ть 'to tell lies' (вр-у, вр-ё-т)
> жа́ждать 'to thirst' (жа́жду, жа́ждет)
> ждать 'to wait' (жду, ждёт)
> жрать 'to guzzle' (жру, жрёт)
> ора́ть 'to bawl' (ору́, орёт)
> рвать 'to tear' (рву, рвёт)
> ржать 'to neigh' (ржу, ржёт)
> соса́ть 'to suck' (сосу́, сосёт)
> стона́ть 'to groan' (стону́, сто́нет)

The only verb in -г- in this group presents the normal mutation of г to ж (see p. 184):

> лгать 'to lie' (лгу, лжёшь, лжёт)

The only verb in -к- retains the к, abnormally:

> ткать 'to weave' (тку, ткёшь, ткёт)

2. PRESENT AND INFINITIVE STEMS OF DIFFERENT STRUCTURE

The difference, apart from the suffix -a-, is occasioned by:

(1) the presence of a mobile vowel, -o- or -e-, in the present stem:

> зв-а-ть 'to call' (зов-у́, зов-ёт)
> брать 'to take' (беру́, берёт)
> драть 'to flay' (деру́, дерёт)

(2) the presence of different consonants in the two stems:

> е́х-а-ть 'to go otherwise than by foot' (е́д-у, е́д-е-т)

3. STEMS WHOSE FINAL CONSONANTS DIFFER
    THROUGH ALTERNATION

This group includes some sixty verbs. The present stem
may end only in ч, ш, ж, щ, and *soft* л. Some of these verbs
tend to become assimilated to the more regular class III,
sometimes with slight change of meaning. These recent
parallel forms are listed. The alternations are the following:

к:ч   кли́кать 'to call' (кли́чу, кли́чет)
        мурлы́кать 'to purr' (мурлы́чу, мурлы́чет; and
            also: мурлы́каю, мурлы́кает)
        пла́кать 'to weep' (пла́чу, пла́чет)
        скака́ть 'to skip, to gallop' (скачу́, ска́чет)
        ты́кать 'to poke' (ты́чу, ты́чет; and also ты́каю,
            ты́кает)

г:ж   бры́згать 'to splash' (бры́зжу, бры́зжет; and
            also: бры́згаю, бры́згает)
        дви́гать 'to move' (дви́жу, дви́жет; and also:
            дви́гаю, дви́гает)

х:ш   бреха́ть 'to yelp, to tell lies' (брешу́, бре́шет)
        колыха́ть 'to sway' (колы́шу, колы́шет)
        маха́ть 'to wave' (машу́, ма́шет)
        паха́ть 'to plough' (пашу́, па́шет)

т:ч   This group is composed of verbs expressing
            mainly various types of sound:
        бормота́ть 'to mutter' (бормочу́, бормо́чет)
        грохота́ть 'to crash, to roar' (грохочу́, грохо́чет)
        клокота́ть 'to bubble' (клокочу́, клоко́чет)
        лепета́ть 'to babble, to prattle' (лепечу́,
            лепе́чет)
        лопота́ть 'to mutter' (лопочу́, лопо́чет)
        мета́ть 'to throw' (мечу́, ме́чет)
        пря́тать 'to hide' (trans.) (пря́чу, пря́чет)
        рокота́ть 'to murmur' (рокочу́, роко́чет)
        топта́ть 'to tread' (trans.) (топчу́, то́пчет)
        хлопота́ть 'to bustle, to take trouble' (хлопочу́,
            хлопо́чет)

хохота́ть 'to guffaw' (хохочу́, хохо́чет)

шепта́ть 'to whisper' (шепчу́, ше́пчет)

щебета́ть 'to twitter, to chirp' (щебечу́, щебе́чет)

щекота́ть 'to tickle' (щекочу́, щеко́чет)

т:щ   клевета́ть 'to slander' (клевещу́, клеве́щет)

ропта́ть 'to murmur' (ропщу́, ро́пщет)

скрежета́ть 'to grit the teeth' (скрежещу́, скреже́щет)

трепета́ть 'to tremble' (трепещу́, трепе́щет)

д:ж   глода́ть 'to gnaw' (гложу́, гло́жет)

ст:щ   блиста́ть 'to shine' (блещу́, бле́щет); note the difference in the root-vowel (and also: блиста́ю, блиста́ет)

свиста́ть 'to whistle' (свищу́, сви́щет)

хлеста́ть 'to whip' (хлещу́, хле́щет)

ск:щ   иска́ть 'to seek' (ищу́, и́щет)

плеска́ть 'to splash, to lap' (плещу́, пле́щет)

полоска́ть 'to rinse' (полощу́, поло́щет)

ры́скать 'to scour about' (ры́щу, ры́щет; and also: ры́скаю, ры́скает)

с:ш   писа́ть 'to write' (пишу́, пи́шет)

пляса́ть 'to dance' (пляшу́, пля́шет)

чеса́ть 'to comb' (чешу́, че́шет)

теса́ть 'to hew, to trim' (тешу́, те́шет)

з:ж   вяза́ть 'to bind, to knit' (вяжу́, вя́жет)

(с)каза́ть 'to tell' (скажу́, ска́жет) and all other compounds with the same root

лиза́ть 'to lick' (лижу́, ли́жет)

ма́зать 'to smear' (ма́жу, ма́жеть)

низа́ть 'to string' (нижу́, ни́жет)

обяза́ть 'to bind, to oblige' (обяжу́, обя́жет)

ре́зать 'to cut' (ре́жу, ре́жет)

п:пл   ка́пать 'to drip, to drop' (ка́плю, ка́плет; and also: ка́паю, ка́пает)

сы́пать 'to strew' (сы́плю, сы́плет)

трепа́ть 'to worry' (треплю́, тре́плет)

щипа́ть, 'to pinch' (щиплю́, щи́плет; and also: щипа́ю, щипа́ет)

б:бл   колеба́ть 'to shake' (колеблю́, коле́блет)

м:мл   дрема́ть 'to doze' (дремлю́, дре́млет)

The two verbs in -л- are irregular:

слать 'to send' changes с- to ш-: шлю, шлёт

стлать 'to spread' inserts an -е-: стелю́, сте́лет

4. STRESS

The verbs of groups 1 and 2 have a fixed final stress, except жа́ждать and е́хать which have an initial stress, and стона́ть which has a mobile stress.

The verbs of group 3 have either a mobile stress or, rarely, a non-final fixed stress.

III. SECOND CLASS: VERBS IN -НЕ-/-НУ-

The present of these verbs is no different from that of the first class; the stem ends always in a suffixal -н-. The infinitive has the suffix -у- in addition to this same -н- and always ends in -нуть. These characteristics make the second class a well-defined unit. The verbs of this class have no present gerund.

In the past tense of certain verbs of this class the -ну- may be dropped.

A. *VERBS WHICH RETAIN THE SUFFIX -НУ- IN ALL FORMS OF THE INFINITIVE STEM*

These verbs for the most part indicate instantaneous action (see p. 252) and are perfective. The stem preceding the -н- may be either consonantal (пры́г-ну-ть 'to leap') or vocalic (тро́-ну-ть 'to touch'). The past participle passive ends in -нутый.

Example: крик-ну-ть 'to cry out':

Singular	*Plural*
1. крик-н-у	1. крик-н-е-м
2. крик-н-е-шь	2. крик-н-е-те
3. крик-н-е-т	3. крик-н-ут

Imperative крик-н-и

Past tense крик-ну-л; past part. act. крик-ну-вший; past part. pass. крик-ну-тый

Examples of verbs conjugated like крикнуть are:

дро́гнуть 'to shudder'	ру́хнуть 'to collapse'
кольну́ть 'to prick'	шагну́ть 'to step'
косну́ться 'to touch'	улыбну́ться 'to smile'
вы́нуть 'to take out'	ки́нуть 'to throw'
ду́нуть 'to blow' (once)	плю́нуть 'to spit'

This group includes four imperfectives:

гнуть 'to bend'	тону́ть 'to drown' (intr.)
льнуть 'to stick' (intr.)	тяну́ть 'to pull'

The stress is fixed, either on the root or on the suffix. It is mobile in only three verbs:

тону́ть 'to drown' (тону́, то́нет)
тяну́ть 'to pull' (тяну́, тя́нет)
мину́ть 'to pass' (ми́нет; the 1st pers. sing. does not occur)

This group A has a limited degree of productivity in furnishing instantaneous perfectives to imperfectives of duration (see also p. 213):

резну́ть 'to cut' (once) (imp. ре́зать)
хвастну́ть 'to boast' (once) (imp. хва́стать)
рискну́ть 'to risk' (once) (imp. рискова́ть)

B. *VERBS WHICH MAY DROP THE SUFFIX* -НУ- *IN CERTAIN FORMS OF THE INFINITIVE STEM*

These verbs, which always have monosyllabic stems, are employed mostly with prefixes, in which case the absence of the suffix -ну- is almost regular in the past tense and the past participle active. With simple verbs (not frequently employed) the suffix -ну- tends to be introduced in all forms of the infinitive stem.

The verbs of this group are intransitive and imperfective (when simple) of inceptive force. *This group is quite dead.*

The present tense of this group is indistinguishable from that of group A:

> мёрзнуть 'to be cold, freeze':
>> present tense мёрзну, мёрзнет
>> imperative мёрзни
>> past tense мёрз, мёрзла, мёрзло, мёрзли
>> past. part. act. мёрзший and мёрзнувший
>> past gerund мёрзнув
> распу́хнуть 'to swell'
>> past tense распу́х, распу́хла, распу́хло, распу́хли
>> past part. act. распу́хший

The following verbs belong to this group:

блёкнуть 'to fade'	ки́снуть 'to become sour'
ви́снуть 'to hang' (intr.)	кре́пнуть 'to grow stronger'
вя́знуть 'to stick' (intr.)	мо́кнуть 'to be soaked'
вя́нуть 'to wither'	па́хнуть 'to smell' (intr.)
га́снуть 'to die down'	сле́пнуть 'to go blind'
ги́бнуть 'to perish'	со́хнуть 'to dry' (intr.)
гло́хнуть 'to go deaf'	сты́нуть 'to become cold'
зя́бнуть 'to be frozen'	ча́хнуть 'to waste away'

Without prefixes all these verbs are frequently used in

the present, but scarcely in the past tense. With prefixes they are currently employed in all tenses and forms.

The following verbs are used only when prefixed:

отве́ргнуть 'to reject, repudiate' (also with из-, низ-, опро-, по-, под-, с-)

привы́кнуть 'to get used' (also with об-, от-, с- + ся)

воскре́снуть 'to rise from the dead'

умо́лкнуть 'to fall silent' (also with за-, приу-, с-)

размя́кнуть 'to grow soft' (also with от-, с-)

дости́гнуть 'to reach' (also with за-, на-, по-)

исся́кнуть 'to run dry'

исто́ргнуть 'to extort' (also with от-)

зати́хнуть 'to calm down' (also with при-, с-, у-)

исче́знуть 'to disappear'

The verbs of the group B have a consonantal stem before the suffix -н- except

вя́нуть 'to wither', past part. act. (у)вя́дший

сты́нуть 'to become cold', past part. act. (о)сты́вший (see p. 203)

The stress is fixed and always falls upon the root.

IV. THIRD CLASS: VERBS IN -E- WITH VOCALIC STEM

This class is characterized by a *yod* which is inserted, necessarily, between the present stem and the connecting vowel or the vocalic endings of the present group. The *yod* does not occur in the infinitive group, all the endings of which begin with a consonant. Orthographically, the *yod* is incorporated in the vowels е, ё, я, ю: де́лает 'he does' = *d'éla-je-t* (pronounced *d'élǝit*, see p. 168).

The verbs of the Third Class are all imperfectives.

A. *INFINITIVE STEM WITHOUT SUFFIX*

I. PRESENT AND INFINITIVE STEMS IDENTICAL IN STRUCTURE

The final vowel of the stem may be -a, -e, -y, -и.
Example: ду́ма-ть 'to think'

Singular	*Plural*
1. ду́ма-ю	1. ду́ма-е-м
2. ду́ма-е-шь	2. ду́ма-е-те
3. ду́ма-е-т	3. ду́ма-ют

The verbs with stems in -a- (or -я-) are numerous. In addition to two primary verbs (знать 'to know' and сия́ть 'to shine') this group includes an unlimited number of verbs derived either from nouns (see p. 263), such as:

> обе́дать 'to dine'
> ка́шлять 'to cough'
> разбо́йничать 'to be a highway robber'

or from other verbs; all suffixal imperfectives (see pp. 215–21) belong to this category, such as:

извеща́ть 'to inform'	переде́лывать 'to alter'
обвиня́ть 'to accuse'	подпи́сывать 'to sign'
открыва́ть 'to open'	собира́ть 'to gather'

These verbs in -a- form one of the most productive classes of the Russian verbal system.

The verbs in -e- also constitute a living class (see p. 264), though much less so than that of the verbs in -a-:

греть 'to warm'	желте́ть 'to grow yellow'
уме́ть 'to be able'	тверде́ть 'to harden' (intr.)

The verbs in -y- and -и- are entirely unproductive and are represented only by a few isolated examples:

> дуть 'to blow' (ду́ю, ду́ет)
> гнить 'to rot' (гнию́, гниёт)

2. PRESENT AND INFINITIVE STEMS OF DIFFERENT STRUCTURE

This group includes a few primary verbs in which the root vowel of the infinitive differs from that of the present stem. The differences are the following:

ы:о	выть 'to howl' (во́ю, во́ет)
	крыть 'to cover' (кро́ю, кро́ет)
	мыть 'to wash' (мо́ю, мо́ет)
	ныть 'to ache, to whine' (но́ю, но́ет)
	рыть 'to dig' (ро́ю, ро́ет)
и:е	брить 'to shave' (бре́ю, бре́ет)
е:о	петь 'to sing' (пою́, поёт)

3. STRESS

The verbs of group A have a fixed, non-final stress which falls either on the root or on the final vowel of the stem. Final stress occurs in only two verbs:

гнить 'to rot'   петь 'to sing'

B. *INFINITIVE STEM WITH SUFFIX*

1. THE SUFFIX -я-

Only a small number of verbs have the suffix -я-, which is entirely unproductive, as:

ла́-я-ть 'to bark' (ла́-ю, ла́-е-т)
та́ять 'to melt' (та́ю, та́ет)
ве́ять 'to blow, to winnow' (ве́ю, ве́ет)
ре́ять 'to hover' (ре́ю, ре́ет)
се́ять 'to sow' (се́ю, се́ет)
смея́ться 'to laugh' (смею́сь, смеётся)
чу́ять 'to feel' (чу́ю, чу́ет)

2. THE SUFFIX -ва́-

This suffix is limited to three groups of verbs:

да-ва́-ть 'to give' (да-ю́, да-ё-т), with its compounds

вставáть 'to stand up' (встаю́, встаёт), and the other compounds from the same root: доставáть 'to obtain', уставáть 'to grow tired', &c.

узнавáть 'to recognize' (узнаю́, узнаёт), and the other compounds from the same root: признавáть 'to acknowledge', сознавáть 'to realize', &c.

In all these verbs the forms without -вá- are limited to the present tense and to the present participle active:

даю́щий, встаю́щий, узнаю́щий.

On the other hand, the suffix -вá- has established itself in the present participle passive:

давáемый, доставáемый, узнавáемый,

and in the present gerund:

давáя, вставáя, узнавáя.

3. VERBS IN -у-/-ова-

These verbs have a present stem in -у- (-ю-) and an infinitive stem in -ова- (-ева-). In this latter group, the -ов- (-ев-) belongs to the stem and corresponds to the -у- (-ю-) of the present stem, while the -а- is a suffix.

This type includes a few primary verbs, such as:

ковáть 'to forge' (кую́, куёт)
плевáть 'to spit' (плюю́, плюёт)
жевáть 'to chew' (жую́, жуёт)

These verbs have a fixed final stress.

The vast majority of verbs of this type are derived forms. The type is extremely productive:

торговáть 'to trade' (торгу́ю, торгу́ет)
совéтовать 'to advise' (совéтую, совéтует)
филосóфствовать 'to philosophize' (филосóфствую, филосóфствует)
интриговáть 'to intrigue' (интригу́ю, интригу́ет)

ликвиди́ровать 'to liquidate' (ликвиди́рую, ликви-
ди́рует)

маскирова́ть 'to mask, camouflage' (маскиру́ю,
маскиру́ет)

The type in -ю-/-ева- is less common:

горева́ть 'to grieve' (горю́ю, горю́ет)
штемпелева́ть 'to stamp' (штемпелю́ю, штемпелю́ет)
ночева́ть 'to pass the night' (ночу́ю, ночу́ет)

The derived verbs in -у-/-ова- have a fixed stress, which
may fall either on the root or on the suffix (-у́-/-ова́-).
Verbs in -ю́-/-ева́- have only the latter stress.

V. FOURTH CLASS: VERBS IN -И-

The verbs of this class display the same consonantal
alternations as those of the last subdivision of the first class
(I B 3, see p. 189). The modified consonant occurs only in
the 1st pers. sing. of the present tense. The consonants л,
р, and н are soft in the 1st pers. sing. and the 3rd pers. pl.
Three different suffixes may occur in the infinitive stem.

A. *INFINITIVE STEM WITH SUFFIX* -И-

I. CONSONANTAL STEM

Example: кра́с-и-ть 'to paint, dye, adorn'.

Singular	Plural
1. кра́ш-у	1. кра́с-и-м
2. кра́с-и-шь	2. кра́с-и-те
3. кра́с-и-т	3. кра́с-я-т

In the past participle passive of verbs of this group the
suffix -и- is replaced by -е- and the final consonant of the

stem undergoes the same modification as in the 1st pers.
sing. of the present tense: кра́ш-е-нн-ый. It is to be observed, however, that the large number of verbs in -дить
which have a Church Slavonic past participle passive in
-ждённый never take -жду, but only -жу, in the 1st pers.
sing. of the present:

> предупреди́ть 'to warn':
> предупрежу́, предупреждённый

Like кра́сить are conjugated, for example:

т : ч	плати́ть 'to pay' (плачу́, пла́тит)
т : щ	запрети́ть 'to forbid' (запрещу́, запрети́т)
д : ж	ходи́ть 'to walk' (хожу́, хо́дит)
ст : щ	чи́стить 'to clean' (чи́щу, чи́стит)
з : ж	грози́ть 'to threaten' (грожу́, грози́т)
б : бл	люби́ть 'to love' (люблю́, лю́бит)
в : вл	лови́ть 'to catch' (ловлю́, ло́вит)
м : мл	корми́ть 'to feed' (кормлю́, ко́рмит)
п : пл	купи́ть 'to buy' (куплю́, ку́пит)

> пили́ть 'to saw' (пилю́, пи́лит)
> кури́ть 'to smoke' (курю́, ку́рит)
> вини́ть 'to accuse' (виню́, вини́т)
> служи́ть 'to serve' (служу́, слу́жит)
> учи́ть 'to teach' (учу́, у́чит)
> туши́ть 'to extinguish' (тушу́, ту́шит)
> тащи́ть 'to drag' (тащу́, та́щит)

This group is productive. It receives a steady flow of new
formations from nouns, usually with prefixes (see p. 266),
as:

вы́школить 'to train'	прове́трить 'to air'
окружи́ть 'to surround'	удо́брить 'to fertilize'

The stress may be mobile, but in the majority of cases
(and, in particular, in all the denominatives) it is fixed
either on the root or on the final syllable.

2. VOCALIC STEM

This group is very restricted and is entirely unproductive:

кле́ить 'to stick' (tr.) (кле́ю, кле́ит)
поко́иться 'to rest upon' (поко́юсь, поко́ится)
сто́ить 'to cost' (сто́ю, сто́ит)
стро́ить 'to build' (стро́ю, стро́ит)
та́ить 'to hide' (таю́, таи́т)

B. *INFINITIVE STEM WITH SUFFIX* -E-

This group, which is not productive, includes some forty verbs. Verbs of this type always have a consonantal stem. The most usual are:

т : ч	верте́ть 'to turn, to twist' (верчу́, ве́ртит)
	лете́ть 'to fly' (лечу́, лети́т)
д : ж	ви́деть 'to see' (ви́жу, ви́дит)
	ненави́деть 'to hate' (ненави́жу, ненави́дит)
	оби́деть 'to offend' (оби́жу, оби́дит)
	сиде́ть 'to sit' (сижу́, сиди́т)
	галде́ть 'to make a din' (1st pers. not used, галди́т)
	смерде́ть 'to stink' (1st pers. not used, смерди́т)
ст : щ	блесте́ть 'to shine' (блещу́, блести́т)
	свисте́ть 'to whistle' (свищу́, свисти́т)
с : ш	висе́ть 'to hang' (intr.) (вишу́, виси́т)
	зави́сеть 'to depend' (зави́шу, зави́сит)
б : бл	скорбе́ть 'to grieve' (скорблю́, скорби́т)
м : мл	шуме́ть 'to make a noise' (шумлю́, шуми́т)
п : пл	скрипе́ть 'to creak' (скриплю́, скрипи́т)
	сопе́ть 'to sniff' (соплю́, сопи́т)
	терпе́ть 'to endure' (терплю́, те́рпит)
	храпе́ть 'to snore' (храплю́, храпи́т)

л   велéть 'to command' (велю́, вели́т)
       болéть 'to ache' (1st pers. not used, боли́т)
р   горéть 'to burn' (intr.) (горю́, гори́т)
       смотрéть 'to look' (смотрю́, смо́трит)
н   звенéть 'to ring' (intr.) (звеню́, звени́т)

The stress is usually fixed, and final. It is not final in: ви́деть, ненави́деть, оби́деть, зави́сеть.

Three verbs have a mobile stress: вертéть, терпéть, смотрéть.

C. *INFINITIVE STEM WITH SUFFIX* -A-

1. CONSONANTAL STEM

This group, which is not productive, includes some twenty-five verbs. Most of them denote sounds. The stem may end only in ч, ж, щ, ш:

бренчáть 'to jingle, to thrum' (бренчу́, бренчи́т)
бурчáть 'to grumble, to rumble' (бурчу́, бурчи́т)
ворчáть 'to grumble, to growl' (ворчу́, ворчи́т)
журчáть 'to ripple' (журчу́, журчи́т)
звучáть 'to sound' (звучу́, звучи́т)
кричáть 'to shout' (кричу́, кричи́т)
молчáть 'to be silent' (молчу́, молчи́т)
мчать 'to whirl along' (мчу, мчит)
мычáть 'to mow' (мычу́, мычи́т)
рычáть 'to roar' (рычу́, рычи́т)
стучáть 'to knock' (стучу́, стучи́т)
торчáть 'to stick out' (торчу́, торчи́т)
урчáть 'to rumble' (урчу́, урчи́т)

брюзжáть 'to grumble' (брюзжу́, брюзжи́т)
визжáть 'to scream' (визжу́, визжи́т)
держáть 'to hold' (держу́, дéржит)
дребезжáть 'to jar' (дребезжу́, дребезжи́т)
дрожáть 'to tremble' (дрожу́, дрожи́т)
жужжáть 'to buzz' (жужжу́, жужжи́т)

лежа́ть 'to lie' (лежу́, лежи́т)

вереща́ть 'to squeal' (верещу́, верещи́т)
пища́ть 'to squeak' (пищу́, пищи́т)
треща́ть 'to crack, to crackle' (трещу́, трещи́т)

дыша́ть 'to breathe' (дышу́, ды́шит)
слы́шать 'to hear' (слы́шу, слы́шит)

The stress is usually fixed and final. It is initial in слы́шать and mobile in держа́ть, дыша́ть.

2. VOCALIC STEM

Only two verbs of this type have vocalic stem:

стоя́ть 'to stand' (стою́, стои́т)
боя́ться 'to fear' (бою́сь, бои́тся)

VI. VERBS WHICH COMBINE FEATURES OF DIFFERENT CLASSES

Very few verbs remain outside the four classes.

1. THE TWO STEMS BELONG TO DIFFERENT CLASSES

(1) Present of Class I, infinitive with suffix -e- (Class III or IV):

реву́, ревёт, inf. реве́ть 'to roar'

(2) Present of Class I, infinitive with suffix -и- (Class IV):

ушибу́, ушибёт, inf. ушиби́ть 'to hurt' (tr.);

the past tense, however, belongs to Class I: уши́б; similarly the other compounds from the same root, like ошиби́ться 'to make a mistake'.

(3) Present of Class II, infinitive without the suffix -ну- (Class III):

де́ну, де́нет, inf. деть 'to put'
ста́ну, ста́нет, inf. стать 'to become, to begin'

стыну, стынет, inf. стыть 'to grow cold' (a regular infinitive, стынуть, is also employed, see p. 193)

(4) Present of Class II, infinitive without the suffix -ну- (Class I):

> достигну, достигнет, inf. достичь 'to attain'

(5) Present of Class IV, infinitive of Class I:

> сплю, спит, inf. спать 'to sleep'
> гоню, гонит, inf. гнать 'to drive'

2. THE COMBINATION OCCURS WITHIN THE PRESENT TENSE

(1) The verb хотеть 'to wish':

Singular	*Plural*
1. хочу	1. хотим
2. хочешь	2. хотите
3. хочет	3. хотят

The singular is of Class I B 3 (the 1st pers. could also be of Class IV). The retreat of the stress in the 2nd and 3rd pers. sing. is to be noted. The plural belongs to Class IV. The infinitive group also belongs to Class IV.

(2) The verbs бежать 'to run', чтить 'to honour':

Singular	*Plural*
1. бегу, чту	1. бежим, чтим
2. бежишь, чтишь	2. бежите, чтите
3. бежит, чтит	3. бегут, чтут

The 1st pers. sing. and 3rd pers. pl. belong to Class I, the other persons to Class IV. The infinitive belongs to Class IV.

VII. ISOLATED VERBS

This group consists of three verbs which, besides the absence of the connecting vowel, present other peculiarities, in particular a final -м in the 1st pers. sing.

(1) The verb дать 'to give' (perfective):

Singular	*Plural*
1. дам	1. дадим
2. дашь	2. дадите
3. даст	3. дадут

Imperative дай

The infinitive group is regular:

> past tense дал, дала́, да́ло, да́ли
> past part. act. да́вший
> past part. pass. да́нный
> past gerund дав, да́вши

(2) The verb есть 'to eat' (imperfective):

Singular	*Plural*
1. ем	1. едим
2. ешь	2. едите
3. ест	3. едят

Imperative ешь

Pres. part. act. едя́щий

Pres. gerund (rarely used) едя́

Infinitive group:

> past tense ел, е́ла, е́ло, е́ли
> past part. act. е́вший
> past part. pass. (съ)е́денный
> past gerund ев, е́вши

(3) The verb быть 'to be'. What survives of the present tense of this verb belongs to the same type. This verb has three stems:

(*a*) The only survival of the present stem is the 3rd pers. sing., есть, which is used for all persons in the rare cases when it is employed. The old 3rd pers. pl., суть, is a literary and extremely rare form. The pres. part. act., сущий, is now a pure adjective with the meaning 'real'.

(*b*) The stem буд- supplies a future (more exactly a perfective present-future, but the notion of aspect is no longer perceptible in this verb):

Singular	*Plural*
1. бу́ду 'I shall be'	1. бу́дем
2. бу́дешь	2. бу́дете
3. бу́дет	3. бу́дут

This form serves as auxiliary in the future tense of imperfective verbs (see p. 179).

The same stem serves to form the imperative будь and the present gerund бу́дучи. The pres. part. act. (perf.) бу́дущий is now a pure adjective with the meaning 'future'. All the forms derived from the stem буд- belong to Class I.

(*c*) The stem бы- supplies the entire infinitive group:

inf. быть
past tense был, была́, бы́ло, бы́ли
past part. act. бы́вший
past part. pass. (забы́тый 'forgotten')
past gerund бы́вши

The perfective compounds of быть, such as:

забы́ть 'to forget'	прибы́ть 'to arrive'
добы́ть 'to procure'	пробы́ть 'to stay'

have only the stems буд- and бы-.

XII

Verbs: Aspects

I. THE NOTION OF ASPECT

THE Russian verb system is dominated by the *aspect*. Aspect is the manner of considering the action expressed by the verb. This may be considered either as action in progress and unlimited or as limited, completed action. Verbs of uncompleted action are called verbs of *imperfective aspect* or *imperfective* verbs; verbs of completed action are called verbs of *perfective aspect* or *perfective* verbs.

Every Russian verb is either *imperfective* or *perfective*.

The contrast between uncompleted and completed action is expressed most frequently in the difference between the action itself (imperfective verbs) and the result of the action (perfective verbs). But it may appear in other variants, such as the difference between action attempted and action performed, habitual action and single action, action in general and action in particular. A few examples may serve to illustrate these functions of aspect:

> Колу́мб был сча́стлив не тогда́, когда́ откры́л Аме́рику, а когда́ открыва́л её

> 'Columbus was happy, not when he had discovered America, but when he was in the course of discovering it' (DOSTOEVSKY, *The Idiot*, III. 5):

it was not the result of completed action (perfective verb откры́л) which made Columbus happy, but the action itself in its development (imperfective verb открыва́л).

Что же де́лал Бе́льтов в продолже́ние э́тих десяти́
лет? Всё и́ли почти́ всё. Что он сде́лал? Ничего́,
и́ли почти́ ничего́

'What did Beltov do during these ten years? Everything, or almost everything. What did he achieve?
Nothing, or almost nothing' (Herzen, *Who is to
blame?*):

contrast between past imperf. де́лал (action attempted)
and the past perf. сде́лал (action performed).

Во лжи рече́й мои́х глаза́ ули́кой бы́ли:
Я вас обма́нывал, но мог ли обману́ть?

'My eyes revealed the untruthfulness of my words:
I tried to deceive you, but could I do so?'
(Prince Vyazemsky, *Conversation of 7 April 1832*):

contrast between the past imperf. обма́нывал (action
attempted) and the perf. infin. обману́ть (action performed).

С сы́ном одна́ко он употреби́л ту диплома́тию,
кото́рую употребля́л в ва́жных слу́чаях

'With his son, however, he resorted to the diplomacy
to which he used to resort in important cases'
(L. Tolstoy, *War and Peace*):

contrast between the past imperf. употребля́л (habitual
action) and the past perf. употреби́л (single action).

The notion of aspect, while in principle independent of
that of tense, nevertheless exerts an influence upon the
tense forms.

The *present*, which expresses action in its development,
is proper only to imperfective verbs. The present form of
perfective verbs has *future* force, which is natural, since the
completion of an action which is taking place at the present
time can be envisaged only in the future. This is the reason
why the forms

стро́ю 'I build'
стро́ит 'he builds' (*imperf.*)

have present force, while

> постро́ю 'I shall build'
> постро́ит 'he will build' (*perf.*)

have future force.

The present form of perfective verbs may have still other values, but these are never those of the present proper (see p. 230). Perfective verbs have no present tense proper.

On the other hand, the imperfective has, in addition to a present tense, also a *future of development* which is an analytical form:

> бу́ду стро́ить 'I shall build'
> бу́дет стро́ить 'he will build'

Only imperfective verbs have this compound future.

The same distinction as exists in the future between the imperf. бу́ду стро́ить and the perf. постро́ю is marked in the past tenses:

> стро́ил (*imperf.*)
> постро́ил (*perf.*)

The *past imperfective* corresponds to the English past continuous and frequentative ('used to') forms, while the *past perfective* is equivalent, generally speaking, to the other English past tenses.

As the real present tense exists only in imperfective verbs, only these form the *present participles* and the *present gerund*:

> стро́ящий, стро́имый, стро́я

The present-future of perfective verbs has no participial form corresponding to it. Certain perfective verbs of Classes I and IV do however admit a present gerund form, which then has the force of a past gerund:

> принеся́ = принёсши 'having brought'
> поговоря́ = поговори́в 'having spoken'

On the other hand, both imperfective and perfective verbs form *past participles*, active and passive:

стро́ивший, стро́енный
постро́ивший, постро́енный

It is to be observed, however, that the past part. pass. of imperfective verbs is very little employed.

The *past gerund* is limited usually to perfective verbs:

постро́ив 'having built'

and to those imperfective verbs which have no present gerund (see p. 179).

The notion of time, in a Russian verb, is expressed only in the indicative. It is given its full force, moreover, only in the personal forms and is obscured in the participles and gerunds (see p. 232). The other moods possess no temporal value. In other words, the problem of the relation between tense and aspect does not exist for the infinitive, the imperative, and the various modal forms, in which, for this reason, the distinction between the two aspects is all the clearer.

The preceding remarks may be illustrated by the following table, for the verb 'to build'.

	Imperfective verb	*Perfective verb*
Present	стро́ит	—
Future	бу́дет стро́ить	постро́ит
Pres. part. act.	стро́ящий	—
Pres. part. pass.	стро́имый	—
Present gerund	стро́я	—
Imperative	строй	постро́й
Infinitive	стро́ить	постро́ить
Past tense	стро́ил	постро́ил
Past part. act.	стро́ивший	постро́ивший
Past part. pass.	стро́енный	постро́енный
Past gerund	—	постро́ив

II. FORMATION OF ASPECTUAL PAIRS

Because of this twofold manner in which it may be envisaged, the action of the verb can be expressed completely in Russian only by means of a *pair of verbs* of identical meaning, but of which the one is imperfective, the other perfective.

As a general rule, the verbs of the aspectual pair are not only formed from the same root but are derived one from the other. With the help of certain morphological means an imperfective verb may become a perfective, and a perfective verb may become an imperfective.

These means, which it is essential to know, are the verbal prefixes and suffixes.

There are two principal kinds of aspectual pairs.

In the one, the imperfective forms the basic element, and the perfective is derived from it:

стро́ить (*imperf.*) / постро́ить (*perf.*) 'to build'

In the other, the relation is reversed, and the perfective is the basic element of the pair:

устро́ить (*perf.*) / устра́ивать (*imperf.*) 'to arrange'

A distinction should therefore be drawn in the first place between *imperfective/perfective pairs* and *perfective/imperfective pairs*.

Beside these two types of pairs, in which one of the elements derives from the other, there exists a third, in which the two verbs do not proceed one from the other but are associated by usage.

III. IMPERFECTIVE/PERFECTIVE
PAIRS

1. SIMPLE IMPERFECTIVE/PERFECTIVE WITH PREFIX

In the vast majority of cases simple verbs are imperfective. By a simple verb is meant one which is not felt to be derived from another verb.

The addition of a verbal prefix to a simple verb renders it perfective. The verbal prefixes, which have their own particular meanings, modify that of the verb. Thus, the verb дѣлать 'to do, make', occurs in the following combinations with prefixes:

> вы́делать 'to manufacture'
> доде́лать 'to complete'
> заде́лать 'to stop up, wall up'
> наде́лать 'to commit, cause, make a certain quantity'
> обде́лать 'to mount, set, arrange, urinate upon'
> отде́лать 'to complete, adorn'
> переде́лать 'to alter'
> подде́лать 'to counterfeit'
> приде́лать 'to adjust, add, fix'
> разде́лать (под) 'to imitate' (in painting)

For the values of the verbal prefixes, see p. 253.

All the verbs enumerated are perfectives; but this aspectual function of the verbal prefix is only an incidental feature of its essential function, which is of a lexical nature. It is obvious that the diversity of meaning of the verbs with prefixes attached does not permit the simple verb to form an aspectual pair with any one of them: while all these verbs have the same root as the simple verb, their meanings are different.

However, in certain cases the proper meaning of the verbal prefix may be reduced to such an extent that it becomes a mere means of perfectivation, a grammatical instrument. In the case of the verb дѣлать for example, the prefix c- adds nothing to the meaning of the verb, with the result that the verbs дѣлать and сдѣлать form a true imperfective/perfective pair, and that for all meanings of both verbs.

Other prefixes also may shed their proper meanings to become mere means of perfectivation.

The verbal prefixes c- and по- lose their meaning more frequently than the rest:

> умѣть/сумѣть 'to be able'
> жечь/сжечь 'to burn' (trans.)
> фабриковать/сфабриковать 'to manufacture'
> строить/построить 'to build'
> нравиться/понравиться 'to please'
> щадить/пощадить 'to spare'

Next in order of frequency comes о-/об-:

> слѣпнуть/ослѣпнуть 'to become blind'
> радовать/обрадовать 'to rejoice' (trans.)

The verbal prefixes за-, у-, на-, вз- lose their meaning more rarely:

> ржавѣть/заржавѣть 'to rust'
> тонуть/утонуть 'to drown' (intr.)
> писать/написать 'to write'
> потѣть/вспотѣть 'to sweat'

The verbal prefixes из-, вы-, при-, про-, раз- may lose their meaning on occasion:

> печь/испечь 'to bake'
> купаться/выкупаться 'to bathe' (intr.)
> готовить/приготовить 'to prepare'
> телеграфировать/протелеграфировать 'to telegraph'
> плавить/расплавить 'to melt' (trans.)

The verbal prefixes в-, до-, над-, от-, пере-, под- always retain their meanings and transmit them to the verbs.

A verb may have only one prefix without meaning, and

this prefix varies from verb to verb. It should not be forgotten that this phenomenon is exceptional and does not
apply to the majority of simple verbs. The verb compounded with a prefix does not, in most cases, serve, even
approximately, as the perfective form of the simple verb.
Verbs whose prefixes are in all cases meaningful are, for
example:

пилить 'to saw'   качать 'to swing'
копать 'to dig'   бежать 'to run'

It is obvious that the addition of prefixes is not an ade-
quate means of forming the perfectives of simple verbs.

2. SIMPLE IMPERFECTIVE/PERFECTIVE WITH SUFFIX

The addition of a prefix is not the only means of forming
the perfective form of a simple verb. This may be done
also with the help of the suffix -ну-.

The original function of the suffix -ну- was to form verbs
of instantaneous or single action. It has gradually adapted
itself to its aspectual function, although the adaptation is
incomplete, for the reason that the suffix still retains some
of its old force:

скользить/скользнуть 'to slip'
дуть/дунуть 'to blow'
прыгать/прыгнуть 'to jump'
рисковать/рискнуть 'to risk'

This means of perfectivation has a limited field of application.

IV. PERFECTIVE/IMPERFECTIVE PAIRS

1. Perfective with Prefix/Imperfective with Suffix

The addition of verbal prefixes, as has been seen, is an
inadequate means of forming aspectual pairs. Only one of
the many compound forms of a simple verb can provide it

with an appropriate perfective, and that on condition that the prefix strips itself completely of its meaning. The overwhelming majority of perfectives with prefix do not find their respective imperfectives in the simple verb. To supply the imperfective in these cases the language has recourse to another device: while retaining the prefix (without, therefore, changing the meaning of the verb) it derives an imperfective from the perfective by providing the latter with a special suffix:

perf. переде́лать 'to alter'
imperf. переде́лывать

The suffix does not affect the lexical meaning but serves as a mere means of imperfectivation. The prefix, on the other hand, retains its lexical meaning entire and has no effect on the aspect. This method is extremely convenient and has spread to such an extent that the pair consisting of *perfective with prefix/imperfective with suffix* is now the *typical aspectual pair*.

This method is the more frequent for the reason that the first element of the pair, the perfective with prefix, comprises three vast groups of verbs:

(1) simple verbs with prefix, examined above:

доде́лать, отде́лать, &c.;

(2) verbs derived from other verbs, and more particularly verbs derived from nouns, and not existing without a prefix (see p. 265):

привы́кнуть 'to become accustomed'
урезо́нить 'to bring to reason';

(3) simple perfectives with prefix (see p. 220):

отбро́сить 'to reject'

The overwhelming majority of Russian verbs, therefore, form aspectual pairs of this type.

To form the imperfective of a perfective with prefix,

Russian employs two suffixes, one practically dead (-á-, -я́-, which may also appear in the form -вá-) and the other productive (-ыва-, which appears as -ива- after a vowel or soft consonant). Imperfective verbs with these suffixes all belong to the third class.

I. THE SUFFIX -á-/-я́-

This suffix, which is *nearly dead*, occurs principally in unproductive types of verbs. *It is always stressed*. It is found in three classes of verbs.

(a) Classes I and II

The verbs of Class I (with the exception of group B 3) know practically no other suffix than -á-:

> спасти́/спасáть 'to save'
> вы́пасть (вы́паду)/выпадáть 'to fall out'
> помóчь (помогу́)/помогáть 'to help'
> пережи́ть (переживу́) / переживáть 'to survive'
> рассы́пать (рассы́плю) / рассыпáть (рассыпáю) 'to spread'

In this last verb the distinction between the aspects in the infinitive is expressed only by the difference in stress (for a similar distinction in the present tense in the compounds of знать, see p. 217).

The same suffix -á- is normal also in the unproductive subdivision of verbs in -нуть (Class II B). The suffix -ну- is dropped in the imperfective:

> привы́кнуть/привыкáть 'to become accustomed'
> исчéзнуть/исчезáть 'to disappear'
> угáснуть/угасáть 'to go out' (of lights, fires)

In some cases the final consonant of the stem disappears before the suffix -ну-:

> увя́нуть/увядáть 'to fade'
> раздви́нуть/раздвигáть 'to move apart' (trans.)

In both classes the roots of certain groups of verbs present, as between perfective and imperfective, the alternations zero/и and zero/ы and, in the present tense, the further alternations е/и and о/ы.

These alternations are the result of an old lengthening of the root vowel in the imperfective:

> начáть (начнý) / начинáть 'to begin'
> прижáть (прижмý) / прижимáть 'to squeeze'
> умерéть (умрý) / умирáть 'to die'
> вы́брать (вы́беру) / выбирáть 'to choose'
> прервáть (прервý) / прерывáть 'to interrupt'
> заснýть/засыпáть 'to fall asleep'
> издóхнуть/издыхáть 'to die' (of animals)

(b) Class IV

The most numerous group which makes use of the suffix -á- is that of verbs in -ить (verbs in -еть of Class IV do not, as a general rule, form their imperfectives in -á-). With these verbs the suffix has even retained some degree of vitality. Before this suffix the same consonantal alternations come into play as in the 1st pers. sing. (see p. 199); after the consonants н, л, р, which are always soft, the suffix is written -я́-. For example:

> укрáсить/украшáть 'to adorn'
> поразúть/поражáть 'to strike'
> встрéтить/встречáть 'to meet'
> угостúть/угощáть 'to treat, entertain'
> опередúть/опережáть 'to outstrip'
> освободúть/освобождáть 'to set free'
> затопúть/затопля́ть 'to flood'
> проявúть/проявля́ть 'to manifest'
> вы́яснить/выясня́ть 'to clear up'
> умалúть/умаля́ть 'to diminish'
> оперúться/оперя́ться 'to grow feathers'
> излучúть/излучáть 'to radiate'
> улýчшить/улучшáть 'to improve'

вооружи́ть/вооружа́ть 'to arm'
обобщи́ть/обобща́ть 'to generalize'

It is unusual for the final consonant of the stem of a verb in -ить not to undergo alternation in the imperfective form. Such exceptions are almost exclusively labials, as in:

переруби́ть/переруба́ть 'to cut in two'
поступи́ть/поступа́ть 'to act'
вы́купить/выкупа́ть 'to redeem'

Apart from the three types which have been examined the suffix -á-/-я́- occurs only very exceptionally.

2. THE SUFFIX -ва́-

The suffix -ва́- is no more than a variant of the suffix -á-. Completely dead, it is utilized for primary verbs with vocalic stem (in -и-, -ы-, -у-, -е-, -а-) and for a few verbs in -е- derived from nouns and adjectives:

уби́ть/убива́ть 'to kill'
сбрить/сбрива́ть 'to shave off'
откры́ть/открыва́ть 'to open'
наду́ть/надува́ть 'to inflate'
заболе́ть/заболева́ть 'to fall ill'
обалде́ть/обалдева́ть 'to be dumbfounded'

The verbs in -ва́ть derived from дать 'to give', стать 'to stop, stand', and знать 'to know' have the suffix -ва́- only in the infinitive group of the imperfective (see p. 196):

переда́ть (переда́м) / передава́ть (передаю́) 'to transmit'
отста́ть (отста́ну) / отстава́ть (отстаю́) 'to be behind'
призна́ть (призна́ю) / признава́ть (признаю́) 'to acknowledge'

In the compounds of знать, in the present tense, the distinction of aspects is marked only by the difference of stress.

3. THE SUFFIX -ыва-/-ива-

The suffix -ыва- (-ива- after vowel or soft consonant) is, of all the suffixes used to form the imperfective, the only one which is still living. As a productive suffix, it tends to associate itself particularly with the productive types of verbs, but it extends also to other groups, supplanting the old suffix -á-.

All verbs in -ыва-/-ива- *have a fixed stress which falls on the syllable immediately preceding the suffix* -ыва-/-ива-. The suffix -ыва- is normally pronounced -*əvə*-.

This suffix occurs with verbs of all the classes.

(a) Class III

The suffix -ыва- is particularly frequent with verbs in -ать:

выдумать/выдýмывать 'to invent'
распечáтать/распечáтывать 'to unseal'
переде́лать/переде́лывать 'to alter'
проигрáть/проигрывать 'to lose'
заковáть/закóвывать 'to enchain'
осме́ять/осме́ивать 'to mock'

Of the verbs in -ать with compound suffixes (-овать, -ировать, -изи́ровать, -ствовать, -ничать, see p. 263) the only ones which may form an imperfective in -ыва- are those which take the stress on the final -áть:

перестраховáть/перестрахóвывать 'to re-insure'
разворовáть/разворóвывать 'to plunder'
завоевáть/завоёвывать 'to conquer'
расформировáть/расформирóвывать 'to disband'

It follows that verbs in -изи́ровать, -ничать, and -ствовать, which never take the stress in the final syllable, do not form imperfectives in -ыва-.

(b) Class IV

As with the suffix -á-, the final consonant of the stem undergoes the normal alternation:

спроси́ть/спрáшивать 'to ask'

(For the change of -o- to -á- see paragraph (*e*) below, p. 220)

> обесче́стить/обесче́щивать 'to dishonour'
> нама́гни́тить/намагни́чивать 'to magnetize'
> останови́ть/остана́вливать 'to stop' (trans.)
> зашпи́лить/зашпи́ливать 'to pin'
> подыто́жить/подыто́живать 'to sum up'
> присво́ить/присва́ивать 'to appropriate'
> присмотре́ть/присма́тривать 'to look after'
> просиде́ть/проси́живать 'to remain sitting'
>   (for a certain time)
> задержа́ть/заде́рживать 'to detain'
> отстоя́ть/отста́ивать 'to defend'

With certain verbs in -ить the consonantal alternation does not occur:

> схвати́ть/схва́тывать 'to seize'
> закуси́ть/заку́сывать 'to have a snack'

The utilization of the two suffixes -á-/-я́- and -ыва- with verbs in -ить leads in some cases to the simultaneous existence of two imperfectives for the same perfective:

> накопи́ть/накопля́ть and нака́пливать 'to amass'
> засори́ть/засоря́ть and заса́ривать 'to block up'
> простуди́ться/простужа́ться and просту́живаться
>   'to catch cold'

The tendency is for the forms in -ыва- to displace those in -á-.

(*c*) *Class I*

The only verbs of this class which normally admit the suffix -ыва- are those with stems the final consonants of which are subject to alternation (B 3), and verbs in -оть:

> переписа́ть/перепи́сывать 'to rewrite'
> обыска́ть/обы́скивать 'to search'
> рассказа́ть/расска́зывать 'to narrate'

затоптáть/затáптывать 'to trample upon'
приколóть/прикáлывать 'to pin'
вспорóть/вспáрывать 'to rip up'

Apart from these two groups, the suffix -ыва- occurs only sporadically with verbs of Class I:

присосáться/присáсываться 'to stick to' (by suction)
подкрáсться/подкрáдываться 'to steal up'

(d) Class II

A few verbs in -нуть expressing instantaneous action (a productive type) employ the suffix -ыва-, as in:

взвúзгнуть/взвúзгивать 'to shriek'
захлебнýться/захлёбываться 'to choke' (intr.)
вспрýснуть/вспрýскивать 'to sprinkle'

(e) The alternation o/á in the root

An -o- in the root of the perfective changes to -a- when the syllable in which it occurs is stressed in the imperfective in -ывать:

проглотúть/проглáтывать 'to swallow'
заработáть/зарабáтывать 'to earn'
облокотúться/облокáчиваться 'to lean one's elbows' (on)
вздрóгнуть/вздрáгивать 'to shudder'

and several examples already quoted.

Certain verbs resist this change, as for example:

приохóтить/приохóчивать 'to give a taste for'

The change of -o- to -á- does not take place in the suffixes.

2. Simple Perfective/Imperfective with Suffix

There is in Russian a small, unproductive group of simple perfectives with no morphological element to indicate their perfective value. They constitute pairs with verbs with suffix in exactly the same way as do the perfectives with prefix. As the type is a dead one, the corresponding imperfectives have only the suffix -á- or, very rarely, -вá-.

The basic perfectives are almost exclusively verbs in -ить; the imperfectives, accordingly, normally present the consonantal alternation which is characteristic of these verbs:

кóнчить/кончáть 'to finish'
лишúть/лишáть 'to deprive'
простúть/прощáть 'to forgive'
явúть/явля́ть 'to show'
пленúть/пленя́ть 'to captivate'
удáрить/ударя́ть 'to strike'

In a few verbs consonantal alternation does not occur:

брóсить/бросáть 'to throw'
ступúть/ступáть 'to step'
хватúть/хватáть 'to seize'
пустúть/пускáть 'to let' (the imperfective is due to a false derivation)

To this group may be added a few verbs which were originally compound, but which are now felt as simple verbs, for example:

встрéтить/встречáть 'to meet'
ощутúть/ощущáть 'to feel'
посетúть/посещáть 'to visit'
воскресúть/воскрешáть 'to resuscitate'
осклáбиться/осклабля́ться 'to grin'
околéть/околевáть 'to die' (of animals)

The simple perfectives other than those in -ить are extremely few:

пасть/пáдать 'to fall'
дать (дам) / давáть (даю́) 'to give'
деть (дéну) / девáть (девáю) 'to put'

V. SUPPLETIVE PAIRS

In the aspectual pairs examined so far the perfective is formed from the imperfective or vice versa by means of a comparatively simple mechanism of verbal prefixes and suffixes. In some cases, however, verbs belonging to different series may be associated to form aspectual pairs. The members of these pairs are not connected by the direct links of word-formation, but are merely associated by usage.

Among these suppletive pairs several groups may be distinguished.

1. PERFECTIVE: DETERMINATE WITH PREFIX/IMPERFECTIVE: INDETERMINATE WITH PREFIX

Of the simple imperfective verbs denoting motion a certain number occur in the form of pairs:

> итти/ходи́ть 'to go, walk'
> éхать/éздить 'to go otherwise than by foot'
> нести́/носи́ть 'to carry'
> вести́/води́ть 'to lead'
> везти́/вози́ть 'to transport'
> бежа́ть/бéгать 'to run'
> летéть/летáть 'to fly'
> гнать/гоня́ть 'to drive'
> ползти́/по́лзать 'to crawl'

There are some fifteen verbs of this type, but those apart from the nine listed above present no peculiarities in the matter of aspect.

All these verbs are imperfective. The first verb of each pair, known as the *determinate*, denotes motion tending towards a goal, real or imaginary. The second, known as the *indeterminate*, serves to denote:

(1) motion as such, as also the faculty to perform the particular type of motion;

(2) habitual motion;
(3) motion to a point and back again.

For example:

он е́дет в Ло́ндон 'he is going to London' (now: goal)
он ча́сто е́здит в Ло́ндон 'he often goes to London' (habit)
он вчера́ е́здил в Ло́ндон 'he went to London yesterday' (and returned)

This distinction, which is of a purely lexical nature, disappears when the verbs are combined with prefixes and is replaced by a purely aspectual distinction. The indeterminate with prefix serves as imperfective to the determinate with prefix, which serves as perfective:

Perfective	*Imperfective*
подойти́	подходи́ть 'to approach'
вы́нести	выноси́ть 'to take out, endure'
привести́	приводи́ть 'to bring'
увезти́	увози́ть 'to take away'
вбежа́ть	вбега́ть 'to run in'
взлете́ть	взлета́ть 'to fly up'
догна́ть	догоня́ть 'to overtake'
отползти́	отполза́ть 'to crawl away'

In the case of е́хать/е́здить the aspectual pair is formed not only by the addition of a prefix to each of the two verbs, but also by the addition of the suffix -á- to the indeterminate (with alternation д/ж):

прие́хать (perf.) / приезжа́ть (imperf.) 'to arrive'

This type of formation of aspectual pairs can occur only if both verbs of the pair *determinate/indeterminate* are capable of taking the same prefix in the same sense. If a particular prefix can be employed only with the indeterminate, there is, obviously, no pair; and the indeterminate plus prefix, not having opposite it a determinate plus prefix, becomes

perfective. Thus, the following indeterminates plus prefix
are perfective:

> заходи́ть 'to begin to walk'
> поноси́ть 'to carry for a little'
> уходи́ть 'to harass'

for the reason that the verbs зайти́, понести́, уйти́ do not
exist with the corresponding meanings.

These perfective indeterminates may form imperfectives in their turn. Thus,

> провести́ 'to lead through, spend' (perfective)

finds its imperfective in проводи́ть; but проводи́ть in the
sense of 'to accompany', being without a corresponding
determinate plus prefix, is perfective and forms an imperfective with the aid of the suffix -á-: провожа́ть.

2. FORMATION OF ASPECTUAL PAIRS FROM VERBS WITH THE SAME ROOT

There exist aspectual pairs which have only the root in
common, while differing in respect of all the other morphological elements (prefix, suffix, reflexive particle, alternation) and falling outside the usual pattern of aspectual
derivation, for example:

Imperfective	*Perfective*
сади́ться	сесть 'to sit down'
ложи́ться	лечь 'to lie down'
стоя́ть	стать (ста́ну) 'to stand'
сто́ить	стать (ста́ну) 'to cost'
станови́ться	стать (ста́ну) 'to become'
стреля́ть	вы́стрелить 'to fire a shot'
па́дать	упа́сть 'to fall'
кла́няться	поклони́ться 'to bow'
покупа́ть	купи́ть 'to buy'
скуча́ть	соску́читься 'to miss' (someone)
сомнева́ться	усомни́ться 'to doubt'
подозрева́ть	заподо́зрить 'to suspect'

3. FORMATION OF ASPECTUAL PAIRS FROM ENTIRELY
    DIFFERENT VERBS

Aspectual pairs may be formed by the association of
completely different verbs, for example:

Imperfective	*Perfective*
брать	взять 'to take'
говори́ть	сказа́ть 'to say'
лови́ть	пойма́ть 'to catch'
класть	положи́ть 'to put'
докла́дывать	доложи́ть 'to report'
ворова́ть	укра́сть 'to steal'
находи́ться	очути́ться 'to find oneself, to be'

The causes which have led to the creation of these suppletive pairs are various. The most frequent is the loss of
the normal corresponding element which may either have
dropped out of use or have acquired a different meaning.

VI. VERBS WHICH DO NOT FORM
ASPECTUAL PAIRS

The overwhelming majority of verbs are grouped in
aspectual pairs. There are, nevertheless, an appreciable
number which are not. The action which they express is
in such cases represented either in the imperfective aspect
alone or in the perfective aspect alone. It is only rarely that
the existence of the single aspect is due to the actual
meaning of the verb.

1. Imperfectives without Perfectives

I. SIMPLE VERBS

The bulk of these simple verbs consist of denominative
borrowings from Church Slavonic, of which many end in
-ствовать and -овать (see p. 264):

         му́дрствовать 'to philosophize'
         покрови́тельствовать 'to patronize'

приве́тствовать 'to greet'
уча́ствовать 'to take part'
изоби́ловать 'to abound'
чередова́ться 'to alternate'

To these may be added a few other verbs, such as:

зна́чить 'to mean'   нужда́ться 'to stand in need'
име́ть 'to have'   си́литься 'to strive'

2. VERBS WITH PREFIX

These are almost exclusively Church Slavonic verbs. They tend now to be considered as imperfectives with suffix derived from non-existent or extinct perfectives with prefix:

вымога́ть 'to extort'
обожа́ть 'to adore'
обоня́ть 'to smell' (tr.)
созерца́ть 'to contemplate'
состоя́ть 'to consist'
повинова́ться 'to obey'
подразумева́ть 'to understand'
пресмыка́ться 'to crawl, to grovel'
противоре́чить 'to contradict'
уважа́ть 'to respect'
заве́дывать 'to manage'
заи́скивать 'to curry favour'
отсве́чивать 'to reflect'
просве́чивать 'to shine through'

Some types of imperfectives with suffix possess no corresponding perfectives, viz.:

reflexive verbs with пере- (reciprocity):

перепи́сываться 'to correspond'

verbs compounded with по- frequentative:

попры́гивать 'to hop'

verbs compounded with под- and при- (accompaniment):

подвыва́ть 'to accompany with yells'
припева́ть 'to accompany with the voice'

2. Perfectives without Imperfectives

Isolated perfectives are less numerous than isolated imperfectives. Unlike them, they belong not to the Church Slavonic but to the popular component of the language:

ри́нуться 'to rush'
хлы́нуть 'to gush forth'
очну́ться 'to come to oneself'
нагря́нуть 'to arrive unexpectedly'
перестара́ться 'to overdo it'
погоди́ть 'to wait'
сгла́зить 'to cast a spell on'
устоя́ть 'to resist'

Several types of verbs are limited to the perfective alone:

verbs with за- inceptive:

заспо́рить 'to start to argue'

verbs with по- inceptive:

побежа́ть 'to start to run'

verbs with по- cumulative:

наброса́ть 'to throw in succession'

verbs with от- (cessation):

отобе́дать 'to finish dinner'

reflexive verbs with из- (saturation with a blameworthy quality):

избюрокра́титься 'to become rotten with bureaucracy'

reflexive verbs with раз- (extreme intensification of the action):

разрыда́ться 'to burst into sobs'

VII. VERBS WHICH MAY BE EITHER PERFECTIVE OR IMPERFECTIVE

A number of verbs may be employed both as perfectives and as imperfectives.

1. VERBS IN -овать

The verbs of this group are recent borrowings which, not yet having formed perfectives with prefix, may employ the form in -овать, which was originally imperfective, with perfective force, for example:

> адресова́ть 'to address'
> рекомендова́ть 'to recommend'
> гаранти́ровать 'to guarantee'
> нормирова́ть 'to regulate, ration'
> гармонизи́ровать 'to harmonize'

The same is true of:

> дарова́ть 'to grant, present'
> ночева́ть 'to spend the night'

2. VERBS IN -ить

In the seven verbs of this group, the force of one or other aspect is attached to various shades of meaning of the verb, not to the verb as a whole. These verbs are:

> жени́ть 'to marry' (and   роди́ть 'to give birth to'
>   жени́ться 'to get married') ра́нить 'to wound'
> крести́ть 'to baptize'   ру́шиться 'to collapse'
> казни́ть 'to execute'

To these should be added веле́ть 'to order'.

Verbs: Tense, Mood, Voice

I. TENSES

THE system of tenses within the sentence in Russian is not constructed with reference to the viewpoint of the speaking subject (the 'present understood') as it is in Latin, English, French, and German. For this reason, Russian does not make any distinction between absolute tenses and relative tenses in the finite verb and has no need to observe the sequence of tenses which is the result of that difference. From this it can be understood why Russian manages with only three tenses: present, past, and future. If it requires to express prior or subsequent action in the past or the future, Russian does so with the aid of adverbs or particles.

The meagre tense system is supplemented to some extent by the aspects. This function of the aspects is particularly clear in the present, which, normally, is expressed only by the imperfective form of the verb.

On the other hand, the poverty of the tense system is compensated also by the abundance of modal effects.

1. The Present

I. THE PRESENT IMPERFECTIVE

The present imperfective may be used to indicate:

(1) the ordinary present expressing an habitual or constant action:

> она́ ча́сто игра́ет на роя́ле 'she often plays the piano'

Во́лга впада́ет в Каспи́йское мо́ре 'the Volga flows into the Caspian Sea'

(2) the present continuous:

я сижу́ в кре́сле 'I am sitting in the armchair'

(3) the future, when the sentence contains an indication of time (as in English):

вы́ставка открыва́ется на бу́дущей неде́ле 'the exhibition opens next week'

(4) the perfect and the present perfect continuous:

Алекса́ндр Па́влович живёт в Шотла́ндии уже́ три го́да 'Alexander Pavlovich has lived in Scotland for three years'; жил три го́да would mean that A. P. has already left Scotland

я жду его́ с двух часо́в 'I have been waiting for him since two o'clock'

(5) the historic present:

я подошёл бли́же: смотрю́ и не ве́рю свои́м глаза́м 'I came closer; I looked and could not believe my eyes'

2. THE PRESENT PERFECTIVE

The present form of perfective verbs may be used to indicate, in addition to the future (its normal function), the following types of action:

(1) instantaneous action in the past (the historic present):

толпа́ была́ мра́чная; лишь и́зредка попадётся и сно́ва исче́знет весёлое лицо́ 'the crowd was in a gloomy mood; only here and there a happy face would emerge and disappear again'

(2) potentiality:

да́же ребёнок поймёт э́то 'even a child could understand this'

(3) inevitable or habitual action. This use of the present-future form is frequent in proverbs:

> не обма́нешь, не прода́шь 'if you don't cheat you won't sell'

(4) repeated action (frequentative use). In the following sentence, in which Gorky describes the flooding of the Nizhni-Novgorod fair, the present imperfective and the present perfective are used side by side:

> [я́рмарочный сто́рож] вы́лезет (perf.) из окна́ на кры́шу, ся́дет (perf.) в ло́дку и е́здит (imperf.), смо́трит (imperf.), нет ли где воро́в (*В лю́дях*, XVI) '[the watchman of the fair] climbs out of the window onto the roof, gets into a boat and goes around, to make sure there are no thieves about'

2. The Past

I. THE PAST IMPERFECTIVE

The past imperfective has the value of the imperfect; it corresponds to the English past continuous and the frequentative form ('used to'):

> солда́ты сиде́ли у огня́ 'the soldiers were sitting by the fire'
> по вто́рникам он обе́дал в рестора́не 'on Tuesdays he used to dine in a restaurant'

The past imperfective is generally used to indicate the action and not the result of it, although the action itself may be limited and completed:

> она́ танцова́ла всю ночь 'she danced all night'

Frequently the use of the past imperfective instead of the expected past perfective gives the sentence a slightly vague and sometimes a more polite tone:

> он проси́л вас зайти́ по́сле обе́да 'he asked you to come in the afternoon'

2. THE PAST PERFECTIVE

As the past perfective indicates any action completed in the past, it may be used to express the English past ('I gave'), perfect ('I have given'), and past perfect ('I had given'). When it expresses the perfect, i.e. an action undertaken in the past, the effects of which extend into the present, the past tense of the perfective verb encroaches on the territory of the present and, so to speak, fills the gap left by the lack of a present perfective. This is particularly clear when the past perfective is used in conjunction with the present of an imperfective verb, for example:

> прохо́жий останови́лся (perf.) и смо́трит (imperf.) 'the passer-by stopped and looked' (literally: 'stopped and looks')

The past perfective is frequently replaced by the past imperfective in negative sentences; but this imperfective must not have a too pronounced frequentative force:

> подмели́ вы уже́ ле́стницу? 'have you swept the staircase yet?'
> нет, ещё не подмета́ла 'no, not yet'

3. The Future Imperfective

The future imperfective is not a frequent form in Russian, as it has to compete both with the future perfective and the present imperfective (see p. 230). It is used when an uncompleted and continuous or repeated action has to be expressed in the future:

> до́лго ещё бу́дете вы колеба́ться? 'will you go on hesitating much longer?'

4. Gerund and Participle

If, as has been seen, Russian knows only the absolute value of the tenses in the finite forms of the verbs, the case is different with the gerunds and participles. These constitute the only section of the Russian verb system which admits the notion of relative time, as it exists in English.

I. GERUND

(a) *Present gerund*

The present gerund does not express the absolute present, as the present indicative does, but a relative time, namely: simultaneity with the action of the verb, whether this be present, past, or future:

> смотря́ на пла́н, я вспомина́ю го́род 'looking at the map, I recall the town'
>
> смотря́ на пла́н, я вспомина́л го́род 'looking at the map, I recalled the town'
>
> смотря́ на пла́н, я бу́ду вспомина́ть го́род 'looking at the map, I shall recall the town'

The present gerund may be used also in conjunction with a perfective verb: вспо́мнил, вспо́мню.

It will have been seen that the value of the Russian present gerund coincides with one of the values of the English present participle.

(b) *Past gerund*

If the present gerund expresses simultaneity, the past gerund (perfective) expresses priority, i.e. also a relative time:

> посмотре́в на пла́н, я вспо́мнил го́род 'having looked at the map, I recalled the town'
>
> ... вспо́мню ... '... I shall recall ...'

The main verb may also be imperfective: вспомина́ю, вспомина́л, бу́ду вспомина́ть.

The past gerund imperfective expresses simultaneous action in the past:

> смотре́в на пла́н, я вспомина́л го́род 'looking at the map, I recalled the town'

It therefore has exactly the same force as the present gerund смотря́, and it is for this reason that it is displaced by the latter and is now hardly used (see p. 179).

2. PARTICIPLE

(a) *Present participle*

The temporal value of the pres. part. act. is practically the same as that of the present gerund; it expresses simultaneous action:

> я ви́жу ло́дку, плыву́щую к бе́регу 'I see a boat approaching the bank'
>
> я уви́дел ло́дку, плыву́щую к бе́регу 'I saw a boat approaching the bank'
>
> я уви́жу ло́дку, плыву́щую к бе́регу 'I shall see a boat approaching the bank'

With some verbs the pres. part. act. may denote a permanent quality, outside of any notion of time. The time indicated by the main verb then corresponds to a fraction of the limitless time covered by the participle:

> я не выноси́л шу́ма от проходя́щих поездо́в 'I could not bear the noise of the passing trains'

This applies to all tenses and both aspects.

The pres. part. pass., in the rare cases when it is employed, presents the same characteristics as the active participle:

> он подошёл, возбужда́емый любопы́тством 'he came up, moved by curiosity'

(b) *Past participle*

The past part. act. and pass. of perfective verbs express in the first instance the absolute past, in exactly the same way as the past tense:

> я поднима́ю кошелёк, вы́павший из карма́на 'I pick up the purse which has fallen out of my pocket'

я по́днял кошелёк, вы́павший из карма́на 'I picked
up the purse which had fallen out of my pocket'

я подниму́ кошелёк, вы́павший из карма́на 'I shall
pick up the purse which has fallen out of my pocket'

я чита́ю газе́ты, ку́пленные ва́ми 'I am reading the
newspapers which you bought'

At the same time the past participle expresses prior
action: always, if the main verb is present or future, normally if it is past. For the participle not to express prior
action with a verb in the past tense, special indications are
necessary:

я по́днял кошелёк, пото́м сно́ва вы́павший из
карма́на 'I picked up the purse, which fell out of
my pocket again later on'

Still more explicit indications are required if the past
participle employed with a verb in the future tense is to
express priority in the future (the past in the future).

Past participles of imperfective verbs are used in the
same way, with this difference that the past part. imperf.,
when used with a verb in the past tense, may indicate
simultaneous action:

лю́ди, жи́вшие в Москве́, по́льзовались преиму́-
ществами столи́цы 'people living in Moscow en-
joyed the advantages of a capital city'

II. MOODS

The Russian system of moods is very far from the
rigidity of the classical languages or even from that of such
modern languages as English, French, and German. In the
first place, the modal force tends to be expressed not by the
verbal form itself but by independent particles (see p. 239).
Moreover, the dividing line between the moods tends to be

blurred so that forms proper to one mood are drawn into
the system of another.

The fact that modal differences are expressed more and
more by means of particles leads also to the gradual eli-
mination of the dividing lines between tense and mood.
If a particular particle is associated with only one tense, it
confers on that tense a new shade of meaning and enriches
both the system of moods and that of tenses.

1. Indicative

The indicative is the only mood in Russian in which the
notion of time is present. The indicative expresses mere
action, the normal action of the subject of the sentence;
accordingly, the purely modal force of the verb is reduced
to the minimum.

Because of this modal weakness, the indicative form may
without great difficulty be employed with some of the
meanings of the imperative. The transposition is effected
by means of the appropriate intonation; it is, therefore,
peculiar to the spoken language.

For the indicative to receive another modal value in the
written language, it must be accompanied by a modal
particle or an accessory word (see p. 239).

2. Imperative

I. IMPERATIVE FORCE PROPER

The Russian imperative is devoid of any notion of time
and has only one basic form, as in:

зови́ 'call'   брось 'throw'

This form is that of the 2nd pers. sing., but may also be
employed for the 3rd pers. sing. and pl.:

кто хо́чет слу́шать — слу́шай 'if anyone wants to
listen, let him do so'

всяк го́лову пове́сь 'let everyone bow his head'
(GRIBOEDOV, *Го́ре от ума́*)

In this latter use it often assumes an optative force:

бу́дь они́ про́кляты 'curse them!'
не да́й Бог 'God forbid!'

It may also be employed to express a general injunction:

есть черта́, кото́рой не переходи́ 'there is a line which
must not be crossed'

In familiar and popular usage, this form may also serve
for the 2nd pers. pl.:

держи́ его́, ребя́та! 'Hold him, lads!'

The form in -те is used only for the 2nd pers. pl.:

зови́те 'call'   бро́сьте 'throw'

It is never used for other persons.

As for the past tense (see p. 232), but more regularly,
the presence of a negation entails the use of the imperfective verb instead of the perfective:

возьми́те с собо́й зо́нтик 'take an umbrella'
не бери́те с собо́й зо́нтика 'don't take an umbrella'
не опа́здывайте, пожа́луйста 'don't be late, please'

With a perfective imperative the negation does not
express a prohibition, but a warning, often preceded by the
imperative смотри́те 'take care':

не возьми́те с собо́й моего́ зо́нтика 'don't take *my*
umbrella'
смотри́те, не опозда́йте 'take care not to be late'

2. INCLUSIVE FORM

In place of the imperative of the first person Russian
possesses an *inclusive* form, so called because it includes the
speaker.

The singular of the inclusive form is supplied by the 1st pers. pl. of the future of perfective verbs as well as the present of determinate verbs:

> пока́жем им 'let us show them' (thou and I)
> идём 'let us go' (thou and I)

It may also take the form of the future of imperfective verbs (бу́дем рабо́тать 'let us work'), although the turn of expression with дава́й (see p. 243) is rather more usual in this sense.

To form the plural this form takes the same particle -те which serves to form the 2nd pers. pl. of the imperative proper:

> пока́жемте им 'let us show them' (you and I)
> идёмте 'let us go' (you and I)
> бу́демте рабо́тать 'let us work' (you and I)

This form illustrates both the transposition of an indicative form into the imperative and the purely mechanical manner in which the final -те functions. It must be added that in colloquial usage, the two forms—идём and идёмте —are sometimes confused.

3. SPECIAL MODALITIES OF THE IMPERATIVE

The imperative form is capable of assuming certain modal values which distinguish it from the imperative proper. In these cases only the basic form (never that in -те) is employed, and then serves for both numbers and all three persons.

(a) Arbitrarily imposed obligation

The verb is usually imperfective:

> мы до́ма остава́йся, а вы в кино́! 'So we're supposed to stay at home while you go off to the pictures!'

(b) Arbitrary action (sudden and instantaneous)

This form, which has the value of a past tense, occurs only with perfective verbs:

едва́ он отошёл от бе́рега, как лёд под ним проломи́сь 'he had hardly left the shore when the ice broke under him'

(c) Hypothetical action

Imperatives of this type are equivalent to conditional clauses with е́сли 'if':

загори́сь сара́й ча́сом по́зже, ого́нь бы потуши́ли 'if the barn had begun to burn an hour later, the fire would have been put out'

3. Infinitive

The infinitive may have other values besides those which are normal to it:

(1) that of the inceptive past tense (an essentially popular use, as in French):

вор бежа́ть, да его́ пойма́ли 'the robber started to run, but they caught him'

(2) that of the imperative:

е́хать ры́сью и не остана́вливаться! 'drive at a trot and don't stop!'

4. Words and Particles with Modal Force

There are in Russian a certain number of particles and words which confer various modal values on the verb. As the indicative is the most neutral, the least expressive mood, it is natural that the modal particles should be employed principally with the indicative.

The connexion between the verbal form and the modal particle may be more or less close. Only the combinations which are well established by usage will be examined.

1. THE PARTICLE бы

This particle gives a hypothetical colour, not so much to the verb itself as to the whole clause. It tends to follow the first word of the clause. Since this word, in a hypothetical clause, is frequently a conjunction, бы often fuses with the latter to form a single whole, which is in some cases written as such:

éсли бы 'if'	кáк бы 'as if'
кабы́ 'if'	чтóбы 'in order that'
когдá бы 'if'	дабы́ 'in order that'
лишь бы 'if only'	гдé бы 'wherever'

Whether combined with a conjunction or not, the particle бы may be reduced to б after a vowel (except in кабы́, дабы́).

The particle бы has two principal values:

(1) *Hypothesis proper*

> éсли бы нé было дождя́, травá бы вы́горела 'if it had not rained the grass would have been burnt up'
> во втóрник он бы вас при́нял 'he would have received you on Tuesday'

When it has this value, бы is usually employed with a conjunction.

(2) *Wish*

> постарáйтесь, чтóбы бумáги бы́ли готóвы 'try and see that the papers are ready'
> постыди́лся бы он орáторствовать 'he ought to be ashamed to be speechifying'

The particle бы is normally employed in conjunction with the past tense, which then loses all temporal value. It may, however, also be employed with the infinitive:

> не попáсть бы вам под дождь 'see that you are not caught in the rain'

The particle бы is used even when the hypothetical clause has no verb at all:

> с чего бы это он? 'what can it be that makes him do that?'
>
> нам бы только самую малость 'we want only a trifle'

It will have been observed that the particle бы gives the Russian verb a force corresponding generally to the English conditional and is approximately equivalent to the Greek ἄν.

2. THE WORD бывало

This word is used to indicate repetition in the past of an habitual act. It may be combined with the present-future of perfective verbs (the most usual construction) or with the present or the past tense of imperfective verbs. The resultant combination always refers to past time:

> после бани он бывало сядет пить чай 'it was his custom to sit and drink tea after the bath'
>
> спорим мы бывало целые дни, но дело от этого не подвигалось 'we would argue for days at a time, but it didn't do any good'
>
> моряки бывало бастовали по всякому поводу 'the sailors used to go on strike at the slightest provocation'

The force of бывало may often be conveyed in English by the use of *would*.

3. THE WORD было

This word, usually unstressed, indicates the abandonment of the act, whether it has actually taken place or has merely been begun or simply intended. The essential point is that the act has not led to the expected or intended result. The word было may be combined

(1) with the past perfective; the combination has the force of a past tense:

стáл я бы́ло рисовáть, хотя́ спосо́бностей у меня́ нé
бы́ло 'I took up drawing, although I had no gift for
it' (and I dropped it again)

The same sentence without бы́ло would not have im-
plied abandonment of the study. With the past imperfective the use of бы́ло is virtually limited to the verb хотéть
'to wish':

он хотéл бы́ло лиши́ть себя́ жи́зни, да испугáлся 'he
was on the point of committing suicide, but lost
courage'

(2) with the past participles and past gerund:

останови́вшийся бы́ло мото́р нé был испо́рчен 'the
motor which had stopped was not out of order'
(and it began to go again)
ку́пленные бы́ло вчерá башмаки́ оказáлись малы́
'the shoes we bought yesterday turned out to be too
small' (and we took them back)
согласи́вшись бы́ло стать егó женóй, онá срáзу
раскáялась 'after promising to become his wife,
she immediately regretted it' (and withdrew her
promise)

4. THE PARTICLE -ка

This particle, added to the imperative form, softens the
order and transforms it into an exhortation:

пойди́-ка 'do go'
пойди́те-ка, пойдём-ка, пойдёмте-ка

It may also be added to the 1st pers. sing. of the present-
future of perfective verbs:

пойду́-ка я в цирк 'I think I might go to the circus'

5. THE WORDS дай, давáй

These words have a hortatory force, applied to arbitrary action. They are properly the imperatives of the verb дать (perf.) and давáть (imperf.) 'to give'. They are employed in conjunction only with the first person of the indicative, which is thereby transformed into an imperative, дай with the singular, давáй with the plural: дай, пойдý тудá 'I think I'll go there'; давáй, пойдём тудá 'let's go there'.

The more polite form, давáйте, may be used instead of давáй. On the other hand, дáйте is not used in this sense.

6. THE WORDS пусть, пускáй

These two words, which are properly imperatives of the verbs пустúть (perf.) and пускáть (imperf.) 'to let', may have two different functions:

(1) they combine with the third person of the present imperfective and perfective to form an imperative:

> пусть онú остаю́тся 'let them remain'
> пускáй всё погúбнет 'let everything perish'

(2) with all persons of the present, and also with the conditional form with бы, пусть and пускáй have concessive value:

> пускáй я ошибáюсь, вас э́то не касáется 'even supposing I may be wrong, it has nothing to do with you'
> пусть вы слáбы, борóться всё же нáдо 'weak as you may be, you must struggle'

In the third person, the use of the gen.-acc. instead of the nominative of the personal pronoun intensifies the concessive force of the clause introduced by пусть, пускáй:

> пусть их шýтят 'let them joke'

7. THE PARTICLE да

This particle combines with the third person of the

present imperfective and perfective to form an imperative used in the more elevated style:

да здра́вствует короле́ва! 'long live the Queen!'

8. THE WORD как

This word indicates sudden and unexpected action and is employed in the colloquial style. It is combined with the present-future of perfective verbs and may have the value either of the past tense or (less frequently) of the future:

председа́тель как хва́тит кулако́м по́ столу 'the chairman suddenly thumped the table'

9. THE VERB взять

The verb взять, which properly means 'to take' (perf.), when in the same form as the main verb and linked with it by the conjunctions да, и, да и, serves to indicate sudden and unexpected action (with similar effect to that of the imperative—see p. 238). The verb взять always precedes the main verb, but may be separated from it by other words of the sentence. This construction is limited to perfective verbs, but is possible with all the personal forms of the verb and with the infinitive and with all the moods, including the modal variations expressed by particles. In this last case the particle is detached from the main verb and attached to взять:

а вот возьму́ да не вста́ну 'well, I just won't get up'
по́езд взял да ушёл 'the train suddenly went off'
возьми́ и попроси́ у него́ 'you just go and ask him'
взял бы ты да и попроси́л у него́ 'why don't you just ask him?'
пальто́ возьми́ да и разорви́сь 'his overcoat suddenly tore'
взять бы сейча́с да и вы́купаться? 'what about having a swim right away?'

10. THE VERBAL INTERJECTION

This interjection, which is equivalent to an instantaneous past tense, or, at times, an instantaneous future, is formed from perfective verbs, usually in -нуть, expressing sudden sounds or movements. It is reduced to the monosyllabic root of the verb; in -и- verbs it is terminated by the soft sign:

> ко́шка прыг ему́ на ше́ю 'the cat sprang onto his neck' (from пры́гнуть 'to spring')
>
> цыга́нка хвать её за́ руку 'the gipsy seized her by the hand' (from хвати́ть 'to seize')
>
> шлёп! (from шлёпнуть 'to slap') 'slap!'
>
> бац! (from ба́цнуть 'to strike with a loud noise') 'bang!'

This form is on the border-line between verb and interjection.

III. VOICES

The voices do not present a coherent system. There is nothing even remotely comparable to the voice systems of Greek and Latin.

It is possible to draw only a few basic distinctions in this field.

1. Transitive and Intransitive

The difference between transitive and intransitive verbs is normally not marked by any morphological element.

In two cases only the relation between transitive and intransitive tends to be expressed by a distinction in form:

(1) The addition of a prefix to an intransitive verb may make it transitive. Thus, the intransitive служи́ть 'to serve' gives several transitive compounds, as for example:

> вы́служить пе́нсию 'to earn the right to a pension'
>
> заслужи́ть о́рден 'to win a decoration'

(2) The addition of the reflexive particle -ся, -сь renders a transitive verb intransitive:

бить 'to beat'/биться 'to fight, to strive'
беречь 'to keep'/беречься 'to beware'
кусать 'to bite'/кусаться 'to be apt to bite people'

This phenomenon occurs in all languages which employ the reflexive.

2. Active and Passive

The distinction between active and passive receives morphological expression only in the participles:

видящий, act. / видимый, pass.
увидевший, act. / увиденный, pass.
(from видеть, imperf., and увидеть, perf., 'to see')

Apart from the participles, which alone have a special form for the passive, the passive is expressed in Russian in different ways.

1. THE PASSIVE EXPRESSED BY A REFLEXIVE VERB

This is not a very common turn of expression:

дом строится (строился, будет строиться) 'the house is (was, will be) built'

всё это делается (делалось, будет делаться) очень просто 'all this is (was, will be) done very simply'

In constructions of this type the verb is normally imperfective and the agent is not expressed.

2. THE PASSIVE EXPRESSED BY A PAST PARTICIPLE PASSIVE

This construction is more frequent than the preceding:

дом построен (был построен, будет построен) городом 'the house has been (was, will be) built by the city'

всё э́то сде́лано (бы́ло сде́лано, бу́дет сде́лано)
   о́чень про́сто 'all this has been (was, will be) done
   very simply'

In constructions of this type the participle is perfective
and the agent may be expressed; if it is, it occurs in the
instrumental case.

Sentences of the two types, дом постро́ен and дом был
постро́ен, through the use of the past participle passive,
refer equally to past time. In the former the verb has the
value of the perfect ('has been built'), in the latter, of the
past indefinite, or aorist ('was built'). This is the only case
in which Russian is able to mark such a distinction by grammatical means. In the past perfective the two values have
at their disposal only a single form (see p. 232).

There is, thus, between these two constructions a relationship in the matter both of aspect and of tense, in so far
as the latter is connected with aspect.

However, Russian tends to avoid these constructions,
particularly the first. It replaces them by active or indeterminate constructions, both personal and impersonal (see
pp. 283, 291).

3. Reflexive and Non-reflexive Verbs

Reflexive verbs are formed by means of the particle -ся
or -сь added to the verbal form. The particle -ся occurs
after consonants:

   мы́ться 'to wash oneself'
   мо́ешься (2nd pers. sing. of pres. tense)
   мы́лся (masc. sing. of past tense)
   мо́йся (imperative)

The particle -сь occurs after vowels:

   мо́юсь (1st pers. sing. of pres. tense)
   мы́лись (pl. of past tense)
   мо́ясь (pres. gerund)
   умы́вшись (past gerund)

Only participles take the particle -ся irrespective of the character of the preceding sound:

моющийся (masc.)   моющаяся (fem.)
моющееся (neut.)   моющиеся (pl.)

The final syllables -тся (3rd pers. sing. and pl.) and -ться (infinitive) are pronounced -*ca*, with hard *c* (*ts′* and *t′s′* give *c*, which can only be hard):

моется (*móicə*)   моются (*mójucə*)   мыться (*mýcə*)

The pronunciation -*cca* also occurs.

The с which is not preceded by т may be pronounced either hard or soft. Both pronunciations are correct. Thus:

моюсь (*mójus* and *mójus′*)   мылся (*mýlsə* and *mýls′ə*)

However, the -сь of the present gerund immediately following the stress is always soft:

родя́сь (*rad′ás′*) 'being born'

A certain number of verbs occur only in the reflexive form, as:

боя́ться 'to fear'   смея́ться 'to laugh'
годи́ться 'to be fit'   толпи́ться 'to crowd'

As these verbs do not correspond to any non-reflexive verb, it need hardly be said that the particle -ся has, with them, no particular value.

Other verbs, however, have both a reflexive and a non-reflexive form. In these verbs the particle -ся acquires, consequently, a special value which is not always the same in every case. The reflexive particle serves to form:

(1) reflexive verbs proper (i.e. verbs in which the action returns upon the agent):

бри́ться 'to shave oneself'
бере́чься 'to look after oneself'

(2) passive verbs:

>писа́ться 'to be written'
>разруша́ться 'to be destroyed'

(3) verbs denoting a mental or physical condition of the subject:

>беспоко́иться 'to worry'
>серди́ться 'to get angry'
>интересова́ться 'to interest oneself'

(4) reciprocal verbs (verbs with two or more agents):

>би́ться 'to fight'
>встреча́ться 'to meet'
>проща́ться 'to say good-bye'
>целова́ться 'to kiss'

These four groups exist normally in other languages, as, for example, in French and German. On the other hand, the two following functions of the reflexive are peculiar to Russian:

(5) middle verbs, denoting action of a more personal and intense character:

>стуча́ться 'to knock' (at the door)
>проси́ться 'to ask'
>руга́ться 'to swear, resort to abuse'
>пла́каться 'to weep, wail'
>бода́ться 'to butt'

(6) impersonal use (limited, therefore, to the 3rd pers. sing. and to the neuter if the verb is in the past tense), to indicate action independent of the will of the person to whom the action refers; the noun or pronoun denoting the person, if the person is mentioned, goes into the dative case:

>мне хо́чется 'I feel like'
>де́тям не спи́тся 'the children cannot sleep'
>вам легко́ живётся 'you have an easy life'

писа́телю не рабо́талось 'the writer could not get down to work'

здесь отли́чно хо́дится на лы́жах 'this is a very good place for skiing'

Any verb, apart from those which have only the reflexive form, may be employed in this way.

Verbs: Word-Formation

VERBS may be derived either from other verbs (*deverbals*) or from parts of speech other than verbs: nouns, adjectives, adverbs, particles, &c. (*denominatives*). Foreign verbs borrowed by Russian, as they are not derived from other Russian verbs, may be classed with the denominatives.

The methods of word-formation of the two groups are similar, but their functions are different.

I. VERBS FORMED FROM OTHER VERBS

1. Suffixion

The system of deverbal suffixes is very poor. Moreover, it is reserved almost entirely for the aspectual functions.

I. FREQUENTATIVE SUFFIXES

The suffixes which are used at the present day to form imperfectives, -á-, -вá-, -ыва- (see p. 215), were originally frequentative suffixes, indicating discontinuous action repeated at short intervals. This old function has by now been almost entirely sacrificed to the aspectual function.

These suffixes have retained their frequentative force only in those rare cases where the verb with which they are employed has no corresponding perfective. The verbs of this type are derived from simple imperfective verbs and are used only in the past tense. Their meaning may usually be rendered in English by the expression 'used to'. Some examples follow:

едáл (from ел 'he ate')
живáл (from жил 'he lived')
говáривал (from говорúл 'he said')
úгрывал (from игрáл 'he played')
слы́хивал (from слыхáл 'he heard')

Verbs of this type occur very rarely and constitute popular archaisms.

2. SUFFIXES OF INSTANTANEOUS ACTION

The suffix which expresses single, instantaneous action is -ну- (in the infinitive stem; -н- in the present stem). Nowadays verbs with this perfective suffix normally correspond to imperfective verbs with the suffix -а- (more rarely -е- or -и-, see p. 213). But, even though employed to indicate aspect, the suffix -ну- retains its instantaneous force:

пры́гнуть 'to spring' (пры́гать)
чихнýть 'to sneeze' (чихáть)
пугнýть 'to frighten' (пугáть)
перелистнýть 'to turn over the pages of' (перелистáть, perf. of перелúстывать imperf.)
курнýть 'to smoke' (курúть)

The suffix -ну- shows a certain degree of productivity. In foreign borrowings, apart from рискнýть 'to risk', the use of the suffix -ну- is regarded as vulgar and occurs rarely if at all in the literary language:

кредитнýть 'to credit'
ликвиднýть 'to liquidate'
спекульнýть 'to speculate'

The extended suffix -анý- which occurs parallel with -ну-, has an expressive, often familiar, value:

дерганýть 'to tug' (дёрнуть, дёргать)
резанýть 'to cut' (резнýть, рéзать)

2. Prefixion

The system of word-formation by means of verbal prefixes is very highly developed in Russian.

Russian verbal prefixes are in origin prepositions. The prefixes вз- (воз-), вы-, низ-, пере- (пре-), раз- exist only as prefixes, all the others occur also as prepositions.

The verbal prefixes may retain the concrete, local meaning of the preposition. At the same time, they tend more and more to become abstract and general, and thereby constantly furnish new shades of meaning.

The addition of a prefix usually makes the verb perfective. This, however, is only a secondary function of the prefix. Its normal function is to help to create verbs with new meanings. It is only when the prefix loses all of its proper meaning that it becomes a mere instrument of perfectivation (see p. 211).

In this section the purely lexical value of the verbal prefixes will be examined.

Verbal prefixes ending in a consonant may be followed by a sort of mobile -o- before a stem beginning with a group of consonants.

I. PRODUCTIVE PREFIXES

в- (во-): action directed inwards:

ввози́ть 'to import'	впита́ть 'to absorb'
вбить 'to drive in'	ворва́ться 'to break into'

вз- (вс-, взъ-, взо-) and воз- (вос-, возо-) (this prefix occurs in the second form only in certain verbs of Church Slavonic origin or type):

(1) motion upwards:

взойти́ 'to go up'	вспорхну́ть 'to take wing'
вскорми́ть 'to bring up, rear'	вспоро́ть 'to rip open'
вспаха́ть 'to plough up'	воздви́гнуть 'to erect'

(2) commencement of an action:

вскричáть 'to cry out'   вспугнýть 'to scare'

In the unproductive form воз-:

(3) repetition, renewal (English *re-*):

возроди́ть 'to revive, regenerate'
воспроизвести́ 'to reproduce'

(4) action directed towards or against someone:

восстáть 'to revolt'
вознагради́ть 'to reward'

вы-, always stressed in perfectives:

(1) motion outwards, selection:

вы́гнать 'to drive out'
вы́жить 'to survive, to get rid of'
вы́брать 'to choose'

(2) acquisition by means of a series of actions:

вы́просить 'to obtain by asking'
вы́играть 'to win at gambling'

(3) completion of a process or action:

вы́топтать 'to trample'
вы́родиться 'to degenerate'
вы́спаться 'to have one's sleep out'

до-:

(1) completion of action or attainment of goal:

добрóсить 'to throw up to'
догнáть 'to overtake'

(2) completion of process or action which had been left unfinished:

добри́ться 'to finish shaving'
доби́ть 'to finish off' (a wounded man or animal)

(3) with the reflexive suffix -ся and the preposition до
after the verb, action carried to a negative, absurd
or harmful result:

доигра́ться до слёз 'to play until one is ready to cry'
договори́ться до глу́постей 'to go on talking until
one is talking nonsense'

Verbs compounded with до- are the only verbs which
may undergo a complete fusion with the negative particle
не. In such cases they indicate that the action has not been
performed to the normal or expected extent:

недода́ть 'to give (something) short of the due
amount'
недооцени́ть 'to underestimate'

за-:

(1) action which goes beyond a limit or behind a target:

заки́нуть 'to throw behind'
засла́ть 'to send to a wrong address'

(2) covering, envelopment, or closing:

закопа́ть 'to bury'
заплева́ть 'to spit upon'
заде́лать 'to close, block up, wall up'

(3) action which deviates from its normal course:

занести́ 'to bring in passing'
заде́ть 'to graze'

(4) action which affects only the surface, the edge, or a
limited field:

загоре́ть 'to become sunburnt'
загни́ть 'to rot on one side'

(5) commencement of an action which is not conducted
in any one particular direction:

забе́гать 'to begin to run'
задрема́ть 'to begin to doze'

(6) development of the action to the extreme or to excess:

закорми́ть 'to gorge'
заноси́ть 'to wear out'
засмотре́ться 'to stare'

из- (ис-, изо-):

(1) motion outwards (Church Slavonic; unproductive and literary):

изда́ть 'to utter, publish'
исчерпа́ть 'to exhaust'

(2) action conducted to the extreme (Russian):

измо́кнуть 'to be drenched'
исписа́ть 'to wear out' (a pencil)
       'to fill up' (a sheet of paper)
изне́рвинчаться 'to become overwrought'

на-:

(1) action directed onto an object:

наступи́ть 'to tread on'   намота́ть 'to wind up'

(2) cumulative result:

наворова́ть 'to steal in great quantity'
наобеща́ть 'to promise the moon'
наговори́ться 'to speak one's fill'

над- (надо-):

(1) action which takes place on top of or above something:

надстро́ить 'to build' (something on top of something else)
надписа́ть 'to inscribe, address'

(2) action which affects only the surface or the edge:

надпили́ть 'to make an incision by sawing'
надкуси́ть 'to nibble'

o- and об- (обо-); only об- is productive:

(1) action which envelops the object or which extends to the entire surface:

обвари́ть 'to scald'   описа́ть 'to describe'

(2) distributive action:

одари́ть 'to distribute presents to'

(3) action which passes beside; deprival; cheating:

обогна́ть 'to outstrip'
обве́сить 'to cheat in weighing'

(4) imperfect action:

ослы́шаться 'to mis-hear'
ошиби́ться 'to make a mistake'

от- (ото-):

(1) removal or separation:

оттолкну́ть 'to repulse'
отмы́ть 'to wash off'

(2) compensatory action:

отыгра́ться 'to win back one's losses at gambling'

(3) opening; revelation:

откопа́ть 'to dig up'
отгада́ть 'to guess'

(4) completion:

отрабо́тать 'to finish working'
откорми́ть 'to fatten'

(5) evasion (only reflexive):

отписа́ться 'to make use of written pretexts' (for not doing something)

пере- and пре-; the latter form is Church Slavonic and archaic:

(1) crossing or transfer:

перелéзть 'to climb over'   передáть 'to transmit'
пережи́ть 'to endure'   предáть 'to betray'

(2) surpassing of a limit:

перегрéть 'to overheat'
переборо́ть 'to overcome'

(3) repetition or renewal:

перестраховáть 'to re-insure'
переименовáть 'to re-name'

(4) distributive action:

перебрáть 'to sort out'
перессо́рить 'to set at variance'

(5) separation into two:

перепили́ть 'to saw in two'
перегры́зть 'to gnaw through'

(6) reciprocity (in the reflexive):

перепи́сываться 'to be in correspondence'

по-:

(1) commencement of action in a single direction (with determinate verb):

полетéть 'to start to fly'
поплы́ть 'to begin to swim'

(2) action of short duration (perf.):

покричáть 'to utter a few cries'
поспáть 'to have a nap'

(3) action repeated at intervals (with the suffix -ыва-/-ива-):

пострéливать 'to fire a shot from time to time'

(4) cumulative result:

    поразбива́ть 'to break one after another'

под- (подо-):

(1) action beneath or in the lower part of:

    подложи́ть 'to put underneath'
    подкова́ть 'to shoe' (a horse)
    подчини́ть 'to subordinate'

(2) motion upwards:

    подбро́сить 'to throw into the air'

(3) approach:

    подъе́хать 'to approach'
    подозва́ть 'to call up'

(4) attenuation:

    подсуши́ть 'to dry slightly'
    поджи́ть 'to begin to heal up'

(5) supplementary action:

    подли́ть 'to add' (a liquid)
    подрабо́тать 'to earn additionally'

(6) underhand action:

    подкупи́ть 'to bribe'
    подсмотре́ть 'to spy'

(7) accompaniment (imperf):

    подпева́ть 'to join in' (in singing)

при-:

(1) adjunction; attachment:

    прибежа́ть 'to run up'
    прикова́ть 'to chain to, fasten'

(2) attenuated action:

> припу́дрить 'to powder slightly'
> приоткры́ть 'to half-open'

(3) accompaniment (imperf.):

> припля́сывать 'to dance to' (a tune)

(4) completed action:

> прире́зать 'to murder'
> примири́ть 'to reconcile'

про-:

(1) action directed through something:

> проби́ть 'to transpierce'
> прока́шляться 'to clear one's throat'
> проснуться 'to wake up'

(2) motion past something:

> пробежа́ть 'to run past'
> пропусти́ть 'to let pass'

(3) action performed for a certain length of time:

> проголода́ть неде́лю 'not to eat for a week'

(4) loss, damage:

> пропи́ть го́лос 'to ruin one's voice by drinking'
> прозева́ть слу́чай 'to miss an opportunity'

раз- (рас-, разо-):

(1) dispersion, division:

> разогна́ть 'to disperse'
> разре́зать 'to cut up'
> разли́ть 'to pour out'
> 'размени́ть 'to change' (money)

(2) separation:

расстегну́ть 'to undo' (a garment fastened
  by buttons, &c.)

(3) distribution:

разосла́ть приглаше́ния 'to send invitations'
раскле́ить афи́ши 'to paste up posters'

(4) progressive increase:

разже́чь 'to kindle'
рассмеши́ть 'to make (someone) laugh'
распе́ться 'to warm up' (in singing)

(5) intensity:

расспроси́ть 'to interrogate'
расхвали́ть 'to lavish praise'

(6) annulled action:

разучи́ться 'to unlearn'
разбинтова́ть 'to unbandage'

c- (co-):

(1) combination, collection, connexion:

связа́ть 'to tie together'   созва́ть 'to convoke'
смеша́ть 'to mix'   сочини́ть 'to compose'

(2) removal, departure:

сойти́ 'to descend'
счи́стить 'to clear away'
сорва́ть 'to tear off, to pluck'
сосла́ть 'to banish'

у-:

(1) removal from a given point:

унести́ 'to carry away'
уступи́ть 'to yield'

(2) diminution:

убыва́ть 'to decrease'
усо́хнуть 'to dry up'

(3) attainment of aim:

уговори́ть 'to persuade'
услужи́ть 'to do a service'
узна́ть 'to recognize'

(4) action covering an object:

усе́ять 'to strew'
уку́тать 'to muffle up'

2. UNPRODUCTIVE PREFIXES

These prefixes are Church Slavonic. The verbs with which they are compounded are of literary origin and in most cases dignified in tone:

низ- (нис-, низо-): motion downwards:

ниспада́ть 'to descend, fall'
низложи́ть 'to depose'

пред- (предо-): prior action, putting forward:

предреши́ть 'to decide beforehand'
предложи́ть 'to propose'

To these two prefixes may be added the unproductive forms of those examined above: воз-, о-, пре-.

II. DENOMINATIVE VERBS

1. Suffixion

Unlike deverbal suffixion, which has virtually no function other than to change the aspect of the verb, denominative suffixion serves to create verbs with new meanings.

I. PRODUCTIVE SUFFIXES

The only productive suffixes are those which are identical in the infinitive and the present stems.

The suffix -ова-/-у- is the only alternating suffix of this group.

(1) The suffix -а-/-я- (Class III):

завтракать 'to breakfast'
дичáть 'to grow unsociable'
щеголя́ть 'to flaunt'
áхать 'to say "ah" ' (ax)

The same suffix occurs also in extended forms:

(2) the suffix -ка- in verbs derived from interjections:

хны́кать 'to snivel'
хрю́кать 'to grunt'
кáркать 'to croak'
ты́кать 'to address in the second person singular'

(3) the suffix -нича- in verbs of occupation and behaviour derived from nouns and adjectives and with a pejorative shade of meaning ('to act the ...'); the stress reproduces that of the root words:

вáжничать 'to be pompous'
жáдничать 'to be stingy'
жу́льничать 'to act the sharper'
кокéтничать 'to act the coquette'

(4) the suffix -ова-/-ева- (present -у-/-ю-) in verbs derived from nouns. The stress falls either on the suffix (-овá-/-ý-), an extremely productive type:

голосовáть 'to vote'	бичевáть 'to scourge'
пировáть 'to feast'	воевáть 'to wage war'

including many borrowings:

арендовáть 'to rent'	штурмовáть 'to storm'
интриговáть 'to intrigue'	малевáть 'to paint'

—or on the stem, an unproductive type:

жа́ловаться 'to complain'   сове́товать 'to advise'
сле́довать 'to follow'   чу́вствовать 'to feel'

(5) the suffix -ствова- (present -ству-); the stress is that of the root words:

безмо́лвствовать 'to remain silent'
у́мствовать 'to reason'
филосо́фствовать 'to philosophize'

(6) the suffix -ирова- (present -иру-) serves to Russianize German and French verbs: the stress falls either on the -и- or, more rarely, on the -a-:

дисциплини́ровать 'to discipline'
пози́ровать 'to pose' (intrans.)
эксплуати́ровать 'to exploit'
группирова́ть 'to group'
лакирова́ть 'to lacquer'

(7) the suffix -изи́рова- (present -изи́ру-), with the same functions as the preceding, but also in some verbs of Russian origin:

реквизи́ровать 'to requisition'
большевизи́ровать 'to bolshevize'
украинизи́ровать 'to give a Ukrainian character to'

(8) the suffix -e- (Class III) expresses the fact of becoming something:

глупе́ть 'to become stupid'
камене́ть 'to turn (intr.) to stone'
плеши́веть 'to become bald'
ржа́веть 'to rust'

(9) the suffix -и- (Class IV) serves above all to form factitive verbs:

жени́ть 'to marry' (a man to a woman)
золоти́ть 'to gild'

дура́чить 'to make a fool of'
горди́ться 'to be proud of'

2. UNPRODUCTIVE SUFFIXES

The unproductive suffixes are those which vary as between the infinitive and the present stems. The suffixes treated in this section are those of the infinitive stem.

(1) the suffix -a- (present in -e- without suffix, Class I B 3, see p. 189):

клевета́ть 'to slander'
хохота́ть 'to laugh loudly'

(2) the suffix -á- (present in -ý, -и́шь, Class IV C, see p. 201), with stem ending in ж, ш, ч, щ, in verbs derived from interjections and onomatopoeic words:

рыча́ть 'to roar'   дребезжа́ть 'to jar'

(3) the suffix -é- (present in -ý/-ю́, -и́шь, Class IV B, see p. 200), in the same types of verbs as the preceding group:

храпе́ть 'to snore'   шуме́ть 'to make a noise'

(4) the suffix -ну- (present in -ну, -нешь, Class II B, see p. 193) expresses the fact of becoming, in verbs derived from adjectives:

гло́хнуть 'to become deaf'
кре́пнуть 'to grow strong'

2. Prefixion

To form a verb from a noun or adjective a suffix is always necessary. All the denominatives, therefore, are suffixal verbs. In addition, some denominative verbs exist only in combination with prefixes. These prefixes are therefore to be regarded as elements of word-formation in the same way as the suffixes.

The prefixes to which this applies are the same as in the case of deverbal verbs, excepting до-, над-, низ-, and пред-.

In most cases the prefixes used in the formation of denominative verbs have entirely lost their specific value, or at least a great part of it.

In their overwhelming majority, the denominatives with prefix are verbs in -ить (Class IV A); much more rarely, verbs in -еть (Class III A).

Denominatives with prefix are derived for the most part from nouns, less frequently from adjectives.

In the matter of aspect they are assimilated to perfectives and follow the aspectual system of the deverbal verbs (see p. 214).

Two prefixes are particularly frequent in the formation of denominatives: о- (об-) and у-:

о- (об-) is the principal prefix of denominative verbs. It has no value of its own and furnishes for the most part factitives in -и-:

онемéчить 'to Germanize'	обýглить 'to carbonize'
осуществи́ть 'to realize'	обусло́вить 'to stipulate'
опорожни́ть 'to empty'	обнови́ть 'to renew'
охромéть 'to become lame'	обосо́бить 'to isolate'

The prefix о- is the only one used to form verbs from phrases containing the preposition без 'without', as also from adjectives compounded with без-. Such formations are productive and characteristic of Russian:

обезлéсить 'to deforest', обезлéсеть 'to be deforested' (both derived from the phrase без лéса 'without forest'). Similarly:

обескро́вить 'to bleed white'
обескурáжить 'to discourage'
обезору́жить 'to disarm'
обеззу́беть 'to become toothless'

у- is used to form factitives in which it retains its value of goal attained:

уво́лить 'to dismiss'   уполномо́чить 'to empower'
узако́нить 'to legalize'   усложни́ть 'to complicate'

The other verbal prefixes are much less frequent:

в-	вклини́ть 'to wedge in'
	водвори́ть 'to instal'
вз-	вспыли́ть 'to fly into a passion'
	возвели́чить 'to glorify'
вы-	вы́ветриться 'to crumble away'
	вы́школить 'to train'
за-	зацепи́ть 'to catch against'
	засекре́тить 'to make secret'
из-	излучи́ть 'to radiate'
	измельчи́ть 'to reduce to small pieces'
на-	нашпи́лить 'to pin'
	наловчи́ться 'to become proficient'
от-	отсро́чить 'to postpone'
	отличи́ть 'to distinguish'
пере-	переключи́ть 'to switch'
	переупря́мить 'to outdo in obstinacy'
по-	поручи́ть 'to entrust'
	пони́зить 'to lower'
под-	подыто́жить 'to sum up'
	подрессо́рить 'to mount (something) on springs'
при-	приобщи́ть 'to associate'
	присво́ить 'to appropriate'
про-	прове́трить 'to air'
	продо́лжить 'to continue'
раз-	разоружи́ть 'to disarm'
	разбаза́рить 'to squander'
с-	сооруди́ть 'to construct'
	сплоти́ть 'to join together'

XV

Auxiliary Words

I. PREPOSITIONS

The prepositions, like the adverbs, constitute in Russian a grammatical category the limits of which are not clearly defined. The prepositions are continuously increasing their number at the expense of the other parts of speech, of the adverbs in the first place, but also of the nouns and verbs (gerunds).

This fact makes it possible to distinguish two principal strata of prepositions.

1. Primary Prepositions

These prepositions, some twenty in number, are divided into five groups according to the cases which they govern. Certain prepositions may govern two or even three cases.

I. ACCUSATIVE

The prepositions which govern the accusative form the largest group:

на 'onto, to, for':

> положи́ть на зе́млю 'to put on the ground'
> вид на мо́ре 'a view onto the sea'
> наня́ть на́ год 'to hire for a year'
> купи́ть на два рубля́ 'to buy for two roubles'

в 'into, to, on'; evaluation and comparison:

поéздка в гóрод 'a journey to town'
в тот же день 'on the same day'
в наказáние 'in punishment'
величинóй в кулáк 'the size of a fist'

под 'under':

стать под дéрево 'to stand under the tree'
танцовáть под мýзыку 'to dance to the music'

за 'behind, by':

спрятаться за дом 'to hide behind the house'
за мéсяц до смéрти 'a month before his death'
взять зá руку 'to take by the hand'

о, об 'against':

опирáться о стéну 'to lean against the wall'
удáриться об стол 'to bump against the table'

чéрез 'through, across':

перейти чéрез дорóгу 'to cross the road'
чéрез час 'in an hour'

сквозь 'through':

сквозь огóнь 'through fire'

по 'up to, each' (distributive):

по пятое июля 'to the fifth of July' (inclusive)
по пояс 'up to the waist'
пó три рубля 'three roubles each'

про 'about':

дýмать про болéзнь 'to think about the disease'

с, preposition of evaluation and comparison:

рóстом с бéлку 'about the size of a squirrel'
прошлó с час 'about an hour passed'
с меня хвáтит 'that is enough for me'

The connexion between the accusative and the action of the verb is so close (see p. 159) that the prepositions with local force на, в, под, за, о, че́рез, сквозь indicate only motion, never rest. For the same reason, the accusative after a preposition dependent upon a noun other than a verbal noun is limited to a few phrases of evaluation (see examples with в and c).

2. GENITIVE

The following prepositions govern the genitive:

у 'near, at the house of':

> у мо́ря 'by the sea'
> он живёт у нас 'he lives at our place'
> проси́ть по́мощи у роди́телей 'to ask the parents for help'

до 'up to':

> до го́рода 'as far as the town'
> до вто́рника 'until Tuesday'
> до изнеможе́ния 'to the point of collapse'

от 'away from, from':

> удали́ться от бе́рега 'to go away from the shore'
> от двух (часо́в) до пяти́ 'from two o'clock to five'
> порошо́к от мо́ли 'powder to keep off the moths'
> он проснулся от шу́ма 'the noise woke him up'

из 'out of, from':

> вы́йти из воды́ 'to come out of the water'
> стреля́ть из пу́шки 'to fire the cannon'
> вено́к из цвето́в 'a wreath of flowers'
> молча́ть из тру́сости 'to be silent from cowardice'

c 'down from, from':

> упа́сть со стола́ 'to fall off the table'
> с де́тства 'from childhood'
> с отча́яния 'from despair'

ме́жду 'between' (more frequently with the instrumental, see below):

> ме́жду двух гор 'between two mountains'

без 'without':

> без де́нег 'without money'

для 'for':

> для нас 'for us'

ра́ди 'for the sake of':

> ра́ди нау́ки 'for the sake of science'

3. DATIVE

Only two prepositions govern the dative:

к 'towards':

> подойти́ к две́ри 'to approach the door'
> обрати́ться к наро́ду 'to address the people'
> к ве́черу 'towards evening'
> к на́шему большо́му го́рю 'to our great sorrow'

по 'along, in accordance with':

> итти́ по доро́ге 'to walk along the road'
> не спать по ноча́м 'not to sleep at night'
> по моему́ сове́ту 'on my advice'
> одева́ться по мо́де 'to dress fashionably'
> по рублю́ 'one rouble each'. In this distributive meaning the dative is employed only with the numeral 'one', expressed or understood. With the other numerals по distributive takes the accusative (see p. 269).

4. INSTRUMENTAL

The following prepositions govern the instrumental:

над 'over, above':

> над голово́й 'over the head'
> побе́да над враго́м 'victory over the enemy'

под 'under':

под землёй 'under the ground'
под вла́стью тата́р 'under the domination of the Tatars'
под угро́зой вторже́ния 'under the threat of invasion'

за 'behind, after, at, for':

за стено́й 'behind the wall'
день за днём 'day after day'
за обе́дом 'at dinner'
пойти́ за до́ктором 'to go for the doctor'

пе́ред 'in front of, before':

пе́ред са́дом 'in front of the garden'
пе́ред прогу́лкой 'before the walk'

ме́жду 'among, between':

ме́жду ру́сскими 'among the Russians'
ме́жду на́ми 'among us, between you and me'

с 'with':

брат с сестро́й 'brother and sister'
с раздраже́нием 'with irritation'

The prepositions под and за with the instrumental indicate not motion, as with the accusative, but position. A common feature of the prepositions constructed with the instrumental is that they indicate localization not necessarily involving contact.

5. LOCATIVE

The locative is the only case which is not employed without a preposition. The prepositions which govern this case are five:

на 'on':

на сце́не 'on the stage'
на пра́здниках 'on the holidays'

в 'in':

    в по́гребе 'in the cellar'
    в бу́дущем году́ 'next year'
    в стра́хе 'in fear'

при 'in the presence of, with, in the time of':

    при генера́ле 'with the general'; also, 'in the general's presence'
    прису́тствовать при разгово́ре 'to be present at the conversation'
    при Петре́ Вели́ком 'under Peter the Great'

о, об 'about, on':

    иссле́дование о жи́вописи 'study of painting'
    по́мнить об отъе́зде 'not to forget the departure'

по 'after, on account of':

    по прие́зде 'on arrival'
    тоскова́ть по ро́дине 'to be homesick'

The prepositions на and в with the locative indicate not motion, as with the accusative, but position.

Prepositions ending in a consonant, with the exception of че́рез and сквозь, may take a sort of mobile -о before a group of consonants:

    под меня́ 'under me' (motion)
    подо мной 'under me' (position)

6. USE OF THE PRIMARY PREPOSITIONS

Only the principal meanings of the primary prepositions have been given above. It need hardly be said that these meanings are supplemented, particularly in figurative expressions, by a multitude of secondary shades of meaning which it is impossible to enumerate. As a general rule, in constructions in which the choice of the preposition does not depend entirely on the verb, the original meaning of the preposition tends to be preserved. It is to be observed, however, that the further a prepositional construction departs from the general value of the case governed by the preposition, the more the construction tends to assume an adverbial character. A typical example is that of the preposition по with the dative.

On the other hand, where the choice of the preposition is fixed by the rules governing the use of the particular verb, the preposition tends to lose its original meaning and to become a mere grammatical instrument like the English *to*, without, however, attaining the same degree of abstraction. In the following expressions, for example, the prepositions do not mean very much:

> признавáть за начáльника 'to recognize as chief'
> плáкать по мýже 'to weep for her husband'
> представлять из себя 'to represent'

The prepositions which govern more than one case are, naturally, those which tend most of all to lose their distinctness of meaning.

Not all prepositions nor all the meanings of a particular preposition have the same degree of vitality. Thus, мéжду with the genitive has practically fallen out of use; по with the locative is limited to a few verbs denoting regret (as in two of the examples quoted) and almost exclusively to the singular; по with the accusative, indicating purpose (иттú пó воду 'to go to fetch water'), has been almost eliminated by за with the instrumental (иттú за водóй).

The preposition про (говорúть про войнý 'to talk about the war') is gradually losing ground to о with the locative (говорúть о войнé). Conversely, о is losing its meanings other than that of 'about'; its uses in a temporal sense (о Рождествé 'at Christmas') and with numerals (собáка о трёх ногáх 'a three-legged dog') are already obsolete. Other examples could be quoted.

A prepositional expression contains only one stress. In the vast majority of cases it falls on the noun. Certain prepositions may, however, in certain conditions take the stress themselves; the noun then loses all stress.

2. Secondary Prepositions

This group is constantly being extended by the accession of new prepositions which are furnished principally by three parts of speech: adverbs, nouns, and verbs. In this sense it is possible to say that this group has a certain degree of productivity. It includes a number of forms which occur only as prepositions, but most of them may also be employed as the part of speech which they were originally. As a general rule, every preposition of this group has only one, clearly defined, value.

I. PREPOSITIONS OF ADVERBIAL ORIGIN

This is the most numerous group. It includes four words which are now normally employed only as prepositions:

> против 'opposite, against'
> кроме 'except'
> вместо 'instead of'
> среди 'in the middle of, among'

The others may be employed both as prepositions and as adverbs, as:

близ, возле, около 'near'	после 'after'
вокруг 'around'	прежде 'before'
впереди 'in front' (of)	относительно 'on the sub-
мимо 'past'	ject of'

These prepositions for the most part take the genitive case (this is true of all the examples quoted); some take the dative, as:

вопреки 'in spite of'	подобно 'like'
вслед 'after'	согласно 'according to'
навстречу 'towards'	

2. PREPOSITIONS OF NOMINAL ORIGIN

These are for the most part combinations of primary preposition + noun, as:

вследствие 'because of'   вроде 'of the type of'
ввиду 'in view of'   под видом 'under cover of'

All these prepositions take the genitive.

3. PREPOSITIONS OF VERBAL ORIGIN

The members of this group were originally gerunds, as:

благодаря 'thanks to'   включая 'including'
спустя 'after'   не считая 'not counting'

These prepositions take the same cases as the verbs from which they are derived, except благодаря which takes the dative.

With the secondary prepositions as a whole the tendency is for the construction with the genitive to extend and to become general.

4. COMPOUND PREPOSITIONS

The formation of prepositions is not limited to the groups examined above. A number of primary prepositions are capable of combining with one another or, more frequently, with secondary prepositions, to form new prepositions often of somewhat complex structure. For example:

из-за 'from behind, because of'
из-под 'from underneath'
вслед за 'after'
по отношению к 'in relation to'
несмотря на 'in spite of'
не говоря о 'not to mention'

The case of a noun following a compound preposition is that governed by the final element of the latter. Exceptions are из-за and из-под, which take the genitive.

II. CONJUNCTIONS

The conjunctions, like the prepositions, do not constitute a closed group of words. The dividing line between them and the other parts of speech, particularly the prepositions, the particles and the adverbs, is not clearly defined.

1. PRIMARY CONJUNCTIONS

Within the conjunctions may be distinguished more or less clearly a small number of primary conjunctions, such as:

    и 'and'   да 'and'   а 'and, but'
    но 'but'   и́ли 'or'   и́бо 'for'

2. SECONDARY CONJUNCTIONS

A considerable number of these secondary conjunctions are of pronominal origin, such as:

    что 'that'   как 'as'   чем 'than'
    когда́ 'when'   то́лько 'as soon as'   пока́ 'while'

Others are of various origins:

    е́сли 'if'   е́жели 'if'   хотя́ 'although'
    чуть 'hardly'   едва́ 'hardly'   пусть 'let'

3. COMPOUND CONJUNCTIONS

The conjunctions, particularly those of pronominal origin, may form numerous combinations, either with one another or with the primary prepositions, such as:

           потому́ что, оттого́ что 'because'
           из-за того́ что 'because of the fact that'
           для того́ что 'for the reason that'
           так как 'as, since'
           тогда́ как 'whereas'
           ме́жду тем как 'whereas'
           так что 'so that'

чтóбы 'in order that'
как бы 'however much'
как тóлько 'as soon as'

They may also combine with other words, particularly secondary prepositions and nominal adverbs, to form phrases of considerable complexity, such as:

в видý тогó что 'in view of the fact that'
в сúлу тогó что 'in view of the fact that'
вслéдствие тогó что 'in consequence of the fact that'
по мépe тогó как 'according as'
несмотрá на то что 'in spite of the fact that'
дápoм что 'in spite of the fact that'
подóбно томý как 'just as'
до тех пор покá . . . не 'until'

III. PARTICLES

In addition to the prepositions and conjunctions, the functions of which are clearly defined, there exists a large mass of words of the same, auxiliary, type which give to particular words or entire sentences various shades of meaning, for the most part of a modal character. These particles are of various origins.

The modal particles which form an integral part of the verbal system have already been examined (see p. 239). Besides these, there are a considerable number of particles which are more self-sufficient in respect of their functions, namely:

(1) Particles which indicate the words or thoughts of someone else ('reported direct speech'):

мол, дéскать, де (obsolescent), говорúт (sometimes reduced, when used in this sense, to *grit*):

он, мол, ничегó не знáет 'he says he doesn't know anything'

(2) Emphatic particles:

да́же, уж, и, with the general sense of 'even'
ведь 'after all':

да́же ребёнок поймёт э́то 'even a child could understand that'

же and -то (always enclitic) serve to emphasize the
word they follow:

де́нег-то у него́ и не хвати́ло 'he didn't have enough
money'

(3) Interrogative particles:

ли (see p. 304), ра́зве (when the speaker expects the
answer 'no'), неужѐли (when the speaker hopes to
receive the answer 'no'), бишь (indicating im-
patience at the fact that one has forgotten a word):

ра́зве он у́мер? 'has he really died?'
неужѐли он у́мер? 'can it be that he has died?'
куда́ бишь он уе́хал? 'where was this he went off
to?'

(4) Particles of limitation: лишь, то́лько 'only'.

(5) Particles which express appreciation, whether emo-
tional or logical:

я́кобы, бу́дто-бы 'as if, so-called'
пожа́луй 'I dare say, if you like'
мо́жет быть 'perhaps'
знать 'obviously'
чай 'I think'
аво́сь 'maybe'
небо́сь 'doubtless'

The last four have a colloquial and popular quality.

(6) Particles of introduction and association:

наприме́р 'for example'
зна́чит 'so then, that is to say'

то́-есть 'that is to say'
ста́ло-быть 'so then, consequently'
кста́ти 'by the way, incidentally'
сло́вом 'in a word'
к тому́ же 'moreover'

(7) Particles of comparison, with the general value of 'like' or 'as if' (Lat. *ut ita dicam*):

сло́вно, то́чно, как бу́дто

(8) Particles (used in conversation):
да 'yes'   нет 'no'   спаси́бо 'thank you'

XVI

The Sentence

I. THE SUBJECT

THE subject is normally a noun or a personal pronoun. However, as in most languages, any part of speech may on occasion stand as subject.

The verb may or may not be accompanied by the personal pronoun; in either case the statement, naturally, is a personal one. There is a clear difference in usage between the first and second persons on the one hand and the third person on the other.

1. Subject in First or Second Person

I. INDICATIVE

Although in the present tense the verbal form itself indicates the person, the personal pronoun subject is normally expressed. The rule is, however, less binding than it is in English, and the pronoun may frequently be omitted. This omission is a deviation from the norm; as a general rule its effect is to reinforce the verb and to convey various expressive shades of meaning. The following two lines from Pushkin's *Bronze Horseman* may serve as an example:

Люблю́ тебя́, Петра́ творе́нье,
Люблю́ твой стро́гий, стро́йный вид

'I love you, creation of Peter, I love your stern, shapely aspect'

In the spoken language, which is of its nature more expressive than the written, the omission of the pronoun is at least as frequent as its retention. In dialogue particularly it tends to become the rule:

> Ви́дите ли, сомнева́юсь, что́бы ему́ мо́жно бы́ло помо́чь. — Не счита́ете его́ досто́йным по́мощи? — Пока́ ещё не могу́ сказа́ть

> ' "You see, I doubt whether it's possible to help him." "Don't you think he deserves to be helped?" "I can't say for the moment." '

In replies which consist of the repetition of the verb of the interrogative sentence, it is normal to omit the pronoun:

> По́мните на́шу пе́рвую встре́чу? — Отли́чно по́мню
> ' "Do you remember our first meeting?" "I do very well." '

> Хо́чешь ча́ю? — Хочу́
> ' "Do you want some tea?" "Yes." '

Even the past tense, which requires the expression of the pronoun for the avoidance of ambiguity, may be employed without it in sentences of this type:

> Получи́л ты уже́ отве́т? — Получи́л
> ' "Have you received the reply yet?" "Yes." '

2. IMPERATIVE

In the imperative, unlike the indicative, the use of the verb without the pronoun is normal. Consequently, it is the insertion, not the omission, of the pronoun, which gives the imperative a special expressive shade of meaning which varies according to the context. Speaking very generally, one may say that the pronoun before the verb reinforces the imperative:

> Ты то́лько попро́буй у меня́! 'You just try!'

The effect of the pronoun after the verb, on the other hand, is to soften the imperative:

> не мучьте вы его   'Oh, don't torment him!'

2. Subject in Third Person

Because of the lack of precision of the pronoun of the third person, it may be omitted only in circumstances which preclude all ambiguity. These circumstances are more or less the same as those in which the pronouns of the first and second persons may be omitted in the past tense. For example:

> Он уже проснулся? — Нет, спит ещё ' "Has he woken up yet?" "No, he is still sleeping." '

The omission of the pronoun of the third person plural, where it is not to be understood from the context, gives the statement a force similar to that which is expressed in French by the pronoun 'on' and in German by 'man'. Such statements are often expressed in English by the use of the passive:

> на него смотрят с надеждой 'he is regarded with hope'

The same indeterminate force may also be assumed by other persons, particularly the 2nd pers. sing. (compare the use of 'you' in English). The effect is more colloquial than that of the 3rd pers. pl.:

> сегодня наболтаешь, а завтра раскаиваешься 'today you chatter, but tomorrow you repent'

II. PREDICATE
A. *PERSONAL STATEMENT*
1. Verbal Predicate

The predicate occurs most frequently as some personal form of the verb:

> рыба плывёт 'the fish swims'

The rules for agreement of subject and verb are in general the same as in English.

Only the case of a subject consisting of a numeral or, in general, of a word denoting quantity, presents certain peculiarities. Subjects of this type may have their predicates either in the plural or in the singular. The singular in the past tense takes the neuter form; this latter is, therefore, a construction which has affinities with the impersonal type of construction. The singular tends to be used when the verb is immediately followed by the subject:

> утону́ло (or утону́ли) шесть челове́к 'six people were drowned'
>
> две неде́ли пройду́т (or пройдёт) незаме́тно 'two weeks will pass unnoticed'
>
> блох там оказа́лась (or оказа́лось) у́йма 'it turned out that there were fleas there by the thousand'

The neuter singular must be used with the following words denoting quantity:

> ско́лько 'how much, how many'
> сто́лько 'so much, so many'
> мно́го 'much, many'
> ма́ло 'little, few'
> ско́лько оста́лось де́нег? 'how much money is left?'
> ма́ло люде́й протяну́ло ему́ ру́ку 'only a few people offered to shake his hand'

The same is true for certain approximate estimates:

с деся́ток груш валя́лось под де́ревом 'ten pears or so were lying about under the tree'

2. Non-verbal Predicate

The non-verbal predicate, i.e. the combination of the copula with a complement (noun or adjective) is extremely frequent in Russian.

I. COMPLEMENT IN THE NOMINATIVE

The copula 'to be' is hardly employed except in the past (был) and future (бу́дет). In the present, the copula есть, a form which is valid for all persons (see p. 205), is rare and belongs to the written language. It is sometimes used in definitions:

мысль изречённая есть ложь 'thought uttered is untruth' (TYUTCHEV).

Its use is normal only when the complement is identical with the subject:

де́ньги есть де́ньги 'money is money'

and in the expression:

э́то и есть 'that is what . . . means', as:

э́то и есть война́ 'that's what war means'

As a verb denoting existence, есть 'there is, there are', continues in current use:

в на́ших леса́х есть кабаны́ 'there are wild boars in our forests'

у А́нглии есть флот 'England has a fleet'

In all other cases the copula есть is not expressed, the result of which is the occurrence of purely nominal statements:

а́вгуст жа́ркий ме́сяц 'August is a hot month'

кто вы? — я сто́рож ' "Who are you?" "I am the watchman" '

ли́стья зе́лены 'the leaves are green'

ка́менный ли э́то мост? 'is this a stone bridge?'

дом за́перт 'the house is locked'

In the past and future the use of the copula is obligatory:

ли́стья бу́дут зе́лены 'the leaves will be green'

дом был за́перт 'the house was locked'

The adjective complement is normally in the short form when this form is possible. This is *always* so for the participles passive. The long form, however, tends more and more to be used. In cases where both forms are possible, the temporal or verbal force is stronger in the short form:

я ве́сел 'I am gay' (at the present time)

я весёлый 'I have a gay character'

The adjuncts of the complement tend, naturally, to give it a temporal character and to render the short form preferable:

матро́сы бы́ли пья́ны от во́дки "the sailors were drunk on vodka'

At the beginning of a sentence the adjective complement occurs in the short form:

однообра́зна и грустна́ жизнь ма́ленького челове́ка, и неприхотли́вы его́ ра́дости

'monotonous and mournful is the life of the humble, and modest are their joys'

Adjectives which occur only in fixed phrases are used always in the long form. It is possible to say

генера́л был глух 'the general was deaf'

она́ была́ глуха́ к про́сьбам 'she turned a deaf ear to entreaties' but the long form alone can be used in such expressions, as

глуха́я прови́нция 'a remote province'
глуха́я ночь 'still night'
глуха́я стена́ 'blind wall'
глухо́й согла́сный 'voiceless consonant'

In general, the difference between the long and the short form tends now to lie in meaning rather than in syntax. For the adj. счастли́вый 'happy', for example, the short form is possible only with the original meaning:

де́ти сча́стливы 'the children are happy'

with all other meanings, only the long form can be used:

како́й счастли́вый э́то слу́чай! 'what a lucky chance it is!'
её слёзы счастли́вые 'she weeps from happiness'

Sometimes the difference is very subtle. For 'the water is warm' both вода́ тепла́ and вода́ тёплая may be used; but with an unfavourable meaning (for example, 'too warm for drinking') only the second expression would normally be employed.

2. COMPLEMENT IN THE INSTRUMENTAL

The noun complement may appear also in the instrumental. This occurs only when the copula is expressed, i.e. in the past (был) and future (бу́дет).

Generally speaking, the predicative instrumental indicates a temporary state, while the nominative serves to indicate the permanent state of the subject:

Я — раб, и был рабо́м поко́рным
Прекра́снейшей из всех цари́ц

'I am a slave, and was the humble slave of the fairest of queens' (V. BRYUSOV)

It follows that the adjective complement occurs rarely in the instrumental: the function of the adjective is to qualify the noun apart from any notion of time. Normally, therefore, the instrumental will be encountered only when the context affords definite evidence that the application of the statement is temporary or occasional. For example:

когда́ я был молоды́м 'when I was young'
са́мой споко́йной была́ его́ ло́шадь 'his horse was the calmest of all'

On the other hand, as the noun often indicates action or the relationship between objects, things which are thought of as existing in time, the noun complement is more frequent in the instrumental than in the nominative:

он был не то́лько сотру́дником, но и дру́гом 'he was not only a colleague, but a friend as well'

пе́рвой жено́й инжене́ра была́ англича́нка 'the engineer's first wife was an Englishwoman'

The predicative instrumental in the present without the copula is very rare. It does not occur at all with adjectives; it may be used (instead of the more normal nominative) with nouns denoting occupation and accompanied by an adjunct:

наш сын касси́ром в ба́нке 'our son is cashier in a bank'

The instrumental is much more frequent with certain verbs the specific meaning of which has been weakened and which may be considered as variants of the copula, such as:

стать, станови́ться, сде́латься 'to become'
каза́ться 'to appear to be'
оказа́ться, явля́ться 'to turn out to be'
оста́ться 'to remain'
вы́йти 'to prove to be'

With these verbs, the adjective complement may stand either in the nominative or in the instrumental:

> страна́ стано́вится бедна́ (or бе́дной) 'the country is becoming poor'
>
> он оста́лся недово́лен (or недово́льным) 'he remained dissatisfied'
>
> по́весть вы́шла скве́рная (or скве́рной) 'the story turned out to be a poor one'

With the same verbs, nouns regularly go into the instrumental:

> вероя́тно он ока́жется моше́нником 'he'll probably turn out to be a swindler'
>
> полко́вник каза́лся мальчи́шкой 'the colonel looked a mere boy'

3. OTHER FORMS OF THE COMPLEMENT

Apart from the nominative and instrumental of nouns and adjectives, the complement may, less frequently, assume the most various forms. The copula may be either expressed (past and future) or omitted (present):

(1) noun with preposition:

> Была́ без ра́дости любо́вь,
> Разлу́ка бу́дет без печа́ли
> 'Love was without joy, separation will be without sorrow'
>
> го́сти не в ду́хе 'the visitors are out of humour'
> э́тот чуда́к не от ми́ра сего́ 'this crank belongs to another world'

(2) Noun in the genitive:

> он был ло́вкости необыча́йной 'he was a man of extraordinary skill'
> вы мои́х лет 'you are my age'

(3) Adverb:

> дом его́ был недалеко́ 'his house was not far away'

как вы? 'how are you?'
здоро́вье ничего́ 'the health is not bad'

4. OMISSION OF THE VERBAL PREDICATE

One of the characteristics of the Russian verbal predicate is the readiness with which it may be omitted when either the other elements of the statement or the preceding statement make such omission possible. This occurs in the spoken language:

я к вам с про́сьбой 'I have come to you with a request'
уж я его́ 'I'll show him!'
соба́ка за за́йцем, тот от неё 'the dog dashed after the hare; the hare raced away'
как любо́вник, так топо́р, и бо́льше ничего́, и весь разгово́р 'if your wife has a lover you take an axe, and that's all there is about it, and there's nothing more to be said' (GLEB USPENSKY).

It is sometimes difficult to tell whether a verb of complete predication is to be understood or whether what is involved is a nominal statement, as for example in the following lines from Lermontov:

Под ним струя́ светле́й лазу́ри,
Над ним луч со́лнца золото́й
'Beneath it is the current brighter than azure, above it the golden ray of the sun'

and in:

спра́ва лес, сле́ва река́ 'on the right a forest, on the left a river'

Whatever be the conception behind them, both types furnish many instances of sentences in which no verb is expressed.

B. *IMPERSONAL STATEMENT*

Impersonal statements are very frequent in Russian. The predicate, which is their only essential element, may be expressed by various means.

1. Verbal Predicate

Whatever be the nature of the verbal predicate, it occurs in the third person singular, and in the neuter if it is in the past tense. There are several types of impersonal verbal predicate.

I. IMPERSONAL VERBS

These are almost exclusively verbs denoting natural phenomena and not employed otherwise than impersonally. They exist, therefore, only in the third person singular and the infinitive:

> светáет 'day is breaking'
> бýдет морóзить 'there will be a frost'
> моросúло 'a drizzle was falling'

2. PERSONAL VERBS USED IMPERSONALLY

Many personal verbs are capable of being used impersonally in the third person singular:

> из коридóра дýет 'there is a draught from the corridor'
> самолёт качнýло 'the aeroplane was bumped about'
> у меня́ в прáвом ýхе звенúт 'I have a ringing in my right ear'
> пáхнет винóм 'there is a smell of wine'

If the agent is indicated, it is expressed in the instrumental case:

> лýжу вы́сушило вéтром 'the puddle was dried up by the wind'

поля залило водой 'the fields were flooded'

3. VERBS IN -СЯ

These are non-reflexive verbs which may be employed with -ся in impersonal expressions:

нам не сидится дома 'we can't bear to stay at home' (for other examples, see p. 249)

4. IMPERSONAL USE OF THE PAST PARTICIPLE PASSIVE

The verb in such cases is normally transitive:

ему было приказано явиться утром 'he was ordered to report in the morning'
кругом насорено 'there is dirt everywhere'

With certain intransitive verbs the usage has a definitely popular tone:

много было хожено 'we did a lot of walking'

5. NEGATIVE STATEMENT

Personal statements with the verb 'to be' employed as a verb of existence become impersonal when negatived; the subject goes into the genitive. The negation of есть is rendered by the invariable word нет (in colloquial language often in the form нету):

в доме нет отопления 'there is no heating in the house' (cf. в доме есть отопление)
на вокзале никого ещё не было 'there was nobody at the station yet'

The same construction is employed with a number of other verbs:

с двух часов не проехало ни одного автомобиля 'no car has gone by since two o'clock'
в его смехе не слышалось насмешки 'no note of derision was to be perceived in his laugh'

Negative statements involving the past participle passive belong to the same category:

> бáбьей глýпости предéла не положéно 'there is no limit to women's stupidity' (OSTROVSKY)
>
> о расхóдах ничегó нé было скáзано 'nothing was said on the subject of expenses'

6. INFINITIVE

Statements in which the infinitive is employed as the principal verb are a peculiarity of Russian syntax. The force of such statements is various. Where the agent is expressed, it goes into the dative:

> вам ходи́ть 'your turn to play' (at cards)
>
> кудá девáться от дуракóв? 'where can one escape from fools?'
>
> быть бедé 'a misfortune is bound to happen'
>
> не видáть тебé Москвы́ как свои́х ушéй 'you'll no more see Moscow than you'll see your own ears'

2. Non-Verbal Predicate

This type of impersonal statement is extremely frequent in Russian. The agent, when expressed, goes into the dative. The predicate is a word which has the form either of an adverb in -o or of a noun (unless it is impossible to classify it as a particular part of speech). However, the terms 'adverb' and 'noun' are valid only from the morphological or historical point of view; the syntactical value of the non-verbal predicate is in reality quite different.

I. ADVERBS IN -O

Forms in -o occur frequently as predicates:

> лéтом жáрко 'it is hot in the summer'
>
> что вам угóдно? 'what do you require?'
>
> дéтям вéсело игрáть 'the children enjoy themselves playing'

The forms in -o often have no connexion with the adverbs, and are employed only predicatively:

> на него́ мо́жно положи́ться 'one can rely on him'
> парохо́ду на́до бы́ло верну́ться 'the ship had to turn back'
> по́лно врать-то 'don't tell any more yarns'

2. NOUNS AND OTHER WORDS

Some of these words are only occasionally employed predicatively:

> пора́ бы́ло уходи́ть 'it was time to go'
> охо́та вам спо́рить 'what pleasure do you find in arguing?'
> швейца́ру бы́ло лень отвори́ть дверь 'the doorman was too lazy to open the door'

Other words are employed only predicatively:

> не жаль вам свое́й мо́лодости? 'do you not regret your youth?'
> его́ нельзя́ ви́деть 'he cannot be seen'
> не́зачем бы́ло туда́ и е́хать 'there was no reason to go there at all'

Cf. also such idioms as:

> мне не до шу́ток 'I'm in no mood for joking'

III. SECONDARY ELEMENTS OF THE SENTENCE

I. DIRECT OBJECT

The direct object is expressed, as in most languages, by the accusative (see p. 159):

> я ви́жу доро́гу 'I see the road'
> рабо́чие пьют пи́во 'the workmen drink beer'

In negative statements this accusative is replaced by the genitive, provided that the purpose of the negation is, as it usually is, to preclude the action of the sentence and to suppress the transitivity of the verb:

> я не ви́жу доро́ги 'I don't see any road'
> рабо́чие не пи́ли пи́ва 'the workmen did not drink beer'

This genitive is akin to the genitive of separation (see p. 162).

The genitive may be employed even in constructions in which the direct object depends not immediately on a negative verb but on an infinitive dependent on a negative verb:

> он не хо́чет слу́шать му́зыки 'he does not want to listen to music'

However, in this type of sentence the accusative is more usual.

If the negation does not preclude the action of the sentence the verb continues to be transitive and takes the accusative:

> я не люблю́ свою́ тётку 'I do not like my aunt'
> не бей несча́стное живо́тное 'do not beat the poor animal'

The retention of the accusative takes place properly only with individualized direct objects, usually denoting persons and animals.

The co-existence of these two types of construction gives rise to a certain confusion, and it is not uncommon to find the accusative used instead of the genitive in sentences of the former type.

2. EXTENSIONS OF THE VERB

The system of extensions of the verb in Russian has no unusual features. As in many other languages, they are expressed either by the oblique cases of the noun, with or without preposition, or by adverbs. The chapters on the values of the cases, on the adverb and on the preposition will give an idea of the nature of extensions of the verb in Russian.

IV. WORD-ORDER

In English, which is a language almost without declension, the word-order has syntactical functions which are responsible for its relative rigidity. In Russian the syntactical relations are expressed by the inflexional forms, and the word-order, being freed from syntactical tasks, acquires thereby a great degree of flexibility. This flexibility is not, however, arbitrary but serves to produce important stylistic effects. In certain exceptional cases it may, as in English, express syntactical relations.

1. The Ordinary Sentence

The principle of word-order in Russian may be expressed as follows: *there exists a traditional word-order in which the value of the elements of the sentence is neutralized to the maximum; any modification of this order throws into relief the word which has left its usual place.* As this attribution of emphasis is occasioned in most cases by the whole course of the narrative, the sentence in which the order of words has been inverted is in most cases not a completely independent sentence: its full force can be comprehended only if one is acquainted with what precedes or, more rarely, with what follows, in other words, with the reasons for the inversion. In certain cases, few in number, the order of words may be determined by the requirements of rhythm or by stylistic preference. It is to be observed that non-motivated inversion is readily admitted in verse.

In the following examination of the subject, the loss of

independence will be taken as understood and the rhyth-
mic aspect of the sentence will be ignored. Only the attribution of emphasis to particular words, therefore, will be
dealt with.

I. SUBJECT AND PREDICATE

In the 'neutral' word-order the subject with its extension
comes first, the predicate with its extension second:

> бле́дный солда́т в дли́нной шине́ли не спеша́
> указа́л мне доро́гу в го́род
> 'a pale soldier in a long overcoat unhurriedly told me·
> the way to the town'

If the subject is placed at the end, it is thrown into
relief:

> не спеша́ указа́л мне доро́гу в го́род бле́дный солда́т
> в дли́нной шине́ли
> 'it was a pale soldier in a long overcoat who, &c.'

Cf. also:

> счетово́д оказа́лся уби́йцей
> 'the accountant turned out to be a murderer'

as against:

> уби́йцей оказа́лся счетово́д
> 'the murderer turned out to be the accountant'

The shift of the subject in the first example also brings
out the value of the adjective and the adjectival phrase
which accompany it: the paleness and the dress of the
soldier are thereby emphasized. These same elements may,
however, be emphasized without any change of position of
the subject; it is sufficient for them to shift their position in
relation to the subject (see below).

On the other hand, the fact that the predicate comes at
the beginning of the sentence does not usually throw the
emphasis on to it; the shift of the predicate serves usually

only to indicate the dependence of the sentence on the preceding or following elements. Thus inversion of this type is obligatory with verbs of speaking which introduce direct speech:

смотри́те — вскри́кнула она́ ' "look!" she cried'

Cf. also the use of the definite article in the translation of уби́йцей оказа́лся счетово́д, above ('the murderer', whose identity had already been discussed).

In general, Russian is disinclined to emphasize the verb otherwise than by the intonation. For the same reason, except in statements consisting of only two elements, such as

со́лнце гре́ет 'the sun warms'

it is very unusual for a verb to occupy the last place in the sentence. In the first example in this section such a position of the verb would be entirely unnatural.

The fact that the subject usually occupies the first position in the sentence induces us, in such a sentence as

купа́ться прия́тно 'bathing is pleasant'

to regard the infinitive as the subject and the form in -o as the predicate. Inversion, by which the infinitive takes the second place, turns it into the predicate and renders the statement impersonal:

прия́тно купа́ться 'it is pleasant to bathe'

This is one of the few cases in which the order of words alone determines the value of the elements of the sentence. The position of the substantivized adjective and, on occasion, that of the direct object, constitute the other cases.

2. SECONDARY ELEMENTS OF THE SENTENCE

(a) Words dependent upon nouns

The attributive adjective precedes the noun except in special cases, as, for example, when the adjective assumes the function of a proper name:

Ива́н Гро́зный 'Ivan the Terrible'
Пе́тька Лы́сый 'Bald Peter'

Inversion for the purpose of emphasis is possible but rare. It occurs principally in two cases:

(1) when the adjective qualifies a noun in apposition:

он не доверя́л отцу́, челове́ку легкомы́сленному 'he did not confide in his father, who was an irresponsible man'

(2) in enumerations:

у́лицы напо́лнились солда́тами англи́йскими, америка́нскими и францу́зскими 'the streets filled up with British, American, and French soldiers'

In such cases the adjective tends to assume the character of a noun in apposition.

The regularity with which the adjective precedes the noun is the only means of distinguishing between the adjective proper and the substantivized adjective:

больно́й ни́щий 'a sick beggar'
ни́щий больно́й 'a destitute invalid'

Most possessive and demonstrative pronouns take no stress and may either precede or follow the noun to which they refer:

моя́ жена́ and жена́ моя́ 'my wife'
с его́ судьбо́й and с судьбо́й его́ 'with his destiny'
э́тому до́му and до́му э́тому 'to this house'

Adjectival phrases tend to follow the nouns which they qualify. This is their normal, and in most cases their only possible position. The same applies to the pronoun кото́рый in the sense of 'whose':

солда́т, шине́ль кото́рого . . . 'the soldier whose overcoat . . .'

It is unusual for an adjectival phrase to precede the

noun which it qualifies; to do so it must be in the genitive case:

> высо́кого ро́ста солда́т 'a soldier of lofty stature'

is possible as well as the more normal солда́т высо́кого ро́ста.

It is therefore impossible, in the first example of the preceding section, to interchange the positions of the adjective and the adjectival phrase qualifying солда́т. They may, however, be placed in *apposition* (which requires a special intonation). For this they must be grouped together either before or after the noun:

> бле́дный, в дли́нной шине́ли, солда́т
> or солда́т, бле́дный, в дли́нной шине́ли

The use of apposition entails the attribution of special emphasis. Apposition is always possible for the adjective; an adjectival phrase, on the other hand, is never placed in apposition before the noun except when it is accompanied by an adjective, as in the example quoted. One cannot say: в дли́нной шине́ли, солда́т. Similarly, the expression доро́гу в го́род in the predicate group does not admit of any transposition of its component elements.

The adverb, at any rate when it ends in -o or -и, normally precedes the adjective:

> осо́бенно у́мный 'particularly intelligent'

Inversion intensifies the force of the adverb:

> у́мный осо́бенно 'intelligent in a particular way'

The cardinal numerals precede the word to which they refer. If they follow it, it is to indicate an approximate number:

> де́сять рубле́й 'ten roubles'
> рубле́й де́сять 'ten roubles or so'

This inversion is employed only when the numeral is in the nom.-acc. or in the gen. with negation.

(b) Words dependent upon verbs

The *direct* or *indirect object* follows the verb: . . . указа́л мне доро́гу. . . . . Inversion throws the emphasis onto the direct object. At the same time it normally makes necessary a shift of the subject to the end of the sentence:

> доро́гу в го́род не спеша́ указа́л мне бле́дный солда́т в дли́нной шине́ли

This shift prevents the verb from coming at the end of the sentence, a position which, as has been seen, is not normal in Russian.

The order 'subject–verb–direct object' becomes obligatory and thereby acquires syntactical force whenever the form of the direct object (acc.) coincides with that of the subject (nom.), that is, whenever the direct object is not a fem. sing. or a masc. sing. denoting a person or an animal. Thus, in Marx's formula

> бытие́ определя́ет созна́ние 'being determines consciousness'

the positions of the two nouns could not be reversed without a reversal of the meaning of the sentence.

In impersonal statements the direct or indirect object precedes the verb:

> больно́го лихора́дит 'the patient is feverish'
> автомоби́ль опроки́нуло 'the car overturned'
> де́тям бы́ло ска́зано 'the children were told'

Inversion of this order indicates that the sentence depends on what precedes, exactly as with personal statement.

Personal pronouns if unstressed may either follow or precede the verb (cf. what has been said of the possessive and demonstrative pronouns): указа́л мне and мне указа́л. Even in the case of the pronoun subject, inversion of the type иду́ я 'I am going' serves only to point out the existence of a whole of which this statement is a part; the pronoun я is no more emphasized than it is in the usual form of the expression, я иду́.

The *adverbial extension* of the verb, as in English, possesses a considerable degree of independence in relation to the verb. In the example quoted, the gerund не спеша́ might be placed either before or after the verb. It might also come after мне or even at the beginning of the sentence: не спеша́, бле́дный солда́т. . . . The greater its distance from the verb the more the adverb is thrown into relief.

(c) *Negation*

The negative particle in Russian immediately precedes the word to which it refers. It is associated with it so closely that, when it does not refer to the verb, the sentence does not become negative:

> по́езд не опозда́л 'the train was not late'
>
> по́езд опозда́л не на де́сять, а на два́дцать мину́т 'the train was not ten minutes but twenty minutes late'
>
> его́ воспи́тывали не как короля́ 'they brought him up not in the style of a king'

The difference between the following two sentences is to be noted:

> он не пое́хал в ту сто́рону 'he did not go in that direction'
>
> он пое́хал не в ту сто́рону 'he went in the wrong direction'

(d) *Enclave*

Unstressed particles or other words which are capable of losing or attenuating their stress (adverbs, pronouns, &c.) may be inserted into combinations of words which might have appeared indissoluble. This phenomenon, characteristic of Russian, may be called 'enclave'. Enclave is a feature of the spoken language.

The following are examples of the enclave:

Петра́ же Вели́кого э́то не останови́ло
'however this did not stop Peter the Great'

Анна-то Ива́новна и не заме́тила
'but Anna Ivanovna just didn't notice'

э́то два́дцать пять отсю́да киломе́тров
'it is twenty-five kilometres from here'

девяностоле́тний почти́ стари́к
'an old man getting on for ninety'

в Сове́тском, ка́жется, Сою́зе
'in the Soviet Union, I think'

дешёвый зо́нтик с сере́бряною впро́чем ру́чкой
'a cheap umbrella, though it had a silver handle'

я зайду́ перед са́мым, пожа́луй, обе́дом
'I'll look in probably just before lunch'

душе́вно, так сказа́ть, больно́й
'a mental invalid, one might say'

2. Questions

It need hardly be said that in these expressive sentences an essential part is played by intonation. Sometimes only the intonation can indicate which word carries the weight of the interrogation, and the construction of the sentence is then not different from that which has just been studied.

There is also, however, a word-order proper to this kind of sentence: the emphatic word is placed first. This special word order does not suppress the appropriate intonation:

парохо́д войдёт за́втра в га́вань?
'will a *ship* come into the harbour tomorrow?'

войдёт за́втра парохо́д в га́вань?
'will the ship *come into* the harbour tomorrow?'

за́втра войдёт парохо́д в га́вань?
'will the ship come into the harbour *tomorrow*?', &c.

The addition of the particle ли to the word to which the interrogation refers removes any uncertainty that may exist as to the object of the latter:

за́втра ли войдёт парохо́д в га́вань?

This usage is literary in character, except in the case of indirect questions subordinate to a negative or interrogative statement:

я не зна́ю, войдёт ли за́втра парохо́д в га́вань
'I don't know whether the ship will come into the harbour tomorrow'

What is involved in this case is not the word-order but the syntax of subordination.

V. PUNCTUATION

Russian has the same punctuation marks as English and employs them generally in the same way. The usage is the same in both languages for the following punctuation marks: full stop, semi-colon, colon, question mark, exclamation mark, points of suspension, brackets, inverted commas.

The use of the comma and the dash, on the other hand, shows certain peculiarities. These alone will be examined here.

1. Comma

I. GENERAL OBSERVATIONS

In many cases the use of the comma is the same in both languages, particularly in enumerations and in isolating independent elements of the sentence, such as the names of persons addressed, words in apposition, interjections, particles, isolated words and phrases, interpolations, &c. These cases will not be examined here. The difference in usage comes out most clearly in the general use of the comma between clauses of the same sentence, whether these be subordinate or co-ordinate. If the subordinate clause is inserted into the principal clause, it is always enclosed between two commas.

2. SUBORDINATE CLAUSES INTRODUCED BY CON-JUNCTIONS

The comma is *obligatory* between the subordinate clause and the principal clause:

> я приду́ ве́чером, е́сли успе́ю
> 'I shall come in the evening if I have time'

> когда́ наступи́ла ночь, бегле́ц был уже́ далеко́
> 'when night fell, the fugitive was already far off'

It should be noted in particular that the conjunction что 'that' is *always* preceded by a comma:

> он уви́дел, что оши́бся
> 'he saw that he had made a mistake'

With compound conjunctions of which the second element is что the comma usually stands before the entire conjunction; it may also, however, stand immediately before что in order to emphasize the idea of cause, purpose or time expressed by the subordinate clause, as for example:

> лю́ди умира́ли, потому́ что была́ эпиде́мия
> 'people were dying because there was an epidemic'

> лю́ди умира́ли потому́, что была́ эпиде́мия
> 'people were dying for the reason that there was an epidemic' (and not for any other reason)

3. SUBORDINATE CLAUSES INTRODUCED BY INTERROGATIVE-RELATIVE PRONOUNS AND ADVERBS

The comma is *obligatory* between the two clauses:

скажи́те, что мне де́лать
'tell me what I am to do'

кто был счастли́вей, был умне́й
'he who was happiest was wisest' (Boratynsky)

дере́вня, где скуча́л Евге́ний, была́ преле́стный уголо́к
'the village where Eugene suffered boredom was a charming spot' (Pushkin)

я смотре́л на ме́сяц, кото́рый ме́дленно поднима́лся над дома́ми
'I looked at the moon, which was slowly rising above the houses'

стару́ха приказа́ла тем го́лосом, каки́м говоря́т то́лько с подчинёнными
'the old woman had given the order in the tone of voice which is employed only with subordinates'

The interrogative-relative pronouns may stand not at the very beginning of the subordinate clauses for the reason that they are preceded by prepositions or nouns; the comma then comes before these prepositions or nouns as the case may be:

он не узна́л, в чём его́ обвиня́ют
'he did not find out what he was accused of'

ви́дите го́ру, у подно́жья кото́рой мы остано́вимся?
'do you see the mountain at the foot of which we shall stop?'

4. PHRASES INTRODUCED BY PARTICIPLES

These are closely related to relative clauses introduced by который, какой (in the nominative, accusative, and genitive with negation), and are often interchangeable with them. They are preceded and followed by commas. Thus, the relative clause in the fourth example quoted in the preceding section could be replaced by the equivalent participial expression:

> я смотрел на месяц, медленно поднимающийся (or поднимавшийся, see p. 235) над домами
> 'I looked at the moon, which was slowly rising above the houses'

> перед ним расстилалась бесконечная степь, освещённая солнцем
> 'before him stretched the boundless steppe in the full light of the sun'

5. PHRASES INTRODUCED BY GERUNDS

These phrases perform the same functions as adverbial clauses. They are separated by commas from the rest of the sentence.

> сын смутился, не найдя ответа
> 'the son, finding nothing to say in reply, became confused'

> прощаясь, она расплакалась
> 'when saying goodbye she burst into tears'

6. CO-ORDINATE CLAUSES

Co-ordinate clauses connected by conjunctions such as и, да, а, но, или, &c., are separated by commas; a comma must therefore be inserted between two clauses with different subjects and connected by и:

> хозяин скрылся, и никто этого не заметил
> 'the master of the house had disappeared and nobody had noticed the fact'

суда́ стоя́ли на я́коре, и ча́йки лета́ли над водо́й
'the ships were riding at anchor and gulls were flying over the water'

If, however, the two co-ordinate clauses have an element in common, the comma is not employed:

в порту́ стоя́ли суда́ на я́коре и ча́йки лета́ли над водо́й
'in the harbour the ships were riding at anchor and gulls were flying over the water'

Again, the comma is not inserted if the conjunction и unites two subordinate clauses:

он успе́л лишь уви́деть, что игроки́ вы́шли на по́ле, что им принесли́ мяч и что игра́ начала́сь
'he only had time to observe that the players had gone out onto the field, that they had been brought the ball and that the game had begun'

2. Dash

I. GENERAL OBSERVATIONS

The use of the dash in Russian is much more widespread than in English. It is sometimes nothing more than a substitute for the comma, brackets, or the colon, particularly when used to indicate apposition and parenthesis:

Ива́н Петро́вич — владе́лец велосипе́да — бро́сил-ся вперёд
'Ivan Petrovich, the owner of the bicycle, rushed forward'

In such cases the dash may be combined with a comma:

вот тут то́лько, — да́йте-ка каранда́ш, — не дово́ль-но си́льно поло́жены те́ни
'but in this place—give me the pencil a minute—the shading is not deep enough' (Turgenev)

There are, however, certain cases in which the use of the dash is traditional. At the same time the rules governing its use are far from being as definite and strict as in the case of the comma. Generally speaking, the dash is employed to indicate a more pronounced pause than the comma.

2. NOMINAL STATEMENTS

In a nominal statement in which the copula is not expressed, the dash is used to separate the predicate (complement) from the subject. It serves, so to speak, as substitute for the copula:

> ваш худо́жник — италья́нец
> 'your painter is an Italian'

> война́ — э́то коне́ц всему́
> 'war means the end of everything'

Personal pronouns are not separated from the predicate by a dash:

> он италья́нец
> 'he is an Italian'

Care should be taken not to confuse the dash with the hyphen, which indicates mere apposition:

> ваш худо́жник-италья́нец
> 'your Italian painter' (lit. 'your painter the Italian')

3. STATEMENTS WITH VERB OMITTED

The dash indicates the pause due to the omission of the verb:

> я бро́сился к две́ри, он — к окну́
> 'I rushed to the door, he to the window'

4. CO-ORDINATION INSTEAD OF SUBORDINATION

Frequently in the colloquial style two co-ordinate principal clauses without conjunction are employed where

logically a principal and a subordinate clause might have
been expected. This construction occurs usually in conditional sentences. Normally such clauses are separated by a
dash:

> он засмеётся — все хохо́чут
> 'if he laughs they all guffaw' (PUSHKIN)

> муж и́з дому — жена́ в слёзы
> 'as soon as the husband leaves the house, the wife
> bursts into tears'

5. RESUMPTION OF ENUMERATIONS

The dash sometimes precedes a word of general value,
such as всё, никто́, ничто́, всегда́, везде́, никогда́, when employed to resume an enumeration or to sum up a situation:

> ни сла́ва, ни бога́тство, ни почёт — ничто́ его́ уже́
> не привлека́ло
> 'neither fame nor wealth nor honour—nothing
> attracted him any more'

> он дилета́нт — и всё тут!
> 'he is a dilettante, and that's all there is about it'
> (TURGENEV)

6. DIRECT SPEECH

In Russian, as in French, direct speech is indicated not
by inverted commas, but by a dash.

The sentence meaning 'said he', or something similar,
if it is inserted into the direct speech, is preceded and
followed by a dash:

> — Я и говорю́, са́мое лу́чшее держа́ть его́ в ви́нном
> по́гребе — пробаси́л генера́л. — Увести́ пле́нника.
> ' "That's what I say: the best thing would be to keep
> him in the wine-cellar", the General said in a
> booming voice. "Take the prisoner away." ' (A. N.
> TOLSTOY)

If the direct speech contains a quotation of someone's actual words or thoughts, these are indicated by inverted commas as in English:

> — Проходи́ла сейча́с ми́мо вас, поду́мала: "Дай зайду́ к нему́."

'I was passing by your house just now and I thought to myself, "I think I'll call on him." ' (Dostoevsky, Подросток)

BIBLIOGRAPHY

The following list comprises only a selection of essential works

BIBLIOGRAPHY

B. O. UNBEGAUN, *A Bibliographical Guide to the Russian Language.* Oxford, 1953. Pp. xiv+174 (with the collaboration of J. S. G. Simmons). A selected bibliography with commentary covering 1,073 works.

GENERAL DESCRIPTIONS OF THE LANGUAGE

В. В. ВИНОГРАДОВ, *Русский язык (Грамматическое учение о слове).* Москва-Ленинград, 1947. Pp. 784. The most penetrating and complete analysis of literary Russian.

Л. А. БУЛАХОВСКИЙ, *Курс русского литературного языка,* том I, 5-ое переработанное издание. Киев, 1952. Pp. 446. A completely up to date description of the literary language, and the most balanced work of its type in existence.

А. А. ШАХМАТОВ, *Очерк современного русского литературного языка,* 4-ое издание. Москва, 1941, 288 pages. While devoted mainly to phonology and morphology, this work deals also with the Church Slavonic element in Russian.

W. K. MATTHEWS, *The Structure and Development of Russian.* Cambridge, 1953. Pp. 225. A description of the language, including dialects and history, which is too short to be wholly successful.

GRAMMARS

The most complete grammar is that published by the Academy of Sciences of the U.S.S.R. It is a collective work:

Грамматика русского языка. Том I: Фонетика и морфология. Том II: Синтаксис, часть 1–2. Москва, 1952–4. Pp. 720, 703, 444. [A corrected re-issue began publication in 1960].

Other good grammars are:

ANDRÉ MAZON, *Grammaire de la langue russe,* troisième édition, revue et corrigée. Paris, 1949. Pp. 301 (*Collection de grammaires de l'Institut d'Études Slaves,* V).

ERICH BERNEKER, *Russische Grammatik,* fünfte verbesserte Auflage von Max Vasmer. Berlin 1947. Pp. 155 (*Sammlung Göschen,* 66).

Р. Кошутић, *Граматика руског језика*, I, A (Phonology). Петро-
град, 1919. Pp. lvi+512; II (Morphology). Београд, 1914.
Pp. xvi+276. Although somewhat out of date, this Serbian
grammar is still useful, particularly for phonology.

PHONOLOGY

S. C. BOYANUS, *Russian Pronunciation* . . . together with a *Russian
Phonetic Reader*. London, 1955. Pp. xi+122+vii+200. A brief
but complete description of the literary pronunciation; intonation is also treated.

ORTHOGRAPHY

А. Б. ШАПИРО, *Русское правописание*. Москва, 1951. Pp. 200. The
most convenient work to consult on Russian orthography.

Я. К. ГРОТ, *Спорные вопросы русского правописания от Петра Вели:ого
доныне* (in his Филологические разыскания, 4-ое издание.
С.-Петербург, 1899, pp. 469–869). The most detailed work on
the principles and history of Russian orthography.

А. Б. ШАПИРО, *Основы русской пунктуации*. Москва, 1955. Pp. 398.

SYNTAX

А. А. ШАХМАТОВ, *Синтаксис русского языка*, издание второе. Ленинград, 1941. Pp. 620. The value of this posthumous work, which
is not a convenient reference book, lies in the immense number
of examples which it contains.

А. М. ПЕШКОВСКИЙ, *Русский синтаксис в научном освещении*, 6-ое
издание. Москва, 1938. Pp. 452. The documentation is less
rich than in Shakhmatov's work, but the theoretical portion is
fuller (any edition, beginning with the third, may be consulted).

DICTIONARIES

The Academy of Sciences has published a series of Russian dictionaries, beginning in the eighteenth century. The old editions are
out of date (1789–94, 1806–22, 1847, 1868); the editions of the late
nineteenth and early twentieth centuries were not completed. The
most recent (and not the best) edition is:

Словарь современного русского литературного языка, I–IX (А–пнуть),
Москва–Ленинград, 1950–9. [In progress.]

It is, accordingly, necessary to consult other dictionaries:

В. И. Даль, *Толковый словарь живого великорусского языка*, 4-ое
исправленное и значительно дополненное издание, I–IV.
С.-Петербург-Москва, 1912–14. The third edition does not
differ from the fourth; the first two editions are to be avoided.
Offset editions have been produced in Tokyo in 1934, and in
Paris in 1954. A very rich dictionary, both literary and dialectal.

Толковый словарь русского языка, под редакцией Д. Н. Ушакова,
I–IV. Москва, 1935–40. There are two offset editions made in
1948, one in the U.S.S.R., the other in the U.S.A. This is the
most complete and reliable dictionary of the literary Russian
language of the last 150 years; the stylistic value of the word is
always indicated.

С. И. Ожегов, *Словарь русского языка*, 3-ье издание. Москва, 1953.
Pp. 848. Excellent for rapid reference. Gives phraseology, but
without quotations from authors. New edition in the press.

HISTORY OF THE LANGUAGE

А. И. Соболевский, *Лекции по истории русского языка*, издание 4-ое.
Москва, 1907. Pp. 309. Although out of date and incomplete,
this work gives a great number of examples.

Л. А. Булаховский, *Курс русского литературного языка*, том II:
Исторический комментарий, 5-ое исправленное и дополненное
издание. Киев, 1958. Pp. 488. A history of Russian with reference
to the modern literary language; the only work which gives the
history of the syntactical forms.

П. Я. Черных, *Историческая грамматика русского языка*. Краткий
очерк, изд. 2-ое. Москва, 1954. Pp. 336. A short, and generally
reliable historical grammar.

П. С. Кузнецов, *Историческая грамматика русского языка*. Морфология. Москва, 1953. Pp. 306. A correct historical morphology, but almost devoid of examples.

HISTORY OF THE LITERARY LANGUAGE

Г. Винокур, *Русский язык: исторический очерк*. Москва, 1945. Pp.
190. 'A brief résumé of the evolution of literary Russian, illustrated by a happy selection of texts. There is a French translation
of this work: G. Vinokur, *La Langue russe*. Paris, 1947. Pp. 153
(*Bibliothèque russe de l'Institut d'Études Slaves*, XXII).

В. В. Виноградов, *Очерки по истории русского литературного языка
XVII–XIX* вв. Москва, 1938. Pp. 448. An offset edition of

this work was produced at Leyden in 1949. The only real history of literary Russian which is based upon abundant documentation.

Л. А. Булаховский, *Русский литературный язык первой половины XIX века*, I–II. Киев, 1941–8. Pp. 452, 467. There is a second edition: vol. I, Kiev, 1957; vol. II, Moscow, 1954. A rich store of the forms of literary Russian of the Pushkin period.

ETYMOLOGICAL AND HISTORICAL DICTIONARIES

Max Vasmer, *Russisches etymologisches Wörterbuch*, I–III. Heidelberg, 1953–8. Pp. xlviii+712, 712, vii+697. The completion of this excellent dictionary has made the following work almost valueless:

А. Преображенский, *Этимологический словарь русского языка*, выпуск 1–15 (А–сулея). Москва, 1910–16. Pp. ххх+674+vi+416. The final portion, in which there are several gaps, was published in the *Труды Института русского языка*, I, Москва-Ленинград, 1949, pp. 5–144. The whole work has been reproduced in an offset edition: A. G. Preobrazhensky, *Etymological Dictionary of the Russian Language*. New York, Columbia University Press, 1951. There is also an offset edition published in Moscow in 1958.

Reference may also be made to

И. И. Срезневский, *Материалы для словаря древне-русского языка по письменным памятникам*, I–III, Дополнения. С.-Петербург, 1893–1912. This dictionary covers the period from the eleventh to the fifteenth centuries and does not except in rare cases go beyond it. Even within these limits it is far from complete. There are two offset editions of this dictionary, published in Graz, 1955–6, and in Moscow, 1958.

DIALECTOLOGY

Р. И. Аванесов, *Очерки русской диалектологии*, часть I. Москва, 1949. Pp. 335. With the publication of the second part, this will be the best documented work on Russian dialectology.

П. С. Кузнецов, *Русская диалектология*, изд. 2-ое. Москва, 1954. Pp. 156. A handy first introduction to Russian dialectology.

INDEX

Abandoned act, 241-2.

Abbreviations, 93-94.

Abstract nouns, 77-80.

Accusative, 31, 40, 45, 64, 159, 268-70.

Accusative in negative statements, 295.

Adjectives (short form), 97-110.

Adverbs, 147-57, 289-90.

Alphabet, 1-3.

Alternation:
é/ё, 26-27.
o/á, 27, 220.
и/e, 28, 196.
ы/о, 28, 196.
consonantal, 23-26.
in aspectual pairs, 216.
in verbs, 189-91, 198-9, 200-1.
vocalic, 26-28.

Animate nouns, 31, 40, 45, 64.

Apposition, 300.

Arbitrary act, 238-9.

Aspect, 165, 206-28.

Aspectual pairs, 210-25.

Assimilation of palatalization, 14.

Assimilation of sonority, 13-14.

Attributive adjective, 298-300.

Augmentative adjectives, 118.

Augmentative nouns, 87.

бы, 240-1.

было (modal word), 241-2.

быть, 205.

бывало (modal word), 241.

Cardinal numerals, 136-43.

Cases (system of), 30-31.

Chancery language, xxiv-xxv.

Church Slavonic, xxiv-xxviii, 253, 256, 258, 262.

Collective nouns, 80.

Collective numerals, 143-5.

Comma, 304-8.

Comparative, 104-8.

Compound adjectives, 118-21.

Compound nouns, 89-94.

Compound prepositions, 276.

Concrete nouns, 81-82.

Conditional, 240.

Conjunctions, 277-8.

Consonants, 6-15, 23-26.
hard, 7-13.
soft, 7-13.
voiced, 7.
voiceless, 7.

Copula, 285-90.

Cyrillic alphabet, xxiv-xxvi.

да (modal word), 243-4.

дай (modal word), 243.

Dash, 308-11.

Dative, 159-60, 271.

давай (modal word), 243.

Demonstrative pronouns, 127.

Denominative adjectives, 110, 113-14.

Denominative verbs, 262-7.

Determinate verbs, 222-4.

Determinative pronouns, 127-8.

Deverbal adjectives, 110-11, 115-16.

Deverbal verbs, 251-62.

Diminutive adjectives, 117-18.

Diminutive nouns, 83-87.

Diminutives of Christian names, 87-89.

Direct object, 294-5, 301.

Direct speech, 310-11.

Double aspect, 228.

Double endings in noun declension, 51-55.

ё (use of), 3-5, 9, 11-13, 26-27.

Enclave, 302-3.

Foreign adjectives, 111.

Frequentative suffixes, 250-1.

Future, 179-80.

Future imperfective, 232.

Gender, 31-32.

Genitive, 162-4, 270-1.

Genitive-accusative, 31, 40, 45, 64.

Genitive in negative statements, 292, 295.
Genitive in predicate, 289.
Genitive singular in -y, 52.
Genitive singular with 'two, three, four', 141–3.
Genitive plural in –ев (neuter), 60.
Genitive plural without ending (masc.), 55.
Gerund, 152.
    past, 178–9, 233–4.
    present, 170–1, 233.

Habitual act, 241.
Hypothetical act, 239–40.

Imperative, 171–2, 236–9, 242–4, 282–3.
Imperfective:
    simple, 211–13.
    with suffix, 213–21.
    without perfective, 225–7.
In perfective suffix -á-/-я-, 215–17.
    -вá-, 217.
    -ыва-/-ива•, 218–20.
Impersonal reflexive verbs, 249–50.
Impersonal statement, 291–4, 301.
Impersonal verbs, 291–2.
Inclusive form, 237–8.
Indeclinable nouns, 69–71.
Indefinite pronouns, 129–30.
Indeterminate verbs, 222–4.
Indicative, 236.
Infinitive, 173, 239.
Infinitive in impersonal statements, 293.
Instantaneous act, 252.
Instrumental, 160–2, 271–2.
Instrumental in predicate, 287–9.
Interrogative relative pronouns, 128–9.
Irregular verbs, 202–3.

-ка (verbal particle), 242.
как (modal word), 244.

Locative, 272–3.
Locative singular in -ý, 52–53.

Middle verbs, 249.
Mobile vowel in adjectives, 99.
Mobile vowel in nouns, 41, 45–46, 60–61, 65.

Modal words and particles, 239–44;
Moods, 235–45.

Negation, 302.
Negative pronouns, 129.
Negative statement, 292–3, 295.
Nominal statement, 285–7, 309.
Nominative in predicate, 285–7.
Nominative plural:
    in -á, 53–55.
    in -ья, 56–57.
    in -и (neuter), 59–60.
Non-suffixal derivatives, 72.
Nouns denoting persons, 73–77.
Nouns in -ёнок, 63–64.
Nouns in -ин, 57–58.
Numerals, 136–46.

Old Church Slavonic, xxiii–xxiv, xxvi.
Optative, 240–1.
Optional phonetic simplifications, 14–15.
Ordinal numbers, 145–6.
Orthography, 1–5.

Participle:
    past active, 176, 234–5.
    past passive, 176–8, 234–5, 246–7, 292.
    present active, 169–70, 234.
    present passive, 170, 234.
Particles, 278–80.
Passive verbs, 246–7, 249.
Past imperfective, 231.
Past perfective, 232.
Past tense, 173–6.
Peasant speech, xxviii–xxix.
Perfective:
    simple, 220–1.
    with prefix, 211–20.
    without imperfective, 227–8.
Personal pronouns, 122–4, 281–3.
Phonology, 5–28.
Pluralia tantum, 68–69, 144–5.
Possessive adjectives in -ин and -ов, 101–2, 116–17.
Possessive pronouns, 125–7.
Predicate, 284–90.
    non-verbal, 285–90.
    verbal, 284–5.

Prefixes:
  in nouns, 92–93.
  in adjectives, 120–1.
  in verbs, 253–62, 266–7.
Prepositions, 268–76.
Present imperfective, 229–30.
Present perfective, 230–1.
Present tense, 167–8.
Pronouns, 122–35.
Punctuation, 304–11.
пуска́й (modal word), 243.
пусть (modal word), 243.

Questions, 303–4.

Reciprocal verbs, 249.
Reflexive verbs, 246, 247–50, 292.
Relative adjectives, 111–13.
Relative adjectives in *yod*, 100–1,
  112.
Russian Church Slavonic, xxiv.

Singulative nouns, 80.
Spoken language, xxviii–xxix.
Stress, 17–22.
  in adjectives, 97, 99–100.
  in noun declension, 33, 38, 41–43,
    46–51, 61–62, 65–67.
  in verbs, 168–9, 175–6, 187, 191,
    196, 198, 199, 201, 202.
  mobile, 42–44, 50–51, 61–62,
    66–67.
Subject, 281–3.
Substantivized adjectives, 103–4.
Sudden act, 238, 244–5.
Superlative, 108–9.
Suppletive aspectual pairs, 222–5.
Suppletive plurals, 56–58, 62–64.

Surnames in -ов/-ев and -ин, 102,
  117.

Tenses, 229–35.
Transitive and intransitive, 245–6.

Verb omitted, 290, 309.
Verbal interjection, 245.
Verbal prefixes, 253–62, 265–7.
Verbal stems, 166.
Verbs in -ануть, 252.
  -ать 188–91, 195, 201–2, 252,
    263, 265.
  -а́ть/-я́ть, 215–17, 265.
  -еть, 200–1, 264–5.
  -ировать, 264.
  -ить, 198–200, 216–17, 264–5.
  -изи́ровать, 264.
  -ять, 196.
  -кать, 263.
  -м 204–5.
  -ничать, 263.
  -нуть, 191-4, 215, 252, 265.
  -овать/-евать, 197–8, 263–4.
  -ствовать, 264.
  -ва́ть, 196–7, 217.
  -ывать/-ивать, 218–20, 252.
Voices, 245–50.
Vowels, 15–22.
  close, 15–16.
  open, 15–16.
  long and short, 15.
  unstressed, 18–22.
Vulgar language of the towns, xxix.
взять (as modal verb), 244.

Word-formation, 33–36.
Word-order, 296–304.

Yod, 3–5, 26, 168.